Flat Army

*Creating a Connected and
Engaged Organization*

Dan Pontefract

JOSSEY-BASS
A Wiley Imprint
www.josseybass.com

Published by Jossey-Bass

A Wiley Imprint

Published simultaneously in the United States of America and Canada

www.josseybass.com

Jossey-Bass books and products are available through most bookstores. To contact Jossey-Bass directly, call our Customer Care Department within the US at 800-956-7739, outside the U.S. at 317-572-3986, or fax 317-572-4002.

Wiley publishes in a variety of print and electronic formats and by print-on-demand. Some material included with standard print versions of this book may not be included in e-books or in print-on-demand. For more information about Wiley products, visit www.wiley.com.

Library and Archives Canada Cataloguing in Publication Data

Pontefract, Dan, 1971–

    Flat army : creating a connected and engaged organization / Dan Pontefract.

Includes index.

ISBN 978-1-118-52979-9 (pbk); 978-1-118-52984-3 (ebk);
978-1-118-52983-6 (ebk); 978-1-118-52982-9 (ebk)

    1. Leadership.   2. Industrial management.   3. Organizational change.   4. Organizational learning.   I. Title.

HD57.7.P66 2013   658.4   C2012-908291-0

Production Credits

Cover design: Adrian So

Managing Editor: Alison Maclean

Production Editor: Lindsay Humphreys

Composition: Thomson Digital

Printer: Friesens Corporation

Printed in Canada

1 2 3 4 5 FP 17 16 15 14 13

Enigma

Some men are born to gather women's tears,
To give a harbour to their timorous fears,
To take them as the dry earth takes the rain,
As the dark wood the warm wind from the plain;
Yet their own tears remain unshed,
Their own tumultuous fears unsaid,
And, seeming steadfast as the forest and the earth
Shaken are they with pain.
They cry for voice as earth might cry for the sea
Or the wood for consuming fire;
Unanswered they remain
Subject to the sorrows of women utterly—
Heart and mind,
Subject as the dry earth to the rain
Or the dark wood to the wind.
—Duncan Campbell Scott[1]

For Denise:
May you continue to catch my tears and debunk my fears.
For all the years.
You prove the paradox wrong.

About ASTD

ASTD (American Society for Training & Development) is the world's largest professional association dedicated to the training and development field. In more than 100 countries, ASTD's members work in organizations of all sizes, in the private and public sectors, as independent consultants, and as suppliers. Members connect locally in more than 120 U.S. chapters and with 16 international partners.

ASTD started in 1943 and in recent years has widened the profession's focus to align learning and performance to organizational results, and is a sought-after voice on critical public policy issues. For more information, visit www.astd.org.

Table of Contents

Acknowledgments

SHERPAS

If my life can be thought of as a Himalayan mountaineering expedition, several people have acted as a personal Sherpa along my journey helping me to crystallize the thoughts inside of this book. That is, over time, these folks have had many direct conversations with me about a Flat Army philosophy. Thank you, Brian Reid, Steven Hill, Bob Bucher, Alexandra Samuel, Alison van Buuren, Mike Desjardins, Marcia Conner, Jon Husband, Bert Sandie, Chuck Hamilton, Lynette Van Steinburg, Bryan Acker, John Ambrose and George Siemens. And a special thank-you to Don Loney, the book Sherpa and to Jeremy Hanson-Finger, the editing Sherpa.

INSPIRATIONS

There are agencies in one's life that invoke new intellect or emotions which prompt new ideas and thinking. I am grateful to the many that arouse my curiosities and my penchant for change both in person and from afar. Thank you, Gordon Downie, author of *Coke Machine Glow*; Henry Mintzberg, author of *Managing*; Euan Semple, author of *Organizations Don't Tweet, People Do*; David Weinberger, author of *Too Big to Know*; Andrew McAfee, author of *Enterprise 2.0*; Simon Sinek, author of *Start With Why*; Karie Willyerd, co-author of *20–20 Workplace*; Clay Shirky, author of *Cognitive Surplus*; Daniel Pink, author of *Drive*; Daniel Goleman, author of *Emotional Intelligence;* Charlene Li, author of *Open Leadership;* Amy Edmondson, author of *Teaming;* Carol Dweck, author of *Mindset;* David Shenk, author of *The Genius in All of Us;* Cathy Davidson, author of *Now You See It;* Tom Malone, author of *The Future of Work;* Gary Hamel, author of *The Future of Management;* and Marjorie Kelly, author of *Owning Our Future.*

INTERLOCUTORS

If you are a believer in Flat Army, you are only as good as your network. My thanks go out to the people who have become trusted interlocutors in my own personal sphere of knowledge and sharing. Thanks to Gautam Ghosh, Mike Prokopeak, G Shawn Hunter, Jocelyn Berard, Jack Stepler, Stephen Lamb, Nilofer Merchant, Nancy Slawski, Steven Wheeler, Daneal Charney, Ben Brooks, Rob Cottingham, Eric Andersen, Megan Murray, Bill Jensen, Bill Ives, John Hagel, Mark Fidelman, Alan Lepofsky, Igo Tan, Gina Minks, Holly MacDonald, Harold Jarche, Rawn Shah, Hutch Carpenter, Jacob Morgan, Andrew Bull, Angie Harrop, Anne Marie McEwan, David Porter, Valerie Irvine, Ross Dawson, Jillianne Code, Gordon Ross, Sameer Patel, Thomas Stone, Charles Jennings, Sidneyeve Matrix, J Keith Dunbar, Susan Scrupski, Jon Ingham, Luis Suarez, Lance Dublin, Christian Finn, Clark Quinn, JP Rangaswami, Jay Cross, Charles Jennings, Jane Hart, Aaron Silvers, Chad Walter, Deborah Wickens, Ralph Nakad, Eric Jordan, John Bevacqua, Gordon Vala-Webb, Leslie Castellani, Bruce Duthie, Angela Alini, Jeff Dunmall and Sara Roberts.

LEADERS

You can't write a book about the ideal operating model in an organization without having actual experience; where your thoughts and philosophies are molded and reshaped. Chuck Luttrell gave me my first job as a high school teacher. He allowed me the opportunity to put Education 2.0 into action when it wasn't even on the map back in 1995. Thank you, Chuck. Lorna Shapiro and Ken Takagaki (Associate Dean and Dean of Computing at the British Columbia Institute of Technology) handed me a ticket to reshape things at the higher education level, in 1998 no less as a 27-year-old. Thank you for believing in my Flat Army model even before I knew what Flat Army really was. Isabelle Clements, Wendy van Donkelaar and Jerry Gratton convinced me to join the corporate world in 2002 where I was given the keys to drive a new paradigm in a high-tech software company. Dan Klein then solidified their decision by further empowering me to reach even greater heights after an acquisition. Thank you for believing in me. I currently work at TELUS, and it was Josh Blair, Andrew Turner, Donna McNicol and Helmut Hager who convinced me it was a place ripe for change and where I should hang my hat for a while. Thanks for allowing me the opportunity to help so many team members across the TELUS organization.

COLLEAGUES

My life and beliefs are further shaped by the people I've been fortunate enough to work with in close quarters over the years. The following are Flat Army role models through and through: Natasa Koledin, Deb Arnold, Khalid Shaikh, Laura Jamieson, Jan Seger, Jose Santos, Eric Moeller, Wendy Toh, Megan Smith, Elizabeth Morwick, Melissa Bowyer, Mary Hewitt, Carmen Choy, Tomasz Zima, David Galloway, Janet Wood—and those who were the cool cats at Crystal Decisions, Business Objects, UBI, SAP, and of course everyone at Team TELUS including the L&C Team. Thank you for helping me grow, if not grow up.

STORIES

When I put the call out to several individuals requesting interviews for their views on certain components of Flat Army, there were (thankfully) a few who actually answered the call. Imagine that! One really must appreciate one's network when writing a book. Hat tip for their honesty and their thoughts to Danielle Tomlinson, Shazia McCormick, Tony Bingham, Jeff Maaks, Stan Garfield, Nick Howe, Cam Crosbie, Lisa Brummel, Marguerite Behringer, Rob Sharpe, Matthew Wilder,

Steve Cadigan, Darren Entwistle, Bill Sullivan, Kelly Martin, Dennis Callahan, Karen Kocher, Daniel Kligerman, Jerry Nine, Linda Stone and Evernote (yes, the entire book was written in Evernote). A final thank you to the impressive team at Wiley, including Don Loney, Elizabeth McCurdy, Jennifer Smith, Therese Garnett, Terry Palmer, Josie Krysiak, Robert Bourque, Deborah Guichelaar and Lucas Wilk.

FRIENDS

If you're lucky to have a few people you can call up at any given moment, regardless of time, distance or conversation gap span and talk about anything in the world, you have the very definition of friends. My thanks to Kelsy Trigg, Stephen Yang, Dave Hancock, Lesley Short, Keith Driscoll, Michelle Hollingworth, Kim Morgan, Gerald Lambert, Frances Picherack, Roman Picherack, Jen Dousett, Tristan Jackson, Jen Schaeffers, Alex Bayne, Christine Laur, Maria Miller, Brian Coleman, Paige Kraft, Bryan MacKinnon, Gareth Reid, Patrick Haussmann, John McNaughton, Denise Baker and Cindy Yu for lending me their ears and singing me a song every now and then.

LOVE

Is there anything more to say? Many thanks through the years to my direct family: Nicole, Mia, Roy, Alana, Natasha, Adam, Michelle, Zoe, Rich, Kara, Suzanne, Chris, Madeleine, Tyler, Debbie, Diane, Ron, Jane, Lawrence and the reason I smile every day . . . Claire (www.clairepontefract.com), Cole (www.colepontefract.com), Cate (www.catepontefract.com) and Denise. *"Love is you, you and me. Love is knowing, we can be."*

CHAPTER ONE

THE MONA LISA IS SO SMALL!

Have you ever been to the Louvre in Paris?

There are those who visit the Louvre to revel in the brilliance of art. There are many, however, whose sole purpose is to rush through the first-floor entrance, plowing past the thirteenth-, fourteenth-, and fifteenth-century Italian paintings to remark out loud, "Wow, the Mona Lisa is so small." They then proceed to the next Parisian tourist attraction like the Palais-Royal or the Panthéon, saying afterward to their friends, "Yes, I've been to the Louvre and have seen the Mona Lisa."

Those who rush to view only the Mona Lisa at the Louvre are myopic and foolish and akin to much of what is going wrong with leadership today. The current state of leadership should make us fearful. We can't merely tick the box that states "Mona Lisa" and suggest that we've covered the art world. So which type are you? Do you visit the Louvre to prove you've seen the Mona Lisa? Or do you savor the experience of being present in the other galleries?

Mike Johnson once said, "The ability to engage employees, to make them work with our business, is going to be one of the greatest organizational battles of the coming ten years."[1] It's been nearly a decade since he penned those words in his 2004 book *New Rules of Engagement: Life-Work Balance and Employee Commitment.* They could have been written today—and perhaps in an even more urgent tone. Leadership models—of which there been many of late—have failed people and organizations.

We recognize it's a question of leadership. It's a question of whether we are embracing the desire of employees to actually be treated like adults. It's a question of maturity; leaders cannot fathom the loss of control, yet paradoxically, it's the more creative and less hierarchical leader who is, in fact, empowering his or her team and getting better results.

Organizations realize that success is achieved through effective leadership, but if engaged employees is the primary outcome we desire from effective leadership, then it's a question of whether we are embracing employees' desires, first and foremost to be treated like responsible adults. Traditional leaders struggle with this concept as it represents a loss of control for them, but creative, less hierarchical-minded leaders who empower their employees are getting better results, and in turn, are empowered and emboldened to reach for greater successes with their cohort.

As I thought through this idea, the notion of *Flat Army* came to me. Sounds intriguing, doesn't it?

This book weaves together my thinking around organizations—that they are at an inflection point, and perhaps even a crisis point. When we hear the word "army," we typically picture images of war in our heads. I, on the other hand, think of fishing boats. The word "army" is derived from *armata*, a medieval Latin term used first in 1533 to depict a fleet of things moving together—an armada, if you will. This, to me, is the essence of an army—a group of people striving, leading together to achieve a common goal.

We need to move together again as an organization. Leadership doesn't come from one, it comes from all. This is why the word "flat" comes in front of army. Flat denotes equality and togetherness. In the English language, "flat" can be used in myriad different ways. For purposes of this book—and my central thesis—I use it to define horizontal connectedness.

Flat Army's audacious goal is to give your organization new life. It aims to free you of the bonds of leadership styles and models that continue to exacerbate disengagement levels of employees, worker dissatisfaction and general innovation malaise. It demonstrates how to both flatten and reunite the armada—and thus the fleet of fishing vessels. The elements of social technologies, collaboration, participation, pervasive learning and connected leadership are frameworks to help both the individual and the organization succeed in the years to come.

Flat Army doesn't diss situational hierarchy, but an overarching omnipresent hierarchy across the organization, controlled by principles of command and control, is an illogical and unsuitable model in a time when the employee wants to desperately become part of the fishing boat armada. They no longer want to be left ashore.

> Our people need to move together again, in the armada, as a collective one.

Concepts like engagement, open leadership, empowerment, new learning paradigms and collaborative behaviors are not inescapable diseases on a boat. There is a cure for those stuck in hierarchical hell. There is hope. But through this observation, I must pose a few questions.

It's time we ask ourselves about the root cause of employee disengagement and vacillation. Is the way in which leaders are leading their teams, organizations and people so antiquated and traditional that employees are being forced to ride a wave for which we might coin the term "the corporate crestfallen"? Why aren't organizations and leaders paying enough attention to whether or not an employee actually wants to be at work? If she does, she makes a meaningful contribution and is productive, whereas if she doesn't, she's merely putting in time and collecting a paycheck. And for those who are paying attention and trying to improve engagement and leadership practices, why have employees plateaued in terms of their level of organizational engagement?

According to Gallup, a global human capital consulting firm, overall employee engagement since 2000 has remained at a paltry 30 percent. More shockingly, levels of active disengagement as well as those simply not engaged in their roles have continued to remain flat at 20 percent and 50 percent respectively.[2] Gallup's most recent report, however, issued in 2011, entitled *State of the Global Workforce*, and based on research with over

47,000 employees in 120 countries around the world, tells an even more chilling corporate-engagement tale:

The overall results indicate that 11% of workers worldwide are engaged. In other words, about one in nine employees worldwide is emotionally connected to their workplaces and feels he or she has the resources and support they need to succeed. The majority of workers, 62%, are not engaged—that is, emotionally detached and likely to be doing little more than is necessary to keep their jobs. And 27% are actively disengaged, indicating they view their workplaces negatively and are liable to spread that negativity to others.[3]

Another human capital consulting firm, BlessingWhite, also found in 2008 that 19 percent of employees were disengaged, 52 percent were only moderately engaged, and 29 percent were fully engaged.[4]

For more than a decade, and however you slice it through whatever external consulting firm's data points, roughly 70 percent to 80 percent of any organization has effectively acted in a practice of workplace ambivalence. The employees would rather not be at work, or worse, they're simply participating in some form of corporate coma—a catatonic catastrophe in the organization if you ask me.

Moreover, why aren't leaders actually doing something about the data that haunts their every move? In a report entitled *Global Leadership Forecast* conducted by Development Dimensions International (DDI) with over 14,000 global leaders, DDI's research indicates that

organizations with the highest quality leaders [are] thirteen times more likely to outperform their competition in key bottom-line metrics such as financial performance, quality of products and services, employee engagement, and customer satisfaction.[5]

DDI further asserts that "organizations with higher quality leadership [are] up to three times more likely to retain more employees than their competition; they also [have] more than five times the number of highly engaged leaders."[6]

Maybe it's time leaders started reading the fine print of those internal employee satisfaction surveys.

The disconsolate must be helped. I intend to do this by building a framework for the book around the following points in order to help you and me create some common ground.

- Common engagement at work (the concept of feeling good, included, valued and willing to go above and beyond the call of duty in effort and praise) is a key link to workplace productivity.
- Organizational attachment can be thought of as the emotional, connected and intellectual commitment to an employee's place of work.
- Approximately 70 percent of employees aren't as engaged as they should be at their place of work.
- If an employee is engaged, he is more productive, and by being more productive, business results improve and customers are happier. (The employees tell their friends about how much they love going to work and thus are good ambassadors to the brand, products, services and so on.)
- Leaders are using leadership design models (and engagement methods) incongruent to today's workplace needs.
- Learning is an integral part of engagement, yet, moronically, we continue to stuff employees into a classroom and posit that's where the learning takes place.
- Society has become more technologically connected and in many places more open and collaborative, but the workplace is stuck in a form of organizational ambivalence.

MY FEARS

Why do I care? I care because I fear, but the only power I carry is the power of observation. My observations, ergo, are fearful.

I fear for my children, currently aged 9, 7 and 5, who will be joining the employment ranks in a few short years. I want them to join (or start) a workforce and an organization that espouses heterarchy and situational hierarchy versus a continuous command-and-control mode of operating. I want them not to fear their place of work, but to be raving fans and thus highly engaged, happy and productive employees. I want their careers to be culturally prosperous. I want them to feel as though there is no delineation between the way in which their homes are run (presumably, open, happy and engaging) and their place of work.

I fear for the so-called Millennials—those born between 1982 and 2004—who currently sit at the bottom of the management food chain, if they are employed at all. Theirs is a DNA of curiosity, community and creativity. How long will it be until their frustration level boils over from the ineptness of today's corporate culture and leadership misfits?

I, as someone born in 1971 and thus termed a member of Generation X by fellow Canadian Douglas Coupland, am also fearful for my own generation. In a 2011 press release, the Center for Talent Innovation reports that 37 percent of Gen X employees are looking to leave their current employers within three years.[7] If two out of every five 30- to 45-year-olds want to jump ship, I fear somewhere along the way we've written a story line that has the next generation of potential leaders tuning out.

This brings us to the baby-boomer generation—the cohort also colloquially known as the Woodstock generation. An interesting study published in 2001 suggests that baby boomers are more affected by perceptions of office politics than is the case for Gen X workers, for example, and such perceptions have a negative effect on their job performance.[8] Boomers are known to have a focus on individual achievement; thus, I fear the natural tendency of any baby-boomer–aged leader is to lead through the demonstration of power and will. Excluding an open culture, coupled with a sense of individualism, is perhaps a primary factor in the lack of overall organizational engagement in today's workplace. Granted, the boomers are hitting retirement age, but there is a legacy left behind that is going to handcuff organizations for years to come if we don't do something about it now. The eradication of past bad practice, one could argue, is at the hands of this generation.

Add it all up, and I'm fearful for the current and future state of organizations that don't react positively to this information.

WHOSE JOB IS LEADERSHIP, ANYWAY?

I have more questions.

Regardless of my musings on my kids' future and a mild swipe at the generations in the workplace, how does this current state of leadership actually affect employee engagement? What is the effect of both good and bad leadership as it pertains to organizational health and engagement? Have we reached a point where employees are forced to mutely scream from the hilltops—out of exasperation—indicating current modes of leadership are obsolete for today's world?

From a leadership perspective, who actually is responsible for employee engagement? Who is responsible for the act of leadership? According to Hay Group, another global management consulting firm, 63 percent of CEOs and other members of the top team reckon it's the top leaders in the company who are "chiefly responsible for staff engagement and leadership," but only 38 percent of those outside the C-Suite agree that the top tier is responsible.[9] Now *that* is a disturbing leadership and engagement paradox.

Is job satisfaction correlated to employee engagement? Or is job satisfaction more correlated to life satisfaction?[10] And if job satisfaction is akin to life satisfaction, are leaders paying enough attention to their employees such that they are in fact caring about their lives, connecting in ways that allow them to enact life-work balance and a sense of community, and a sense of belonging with their colleagues? Do today's leaders actually care about the person who is doing the work? Do they even know her name, let alone what provides her with job satisfaction?

Between 1985 and 2005, the number of Americans who stated they felt satisfied with the way life was treating them decreased by roughly 30 percent. Even more shocking was the number of dissatisfied people; this increased by nearly 50 percent. The reasons appear to be related to Americans' declining attachments to friends and family, lower participation in social and civic activities and diminished trust in political institutions.[11]

Rather than life imitating art, is life imitating the organization instead? As levels of employee engagement have dropped and subsequently stagnated over the past thirty years, it's no wonder the perceived quality of life has decreased as well.

This raises the question of whether today's leaders know if members of their direct report teams have children or not. It's cheeky, I know, but it's a valid question. Does leadership equate to cardboard cut-out relationships or is it an engaging and personal liaison opportunity?

If employees are enthusiastic, committed, passionate and generally into their work, isn't it time leaders of any stripe, at any step in the hierarchy chain, acted with more humility and were less parochial? [12]

Does the health of an organization and its overall engagement correlate to productivity, and in return, financial results? Does it correlate to customer loyalty, employee turnover and retention? While the questions may sound rhetorical, why do command-and-control tactics dominate the workspace versus "cultivate and coordinate" tactics as per MIT Sloan School of Management professor Tom Malone's suggestion from his book *The Future of Work*? [13]

Have we not reached, therefore, a professional paradox in the workplace? Shouldn't we be advocating for and developing a more engaged leader?

Has the organization become so blind that, within the underbelly of the top leadership ranks, a professional mutiny is in the works? Perhaps it's already in motion. A mutiny that manifests in human capital contradiction where employees are either punching in their time to simply get through the day or in eternal job searches hunting for the Holy Grail organization that actually cares about their well-being.

And leaders who sit ignorant of the brewing storm continue to commit offenses of managerial misdemeanor.

The job that people perform is central, or at least a large part of their personal identity. Picture yourself meeting someone for the first time at a cocktail party or a community gathering or your child's first soccer practice. What do you inevitably ask within the first two minutes of your initial conversation? "So, what do you do? Where do you work? How long have you been there?"

When your new acquaintance looks sheepish, or, worse, nosedives into an apoplectic rant about his place of work, you might do one of three things:

- Wince, smile and nod, and affirm that his place of work is awful.
- Agree never to buy the company's product or service due to this diabolical repudiation.
- Hold your breath, wait for the conversation to end, and find the nearest safe harbor as soon as you can.

It is time, therefore, to introduce *Flat Army*.

Employees in today's organizations are expecting more from leaders than what is currently being offered. Sadly and paradoxically, 69 percent of executives agree; they too feel engagement and leadership is a problem in their organizations.[14]

It is time to connect the dots between leadership, engagement, learning, technology and collaboration.

ENGAGING DEFINITIONS

The concept of employee engagement itself is amorphous. Contradictory definitions exist across many realms. I've always been fascinated by the term "engagement." It can mean so many things. It can also be interpreted in so many different ways. There are differences in the way engagement is thought of within the corporate world, in academic circles and among consultants. For example, is employee engagement about an outcome—demonstrating loyalty, job satisfaction, and a likelihood to recommend products and services to your neighbor—or is it a psychological state of being focused, driven and dedicated?

On the other hand, organizations that sound the trumpet of annual, quarterly or weekly engagement gimmicks to allegedly improve employee engagement are somewhere between daft and imbecilic. An employee may be tricked with cotton candy once, but she is eventually going to figure out it's only made of sugar and fancy food coloring.

Richard Axelrod refers to it as plug-and-play activities: "Successful employee-engagement practice is not about plugging in a set of tools and techniques that you just read about in some hotshot guru's latest book—and then expecting engaged employees to magically appear."[15]

Cotton-candy gimmicks are also paradoxical; senior leaders might seem to think they're the right thing to do, but employees everywhere see them for what they are, which is fool's gold.

In 2011, Azka Ghafoor, Tahir Masood Qureshi, M. Aslam Khan and Syed Tahir Hijazi from the University of Central Punjab in Lahore, Pakistan, published research entitled "Transformational leadership, employee engagement and performance: Mediating effect of psychological ownership." These professors sought to show that an employee is engaged when he demonstrates what they refer to as "psychological ownership." And more specifically, that when backed by transformational leadership (and leaders), employees thrive on the basis of "self-identity, belongingness, self-efficacy and responsible attitude":

Employee engagement makes employees more accountable and enhances the sense of belongingness. Employee engagement practiced under transformational leadership develops the positivity in behavior that leads to trust and satisfaction that enhances sense of belongingness. The sense of ownership is supported by the perception of citizenship of employees. Once employees feel themselves as part of the organization their self-identity with organization improves. This identity and association with the organization develops commitment in employees and their performance increases.[16]

That is, when an employee feels as though she is a part of something, when there is unequivocal trust in the workplace and when backed by an environment that is positive and coupled by inclusive leadership, that employee will become engaged and ultimately more productive.

There are those, however, who feel engagement is a load of bricks weighing the organization down and ultimately it's all a waste of time. Laurie Bassi and Dan McMurrer in "Does Engagement Really Drive

Results?" suggest the drivers of employee engagement are not uniform across multiple businesses and industries, nor are they correlated to actual business results.[17] They argue engagement cannot be measured equally across the varying functions of an organization or between different business verticals. Furthermore, they purport the current methods in which employee engagement is measured doesn't have much to do with the actual business results of an organization.

In a conversation with thought leader and author of the book *Organizations Don't Tweet—People Do*, Euan Semple said to me:

If someone came up to you, called you an 'employee' and asked you to 'engage' with them, how would you feel? The phrase has its own demise baked into it. If you really want an engaged workforce, treat [people] as fellow grown-ups working together for a shared purpose. Have real conversations with them about your real challenges and take what they say seriously. If you don't they are likely to keep you at arm's length and only give you a fraction of the support they are capable of.[18]

Research also indicates that the correlation between job satisfaction (akin to engagement) and an increase in job performance is a paltry 0.3 percent.[19] Suffice it to say, there are some naysayers out there that believe employee engagement itself is much like uncooked pasta—full of potential energy but ultimately useless.

Karl Fischer, a regional vice president for Marriott International, disagrees with those who are anti–employee engagement. He believes that as employee engagement goes up, so too does employee performance. In his particular example, for hotel sites that demonstrate a highly engaged workforce, hotel revenues increase 12 percent and there is a 9 percent increase in hotel profit margin per compensation dollar. Furthermore, an engaged Marriott employee translates into a 9-percent reduction of guests experiencing problems, and guests are 11 percent more likely to return to a Marriott property when interacting with an engaged employee.[20]

The paradox continues even as we try to define employee engagement itself.

But I'm with Karl on this one. As you'll see through the coming chapters, engagement is in fact linked to leadership; it's that our leadership style is running up against nineteenth- and twentieth-century behavioral relics.

There are big players in the human resources, human capital and talent management consulting space, some of whom are mentioned above, who significantly invested in defining the term "employee engagement"; they provide consultative services to organizations that want to both fix and potentially increase engagement within their organizations. Some also provide employee engagement or satisfaction survey services. This is big business with revenue and profit hinging on the entire employee engagement definition and outcome.

Gallup defines an engaged employee as one who will

work with passion and feel a profound connection to their company. They drive innovation and move the organization forward.[21]

Towers Perrin (now Towers Watson) specifies employees need both the will and the way in which to actually demonstrate engagement. It defines it in the following way:

- *Employees need the will: the sense of mission, passion and pride that motivates them to give that all-important discretionary effort. And they need the way: the resources, support and tools from the organization to act on their sense of mission and passion.*[22]

AON Hewitt defines engagement as the point at which employees

- *speak positively about the organization to co-workers, potential employees and customers;*
- *have an intense desire to be a member of the organization; and*
- *exert extra effort and are dedicated to doing the very best job possible to contribute to the organization's business success.*[23]

AON Hewitt labels the three aforementioned bullets as "say," "stay," and "strive."

Hay Group defines employee engagement as

- *the commitment employees feel toward their organization; and*
- *employees' discretionary effort—their willingness to go above and beyond the call of duty or go the extra mile for the organization.*[24]

At its root, employee engagement and the act of measuring it, acting on it and utilizing it as a measure of organizational health can have whatever definition suits a particular organization. What matters most, however, is the consistency with which action is taken throughout the organization.

After reading their book *The Enemy of Engagement: Put an End to Workplace Frustration—and Get the Most from Your Employees*, I became quite fond of authors Mark Royal and Tom Agnew's definition of engagement:

Though frameworks for understanding engagement vary, the concept is commonly understood to capture levels of commitment and discretionary effort exhibited by employees. Engaged employees can be expected to display high levels of attachment to an organization and a strong desire to remain a part of it. Consequently, engaged employees are more likely to be willing to go above and beyond the formal requirements of the job, contribute organizational citizenship behaviors, pour extra effort into their work, and deliver superior performance.[25]

If an employee has the wherewithal to go above and beyond the call of duty, wants to contribute organizational citizenship behaviors, and will recommend to others how fantastic an organization he or she works at, it really does have to link back to leadership.

Engagement, therefore, and in my opinion, is about whether or not an employee feels trusted by leaders to do the right thing when it counts. When trust is reciprocal between both the leader and the individual employee, that's when we start seeing an engaged employee who feels connected, a part of the solution, and who will finally go beyond the call of duty demonstrating extra effort, positive feedback to friends, willingness to collaborate, mitigated flight risk, etc. That's when the leader becomes open, and thus trusting, to include the employee in discussions, decisions and ideas. It's when the employee is trustful of the leader to actually contribute, to suggest and to also go above the call of duty. It's leadership quid pro quo.

That is the point at which an employee is engaged and will ultimately be a happier and contributing person of the organization—one who will recommend the organization to others.

For the purposes of this book, we define "employee engagement" as follows:

> **Employee engagement:** The state in which there is reciprocal trust between the employee and leadership to do what's right however, whenever and with whomever.

WHY IS ENGAGEMENT GOOD?

The general population of employees is either disengaged or not engaged (totalling roughly 70 percent according to Gallup and others), CEOs and other executives believe engagement is a problem (and something to mitigate), and when compared to performance and business results, there are varying opinions and results.

Is employee engagement a good thing? Should we actually care?

According to various outlets and research, one side of the paradox continues to demonstrate that an organization which remains blind to employee engagement does and will suffer for fools, for there are ample statistics and metrics that prove its worth:

- A highly engaged organization has the potential to reduce staff turnover by 87 percent and can provide a corresponding increase in performance by 20 percent.[26]
- If there is a 1-percent increase in employee engagement such that an employee commits to the most appropriate customer action, it can lead to a monthly increase of 9 percent in sales.[27]

- Companies with an engaged workforce improve operating income by 19 percent while companies with low engagement results see operating income decline by 32 percent.[28]

- An engaged employee has a willingness to do more than expected (39 percent), higher level of productivity (27 percent), better working relationships (13 percent) and more satisfied customers (10 percent).[29]

- Higher employee engagement results in a 50-percent reduction in reportable accidents, from eighteen per one hundred to nine per hundred.[30]

- More than 66 percent of managers who report they are engaged at work also claim high productivity levels.[31]

- Companies with engaged employees have operating margins 5.75 percent greater than those of low-engagement companies; net profit margins are also 3.44 percent more.[32] Some organizations are proud enough to publicly showcase their engagement efforts as well. Take, for example, the Royal Bank of Scotland who found that in retail banking, a 10-percent increase in leadership effectiveness— as measured by a series of questions about direct and divisional managers—ripples into a 3-percent boost to customer satisfaction and a 1-percent reduction in turnover, which saves some $40 million that would be needed to replace workers.[33]

The U.S. General Services Administration organization, a 12,000-plus employee firm with a $26-billion budget that oversees the business of the U.S. federal government, found through an internal study that "workgroups with higher levels of engagement had, on average, 23–26 more highly satisfied and loyal customers, which equated to more than $1 million in revenue" than workgroups with low or slightly engaged employees.[34] Electronics retailer Best Buy, in concert with research partner BlessingWhite, reported in 2008 that stores where employee engagement increased by one-tenth of a point had sales increases of more than $100,000 for the year.[35]

There is ample data to suggest that an increase in employee engagement positively affects morale, satisfaction and retention, but equally important is that business results (revenue, profit and customer satisfaction) seem to also increase.

But every coin has a flipside. The story continues to unfold.

WHY IS DISENGAGEMENT BAD?

Greg Smith used to work for Goldman Sachs.

His twelve-year career at the venerable global investment banking and securities firm culminated with Greg assuming the position of executive director and head of the equity derivatives business for Europe, the Middle East and Africa. On March 14, 2012, Greg left this prestigious post and organization for what can only be referred to as a case of the disengaged employee.

Greg believed, in short, that Goldman Sachs had lost its way with its employees and it was no longer a great place to work—after being a wonderful place to work for many years. The firm became fixated on profit, lost sight of putting the customer first, and in turn began treating employees like numbers instead of people. Leaders became draconian and disengaged employees were the products of their evil-doing. The CEO, Lloyd C. Blankfein, and president, Gary D. Cohn, were called out by Greg as leaders at Goldman Sachs who will be remembered as having "lost hold of the firm's culture on their watch."[36] No longer was Goldman Sachs an employee-first organization; it became a profit-first company and employees like Greg were bearing the brunt of this new leadership style.

Then one day Greg made a decision. Rather than continuing his employment with Goldman Sachs and what was his own level of personal disengagement, Greg decided to quit outright. But, in a demonstration of integrity, Greg wrote an op-ed column in *The New York Times* entitled, "Why I Am Leaving Goldman Sachs." He powerfully articulated his level of frustration with leaders and the new culture at Goldman Sachs:

It might sound surprising to a skeptical public, but culture was always a vital part of Goldman Sachs's success. It revolved around teamwork, integrity, a spirit of humility, and always doing right by our clients. The culture was the secret sauce that made this place great and allowed us to earn our clients' trust for 143 years. It wasn't just about making money; this alone will not sustain a firm for so long. It had something to do with pride and belief in the organization. I am sad to say that I look around today and see virtually no trace of the culture that made me love working for this firm for many years. I no longer have the pride, or the belief. [37]

Not a big deal, you might be saying to yourself. Sure, but what effect did this obviously disengaged employee have at the organization? Perhaps there were situations where Greg was knowingly sabotaging Goldman Sachs customers by decreeing how awful the company had become. We might never know what damage Greg's outpouring might have inflicted indirectly on Goldman Sachs customers or to his peers; however, what did occur once his op-ed column published in *The New York Times* was an astonishing $2.15-billion loss of its market value. Goldman Sachs' shares dropped 3.4 percent after Greg's column was digested by traders, which was the third-largest decline in the eighty-one-company Standard & Poor's 500 Financials Index. If one disengaged employee can cause that type of damage, what do we make of the legions of disengaged or not-engaged employees that indirectly affect the bottom line on a daily basis?

Being an engaged employee seems to be a good thing for the organization, particularly if you are leading the show at Goldman Sachs. I suspect Blankfein and Cohn could have done without the negative and inquisitive press that ensued after Greg's diatribe. They also undoubtedly had to start an internal investigation of sorts to understand whether or not the accusations were in fact true. Regardless, the direct actions to address this rather disengaged employee had both direct and indirect financial costs at Goldman Sachs. How much of Blankfein and Cohn's time was spent on the matter when they could have been meeting with customers?

But what negative effect does a disengaged or not-engaged employee have outside of Greg's example?

According to Psychometrics, an employee who is not within the 30-percent-engaged bracket has 29 percent of his work relationships be coined as dysfunctional (that is, they can't work with others); 25 percent of employees in this bracket have lower productivity when compared to their engaged colleagues; and 17 percent refuse to go beyond the job description. To me, that's a lot of people who couldn't care less about the organization, its customers and the bottom line.

AON Hewitt researched more than 7,000 organizations and found that each disengaged employee costs an organization an average of $10,000 in profit annually.[38] Gallup counters with a statistic suggesting each disengaged employee equates to $2,246 in operating costs.[39] In total, this alone costs U.S.-based organizations over $300 billion in lost productivity, as well as $64 billion in the United Kingdom, $60 billion in France and roughly $6 billion in Singapore.

The paradox of organizational disengagement and financial results is intriguing, if not alarming. Clay Shirky, a professor at New York University and a fellow at the Berkman Center for Internet and Society, writes in *Cognitive Surplus*, "how we treat one another matters, and not just in a 'it's nice to be nice' kind of way: our behavior contributes to an environment that encourages some opportunities and hinders others."[40] Could it be that the way in which leaders treat their employees might encourage or hinder financial impacts such as cost overruns, time gap to close new clients, call center service lag, or cycle time to complete a project?

Is there a Greg Smith lurking in your organization? Is the cotton-candy irony of fake happy employees about to turn your organization upside down?

THE ORGANIZATION VS. LIFE ITSELF

In his book *The Future of Work*, Tom Malone states, "As managers, we need to shift our thinking from command and control to coordinate and cultivate—the best way to gain power is sometimes to give it away."[41] Gary Hamel, in his book *The Future of Management*, opines, "management and organizational innovation often lags far behind technological innovation. Right now, your company has twenty-first-century, Internet-enabled business processes, mid-20th-century management processes, all built atop nineteenth-century management principles. Without a transformation in our management DNA, the power of the Web to transform the work of management will go unexploited."[42]

There is a causal relationship, a deep link between the way in which we are leading our organizations and how society is changing, be it for the good or for the bad. We need to recognize that yesterday's way of leading needs to be improved but it cannot do so unless we look at leadership in a way that incorporates more open concepts, connected learning, social and collaborative technologies as well as the inclusion of people's opinions and ideas. Today, many companies have leadership development programs. But, do those companies have an actual leadership philosophy that speaks to everyone in the organization? We need a philosophy that accommodates and even supports society's shift towards "cultivate and coordinate" and away from "command and control."

Are leadership development programs evolving to include a new attitude, new DNA, or new bedrock that starts first with the notion that everyone at the company is in fact a leader? The change starts with the principal tenet that we need to open our locked doors, tear down the cubicles and invite the entire organization to the table before making decisions or inventing the next new shiny object. Does it flatten the organization and create a more engaged culture or a happier place to work?

Hewitt Associates (subsequently becoming AON Hewitt) conducted the "Cost Reduction and Engagement Survey" in April 2009 with 518 U.S.-based companies. One interesting point resonated with me: "47% of companies surveyed reported a decline in employee trust as a result of the way in which companies have managed cost reductions."[43]

That data point is powerful. Almost half of the organizations indicated employee trust declined due to the cost-reduction measures put in place during the economic hardship that commenced in 2008. This is hardly surprising, as leaders continued to sublimely demonstrate increased command-and-control tactics in a time of crisis. But imagine if there was a leadership philosophy in place that allowed everyone to more fully understand what was happening, why, and ultimately being involved in the generation of ideas? Imagine asking your organization to problem solve ways that would help the company as opposed to treating them simply as a number in the HR database?

Organizational silos occur from apathy, hierarchy, red tape and anachronistic methods of leadership. The decline in trust as per the study above effectively demonstrates the plight of the organization. I can't think of a single benefit when it comes to organizational silos, a lack of trust or a disengaged workforce. It is another example of how we are closing our minds, walling our innovation and foregoing a more productive and networked organization. As leaders, we should not be closing our minds and becoming territorial.

There was reason to Steve Jobs' madness when he forced designers, programmers and producers at Pixar to congregate in the central atrium of its sole building. His leadership mantra and framework forced collaboration, learning and connection between people that otherwise would never have connected. Jobs tore down the silos even if people didn't know it.[44]

We erect fences in our leadership styles, shutting ourselves away from the imaginations of each other. We need to clearly articulate that a collaborative and engaged culture can and will instill openness, imagination, growth, and promotion of ideas and innovation. A reclamation process must begin. We must reclaim our generosity, our openness, our accessibility as individuals. The solution to fenced-in minds is to bring the fences down, united as an organization of unified and connected people.

If the C-Suite is looking for ROI, leaders need not prove it by return on investment, but by return on intelligence, by return on innovation and by return on ideas. The intelligence, innovation and ideas can be returned to the organization through an open culture, engaged workforce, greater profitability and happier customers.

Life is changing; it's time the organization does so as well.

WHY THIS BOOK? WHY "FLAT ARMY"?

Rather unfortunately, I can't locate the source of a quote that I have lived by for many years. My rally cry has always been the following:

We're not here to see through each other; we're here to see each other through.

For the most part, I think the 70 to 80 percent of people in the workplace not engaged or disengaged have a boss, a leadership team or colleagues who tend to see through others rather than seeing each other through. It's as simple as that.

Throughout my career, wherever I've worked and whenever possible, I've tried to employ the adage of being "here to see each other through." My career trajectory has thus far been an unnatural one—and I don't see it becoming dull either. After completing my undergraduate degree at McGill University (where I met my beloved, an educator), I spent the next three years as a high school teacher in northern Quebec and Vancouver, British Columbia. It was during this time that I learned the true definitions of disengagement and engagement.

Picture yourself in a teachers' staffroom where you've just returned from a three-day long weekend after the first week in October and twenty-plus teachers are firmly nested on various couches and chairs. It's a Tuesday at 8:15 a.m., school starts at 8:35 a.m., and you're busy preparing yourself for a day of classes with your young prodigies. A teacher blurts out, "Well, that's one long weekend down—we've got another one in November, two weeks off at Christmas, then it's March break. Easter right after that, two more long weekends . . . and the year is over. We might not as well teach anymore—we're done here."

A chorus of, "You're so right. The year is over," booms across the staffroom and this young teacher, age 24, wonders if apathy is the new black and whether collecting paychecks is truly what employment is really about.

Not all teachers were disengaged or not-engaged, but if I really thought about it, I'd argue no more than 20 percent of the teachers I worked with over those three years were actually engaged. Those who were engaged were true educators, going above and beyond the call of duty and creating learning environments for their students (and those students' parents) that were inspiring and motivating. To this day a handful of those professionals are still in my network, and a couple have become true friends.

My clients were of course the students, and the ecosystem of learning—coupled by technology, writing, innovation, creativity and openness—was something I passionately brought forward in everything I did. For example, after some cajoling with the principal, I not only set up two computer labs both equipped with the latest desktop publishing, graphic design and innovation software, let alone an ISDN Internet line into the school (remember, this is 1996), but I also convinced him that I could teach two new courses, Journalism and Desktop Publishing, and that through these courses the students would mingle, create and collaborate together to issue a monthly newspaper called *The Alphabet Soup*. My belief was learning shouldn't be boxed in and that true learning (and leadership) occurs when open collaboration is at the forefront. Setting up the construct of these classes and the environment itself and then getting out of the way to watch these 16- to 18-year-olds develop some amazing and creative school newspapers was a somewhat unknowing step onto my personal journey of openness, technology, collaboration and learning.

After realizing I had to escape the situation I was in, I ventured into the next career stop—higher education.

Pierre Trudeau once said, "The essential ingredient of politics is timing."[45] If we swapped the word politics for career development, it would help explain how this four-year stint commencing in 1998 began to crystallize my thinking about the ideal and quintessentially engaged organization.

As a 27-year-old, no less, I was handed the keys to a new venture, not even off the ground, that would assist career-changing adults enter the high-tech space as an IT professional, consultant, web developer, technical support representative, administrator and entrepreneur. As an entirely cost recovery venture (i.e., with no money from the government), the team and I set out to transform the way education was happening in higher education, albeit from the perspective of those already in possession of a degree or diploma looking to crack the dot-com world of the late 90s and early 2000s.

What was unique was the way in which we operated the actual education model. Rather than simply employing the spray-and-pray archetype that has riddled our education ranks since the University of Bologna began credentialing students in 1088, we fused each program with real-world projects, business simulations, industry practicum, open leadership modeling and scenarios that induced both pressure and leadership in collaborative and engaging ways.

Sure, the students got knocked around emotionally and mentally. It was my belief that if we were to prepare these career changers for the nuttiness that was occurring inside of dot-com mania, we had better mimic as best as possible what was actually happening. There were tears, and loads of fear, but in the end those graduates are now located throughout the world as shining examples of holistic leaders: able to openly communicate, proactively engage with stakeholders before doing something, and blend technology and collaboration practices with people skills with an absolutely uncanny ability.

Maurice Li is one of those shining examples. He was able to take his previous degree and survive one of the intensive year-long programs we offered, and, since graduation, he has been an ultra-successful venture capitalist partner with Discovery Capital Management Corporation. Maurice took the time to write to me one day, offering a snapshot of my personal leadership style:

You've been the driving force since day one. Your passion for the program was evident every time you spoke, and at all times while performing the duties that your job required of you. During the good times, you saw to it that everyone stayed as happy as possible; and during the rough times, you alone kept things together in the program by virtue of your presence as a stabilizing force. I recognize and appreciate the contribution you have made to my life & career.[46]

The students and the team we put together to operate these intensive world-class, game-changing experiences were highly engaged. Maurice was but one example of future Flat-Army-like leaders we were graduating. The rest of the academic organization, however, seemed to mimic what happens elsewhere; 70 to 80 percent of the academic and administrative staff were disengaged or not engaged.

By 2002, having spent seven years in both high school and higher-education environments, it was time to enter the corporate sector. It was, as they say in Triple-A-baseball language, time to join the show.

I've had the privilege of working with employees, partners, customers and executives for over a decade. My roles and ultimate responsibilities have centered on the fusion of open leadership, social and collaborative technologies, new learning models and engaging cultural practices that enhance the employee, partner and customer experience. I've always tried to emulate an experience that ensured all stakeholders would, as one of my former CEOs, Bernard Liautaud, used to say, "drink our own champagne." That is, if you're going to be an open and collaborative leader, why not help everyone else do the same?

Within the high-tech and telecom verticals where I've lived since 2002, one thing is for certain: Peter Drucker was right when he allegedly said, "culture eats strategy for breakfast." I've been through more acquisitions than I cared to be and whether we were acquiring companies or were being acquired, it's the culture of both organizations that decides whether things proceed smoothly or not. If the cultures are ones where leaders are there to "see through everyone," failure is bound to occur at some point. If, however, the cultures involve those same people being there to "see each other through" the situation, success is ensured from the moment the acquisition press release is dropped.

Since 2008, I have held the position of head of learning and collaboration at TELUS; a 40,000-employee, $10-billion-plus company unleashing the power of the Internet to Canadians from coast to coast to coast. The TELUS CEO, Darren Entwistle, took the time one day in 2012 to pen a personal letter to me thanking me for various deliverables, including the launch of an enterprise-wide leadership framework for all TELUS team members:

The introduction of the TELUS Leadership Philosophy in 2010 created an important shift to a culture that embraces leadership development of all team members through social, informal and formal learning. This philosophy has become the cornerstone of our new leadership culture at TELUS and recognises that everyone has an important voice in our business, which is reflected in our Customers First culture.[47]

We're not here to see through each other; we're here to see each other through. Both of us.

Sadly, I have directly and indirectly seen the dark side of organizations, and quite frankly, it isn't pleasant. When the number of disengaged or not-engaged grows in an organization or team, it's easier to watch reruns of *American Idol*, and we all know how painful that can be. Conversely, when leaders ignore the rank and file, become dramatically hierarchical, or, worse, act in a nuclear micro-management mode, the team and organization, or both, are one step removed from poking themselves in the eye with an ice pick.

Yes, it sounds overly dramatic, but rest assured I've been a part of an amazing run over the past ten years and it's this positive experience that is the point of the next chapters.

Since you have made it this far into the book, you might also be asking yourself, "What's with all the engagement talk, Dan?"

Fair enough.

For me, a disengaged or not-engaged employee is toxic, but I'd bet my last dollar that it has 95 percent to do with the leadership practices of the organization where they work. Those are the type of leaders who are seeing through their people. In a nutshell, it's not good.

On the other hand, an engaged employee—one who demonstrates reciprocal trust, who feels connected and a part of the solution and who will put in that extra effort—is being helped through any given situation by his or her leader. That employee is engaged because the leader demonstrates and practices behaviors that ensure a democratic and connected working environment.

✳   ✳   ✳

Flat Army focuses on five key tenets:

- **Connection:** The behaviors, actions and tactics to become an engaging leader
- **Collaboration:** The behavioral method in which leaders and employees should be operating

- **Participation:** The act of continuously building your network and distribution of knowledge
- **Learning:** The recognition that learning is continuous, community driven, and everywhere
- **Technology:** The tools and processes that cultivate both an engaged and connected organization

The journey through this book defines frameworks, tools, processes and behaviors that help leaders cross the chasm of a closed or hierarchical style to one that is certainly more open, connected, clear and empowering. It is not a book with rapid-fire examples from across the world; rather, it contains more in-depth scenarios—from business leaders, companies, and even history, geography, math and science situations—interspersed with unique analogies, metaphors and existing research to help explain and depict Flat Army concepts. I was once struck by the foreword in Jim Kouzes and Barry Posner's seminal book, *The Leadership Challenge*, where Tom Peters wrote, "*The Leadership Challenge* has lasted, I believe, because (1) it is research-based, (2) it is practical, and (3) it has heart."[48] I'm continually guided by Tom's observation and my hope is *Flat Army* measures up to that yardstick. There are several thousand awful leadership books out there and I didn't want this one falling into that camp. I'd love to know if you agree or not once you finish the book.

Many leaders are operating somewhere between cynical and skeptical. Doubt leads to dysfunction. Dysfunction leads to organizational apathy. There has to be a better way. This book intends to bring forward these concepts; it's time to unite the boats and thus the flotilla. It's time for Flat Army.

CHAPTER TWO
HOW'D WE GET SO RIGID?

Corporations exist to make money. This isn't likely a surprise to you and nor would it be to suggest that some of those same organizations don't really care about your well-being as an employee. As a consequence, many—but not all—managers lead with a singular focus on profits. They are the classic command-and-control type of manager because of the system—the system built on hierarchy, control and profits—and thus the managerial handcuffs.

Stephen Denning, in his book *The Leader's Guide to Radical Management: Reinventing the Workplace for the 21st Century*, opines,

The reality is that most established firms—no matter which business they are in, no matter how sophisticated their products or services, or what the country of origin—are still operating on the assumption that the workplace can and should be built around the central idea of a system of things to produce goods and services.[1]

And in order to ensure those goods and services are produced on time, on budget and at a pertinent level of quality, the only way in which to ensure this occurs is to control the employee. It's a recipe for organizational-engagement disaster.

This chapter is dedicated to an analysis of rigidity. It's an attempt to whip you into a frenzy of disbelief. If this were a fictional book, the chapter would slowly introduce our antagonist whereas the rest of the book sees our protagonist—the Flat Army leader—attempt to capture or kill off the enemy until the closing denouement. I hope it concludes with a positive ending and there's some sort of warm embrace, but you just have to read to the final chapter to find out.

It might be argued that organizations—whether for-profit or not-for-profit—are simply tools. In fact, the word organization pays homage to the Greek word *organon*, which can be loosely translated as an instrument or a tool. If we consider this definition, it's been an awfully long time since we've treated the organization like a tool. Perhaps the organization itself in situ was the original workplace tool.

The word "hierarchy" dates back to the fourteenth century, and as with many terms from long ago, there are religious connotations. *Hierós* is the Greek term for sacred or holy, and *arkhēs* is the term for ruling. Combine these together and you get "head priest" (*hierárkhēs*). Over the years, Latin, French and English derivatives produced similar meanings. By the seventeenth century the term "hierarchy" became linked to the ranks of the clergy, cementing its relationship to religion. Nowadays, hierarchy is found not only in religion but in the military and in the corporate world through defined levels of management power and control.

So if the term organization is rooted in a word for tool and the term hierarchy to a word for head priest, it's no wonder many organizations and teams (though not all) have saddled themselves with such a dysfunctional state of leading. The manager is the priest—all knowing—and the employees have become bit parts of the master's tool—the organization. It's not meant to sound blasphemous and I don't mean to make fun of anyone's religious beliefs. I'm simply taking creative license to the etymology of organization and hierarchy. Many leaders have somehow become so comfortable with the status quo that they do not question why this pyramidal structure and operating practice continues to exist today. Direction and guidance is one thing, but unilateral close-mindedness to the working class just for the sake of it is disheartening. Many organizations have acted this way, treating employees like numbers and not people for decades. Why?

THE GROCERY STORE OF HIERARCHY

I once went into a grocery store with our three goats (that's code for our children) to pick up some dinner. True to form, the 7- and 5-year-olds (at the time) needed to relieve their bladders. I asked someone at the front of the store where the washroom was and was told it was in the back stockroom beside the deli. We made it to the back, crossed the secret stockroom swinging door and found the toilet. As the 7-year-old was doing his thing, I read some notices on the employee bulletin board. There, sadly, sat a computer printout pinned to the board that read as follows:

Dear Employees,

This is a reminder you are not
to use your cell phones
on the floor or on the back
picnic table during your breaks.
You are also forbidden to use
your phone when working on the floor.
Anyone caught using their phone
will be fired after their shift.

The Management

Always being the cheeky one, I set out to test the theory. As the 5-year-old finished her business, the four of us escaped the cavernous stockroom and proceeded to gallivant shopping throughout the store. My 9-year-old has an unfortunate sensitivity to gluten, but for purposes of this test we pretended she was allergic. I know, I'm a horrible person. She is not afflicted with celiac disease and hopefully never will be, but a slight deviation from the truth was necessary to put my theory into practice. We entered Aisle 2 where the snacks were located, including one of our family favorites, popcorn.

Now, I might know that popcorn is gluten free—or at least the brands we buy are—but that doesn't mean the 9-, 7- or 5-year-old do, and it also doesn't mean an unsuspecting worker in the store knows either. So, I set my plan into motion. Perusing the various microwave and kernel popcorn options, I asked out loud to the goats, "Do you know if popcorn is gluten free?" The look of shock that set in on the oldest child's face was priceless (and, yes, I am a horrible father). After convincing the goats I wasn't sure, I enlisted the service of "Damian" who just happened to be walking by and was presumably gainfully employed by the grocery store.

"Excuse me, young man," I asked rather sheepishly. "Do you know if popcorn is gluten free?" With a smile that was ear to ear, young Damian replied, "Actually, I have no idea, sir. Let's check the box."

He patiently and painstakingly looked at five boxes, attempting to solve the mystery. "I can't seem to tell whether these are gluten free or not," he remarked as he put the fifth box back on the shelf. "Normally, these products tell us if they are gluten free or not, so I'm guessing they aren't."

My evil plan now kicked into full gear.

"Good point," I said. "But don't you think I'd know for certain if we checked online at the company's website?"

"You probably could get the answer there," said our astute worker bee. And this is the precise moment when I went in for the hierarchy kill.

"You're not going to believe this," I lied. "I left my phone at home and otherwise I would check. Do you have a phone or a computer where I could find out?"

Young Damian looked around ever so carefully and said, "Well, I'm not supposed to do this but we can use my phone. Let's check the Newman's Own website to be certain."

Pulling out his fancy smartphone, Damian effortlessly navigated his way over to an FAQ chart on the Newman's Own website that indicated all types of popcorn that they produce were in fact gluten free.

"You're a life-saver," I said, giving him a soft punch on the shoulder. "With their mom away at a function, it's movie night with Dad and the requests for popcorn have been unrelenting. Thanks so much."

"No problem at all, sir," said Damian. "Better to be safe than sorry."

We grabbed a couple of boxes of popcorn, put them in the basket, and made our way to the checkout counter. While driving home,

I couldn't help but think what had just happened. Here was a young man, mid-twenties, risking his job—according to the bulletin in the stockroom—to ensure the customer's needs were being met. He knew the act of bringing out his mobile device was forbidden, yet he instinctively knew that it was necessary in order to fix the situation. He wasn't a tool and he wasn't conforming to the draconian hierarchy in place at the grocery store. Damian was empowering himself to bring about great results for the grocery store.

Later that night while the goats were enjoying their movie, I penned a very short letter addressed to The Management of the same grocery store and it read as follows:

Dear [store name] Management,

I visited your fine establishment on July 5 with my three young children. We were seeking gluten-free popcorn and ran into some difficulty understanding which brands were in fact gluten free.

One of your employees, Damian, was of immense help. I had forgotten my mobile phone at home and he was kind enough to use his own to check whether the popcorn we were looking to buy was gluten free or not. Were it not for him I would have had three disappointed children and a possibly unhealthy situation.

It's a great customer-service story and I felt compelled to write you this note. Please pass along my thanks to Damian.

Sincerely,
Dan Pontefract

The moral of the story is that hierarchy is everywhere; command-and-control leadership is still pervasive, yet employees are itching to break free from not being able to help, not being empowered to sort out problems on their own and not being able to proffer ideas that might actually improve the organization itself.

Don't worry—Damian is still gainfully employed at this grocery store. And I popped back into the stockroom one day and saw that the sign had been removed. The ultimate question remains: how'd we get so rigid?

MONARCHY AS A CATALYST?

Do we have the British monarchy to blame for the inception of today's somewhat pervasive corporate management system of command and control? Are the English responsible for the development of modern-day corporate hierarchies? Their football teams may not be historically good at penalty kicks in major competition (male or female) but they sure have done quite a number with hierarchy and iron-fist ruling.

One idea that supports the inception of the modern corporation dates back to 1600 when Queen Elizabeth I sanctioned the creation of the East India Trading Company (EIC) through a Royal Charter. This from the same family monarchy that also established the English Protestant church and instituted the role of supreme governor.

As history informs us, a group of merchants based in London got together and raised roughly £70,000 (£189 million in today's adjusted currency) to set up a trading company with the longish moniker "The Company of Merchants of London trading into the East Indies." One of the more important aspects of this endeavor was that the company and thus its charter members were granted exclusivity on all English trade east of the Cape of Good Hope. Queen Elizabeth I and the monarchy of the day had in fact set in motion the inception of the first corporate monopoly.

Adam Smith, author of *A Wealth of Nations*, wrote in 1776, "Monopoly of one kind or another, indeed, seems to be the sole engine of the mercantile system," which I believe was absolutely prophetic at the time.[2] Perhaps Smith was reviewing and thinking about the inception of the EIC from years past as evidence to his theory.

Those first EIC merchants had combined their original investment to launch the company. In what was obviously a Malcolm Gladwell "tipping point" of corporate history, they flipped the investment by turning it into company stock to create what is now known as the world's first commercial corporation involving stock.

Through its vast army of 250,000 personnel, expansive flotilla of shipping vessels, ruthless business contracts and rigid corporate structure, the EIC conquered India (and other parts of Asia) with its monopoly on trade for the ensuing decades. The EIC acted with jurisdictional powers of a government, yet it was a private company (and monopoly) authorized and commissioned by the monarchy. At the height of its dominance, the EIC ruled over 20 percent of the world's population.

The EIC actually got more powerful over time. Some seventy years after its inception in 1670, the English monarchy and those aligned to the executive hierarchy of the EIC itself were so infatuated with corporate megalomania due to its rich success, they lobbied King Charles II to bolster its control through a series of supplemental royal acts. The king of the day provisioned the EIC with additional powers, including the abilities to mint money, to start wars or make peace, to act as the law in cases of criminal or civil occurrence and to make autonomous decisions on the acquisition of new territories.

Perhaps therefore it was the EIC, through various acts of acceptance and empowerment by the English monarchy, that were factors in our current ways of corporate command-and-control rule. The East India Company itself thrived for 258 years before the British government reined in its rather cavalier corporation to gain full control of all its endeavors. The English monarchy, which sanctioned the EIC, was arguably the root model by which organizations, both at that time and thereafter, measured themselves against in terms of organizational structure. As the EIC grew more powerful, others saw a structure that could make them rich as well.

But what about the monarchy itself? And not simply the British monarchy, but any monarchy across the globe? Centuries ago, monarchies were rooted in the divine right of control and power. Kings, queens, and in other cases, emperors, often sought to preserve their power at whatever the cost. In the transition from the Roman Republic to the Roman Empire, for example, a line of successive emperors helped to consolidate and centralize power at the emperor's throne with veto powers within and away from the senate. Those ruling emperors instilled a hierarchical command-and-control behavior through all their actions to conquer land, and accumulate wealth. Julius Caesar, Octavian and Tiberius are but three examples from that era.

We need only review the etymology of "monarch" to see that it is derived from the Greek *monárkbēs*, which translates to sole ruler, chief or leader. If it helps, the English word "autocrat" comes from the Greek phrase "one who rules by himself." Things are really looking up, aren't they?

WAR GAMES AND THE INDUSTRIAL REVOLUTION

Although hierarchy in the organization may have taken counsel from past emperors and monarchies, there really were scant examples like the EIC for other organizations to effectively mimic. Tom Malone writes, "Prior to the 1800s, few organizations had developed the large, multilevel, centralized hierarchies with which we are familiar today."[3]

One facet of society did inform many leaders and that was the act of war. Throughout the dawn of time, war has sadly been a part of society. Sun Tzu, Napoleon, Arminius, Caesar, Attila the Hun, Edward I, Peter the Great and George Washington, among countless other military commanders, all shared a common bond—a defined (and hierarchical) chain of command was the manner in which they managed their people and troops. It's suggested by academics that the Romans were the ones who actually initiated the command-and-control system.[4] It was this chain of command model that may have helped form the basis of today's organizational structure and operation. Many organizations still to this day relay information, knowledge and intelligence no differently than did the Roman army. It goes up a silo and down a silo and orders are adhered to under the strictest of conditions.

Of course war provided other great examples throughout the first and second Industrial Revolution eras between 1750 and the onset of World War I in 1914. Society was evolving, as was war, and hierarchical managing was being perfected.

Crown corporations from Britain such as the London Company, Hudson Bay Company and Massachusetts Bay Company began to set up operations in North America. The companies were used as a way in which to export wealth back to investors and the monarchy, which had sanctioned them in the first place. As noted English philosopher Thomas Hobbes once wrote, "corporations are chips off the old block of sovereignty."[5]

Right around this period of time a shift in both demographics and life needs was also occurring. The city—an ever-growing consolidation of people—began to exert its influence on citizens through by-laws and other organizational models. Technology innovation also galvanized societal change. Historically, both rural and city folks produced most of their food, clothing and other goods to satisfy their life needs, as had been customary for centuries. The need for large factories or innovative machinery had not yet been felt. But change was in the wind.

As the Crown corporations grew in size and stature, the thirst for cheaper goods in larger quantities and quicker time-to-market delivery needed to be quenched. Many who might have worked on their own farm or in a rural village left to join the industrial revolution and big-city life. As a result, cities got bigger in both Europe and North America, and the population of rural towns and their farmers decreased dramatically.

Those individuals who drove the pioneering days of successful business dealings were not only successful at attaining large profits, they were the pioneers of organizational hierarchy as well. These entrepreneurs might well be called the "industrial capitalists." The insatiable appetite for quicker, better and quantitatively more goods meant there was a requirement for larger and more innovative factories. As the size of the workforce increased, so too did the size of the problems. Owners, entrepreneurs and leaders of said corporations had nowhere to turn to ensure speedy delivery of their goods and increasing profits. As a result, the implementation of warlike hierarchy came into existence to manage the explosive growth.

What it boiled down to was there was no blueprint to run an organization. There was no model to follow. When industrial revolution entrepreneurs—whether migrant Europeans and Crown corporations in North America, or native Europeans and Crown corporations in Europe itself—first set up their companies, they followed hierarchical command-and-control structures modeled after the military, monarchy or the state. It's not as though present-day Flat Army success stories like Zappos, WestJet Airlines or TELUS were around back then.

If command-and-control tactics worked for various armies to conquer land and people, and it worked for the monarchy and the state, why wouldn't it work for entrepreneurs within the industrial revolution to drive revenues, market share and profits? It makes sense for those trying to build businesses and make a buck or two to emulate something that worked very well. I don't knock them, but I do take umbrage with those today who continue to think it's the way in which to lead. It's one thing to study it but another to employ it.

THE DARK SIDE

If ever there was a time to introduce a George Lucas *Star Wars* reference, it's within our pursuit of hierarchy and command-and-control origins. Knowing full well that his movie series required villains, Lucas cleverly introduced a two-prong approach to evil: the master and the apprentice. Personally, I've always felt Frederick Taylor could play a great Emperor Palpatine in our pop culture analogy, but I wasn't around in the late 1900s to save him from the dark side. His management theory sidekick, Henri Fayol, could have played a great Darth Vader, too.

Taylor is historically known for devising *The Scientific Principles of Management,* which he penned in 1911. In layman's terms, this document was a way in which to systematically treat the management of employees as a scientific problem. The result was a doctrine outlining specific recommendations that tagged employees based on skill and knowledge, which then led to purported higher levels of productivity, efficiency and a reduction in effort.

On the other side of the Atlantic was Henri Fayol, born 1841 in Istanbul but known for his successful attempt at breaking down the functions of a management leader into distinct parts while working in France. He pioneered the definition of what he referred to as the "six functions" and "fourteen principles" of management. Fayol advocated organizations had a centralized hierarchical structure where management held distinct responsibilities and accountabilities over its employees. In Fayol's words, "To manage is to forecast, to plan, to organize, to command, to co-ordinate and control."[6]

To this day, this line continues to send shivers down my spine.

What Taylor and Fayol both devised in terms of their rigid management operating structures wasn't necessarily a bad thing, at least for that era. They devised such rigid structures because management was in need of being systematized due to developments in industrial technology. With the industrial revolution operating in hyperdrive, factories being built throughout the Western world, and an insatiable appetite for more revenues and more profits by entrepreneurs, Taylor and Fayol were merely trying to introduce process in a world devoid of efficiency. They were trying to enhance previous organizational models of the monarchy, the Church, the military and corporations before them to another level of efficiency.

Let's first discuss Taylor and then tackle Fayol.

Taylor dispelled the myth of his day wherein most entrepreneurs and leaders felt they could increase the productivity of workers by making them work harder, coupled with the addition of more overall resources. By way of his analysis and subsequent theorem, Taylor pioneered the concept of pitting job or role standards against actual employee performance. This involved finding the optimum way for a given job to be done and determining the expected "standard" times for elements of the job.

The theory behind Taylor's creed was to standardize work processes based on the study of tasks, the detailed training requirements of employees and specific motivation techniques for employees, furthered by an understanding of the time needed to complete tasks within those processes. Based on his observations, Taylor purported productivity and thus output would increase. His work ultimately suggested that the work between management and employees be delineated such that managers did the thinking and employees performed the specific tasks assigned.

Here is one of Taylor's aphorisms, taken from his doctrine *The Principles of Scientific Management*: "In the past, Man has been first. In the future, the system must be first."[7]

A 1979 book entitled *The Emerging Order; God in the Age of Scarcity* by Jeremy Rifkin and Ted Howard cements my point about Taylorism in one short quote: "The management becomes the mind and the workers the body."[8]

This is where Taylor lives on in many of our corporations today. There are so many organizational casualties in play as a result of Taylor's management theory, it's mind boggling. Think about it. Why do so many managers dismiss the psychological and emotional needs of employees, or neglect to take into consideration employee feedback and opinion? Why don't leaders consider the unique strengths of individuals, which combined can make for a better holistic team environment? How many leaders dismiss the birth of a new baby from a team member, acting as if it was irrelevant? How many use bonuses and increased pay as carrots and as the only motivational factors?

What if Taylorism was all a bad dream? What if it was a deceitful model from the onset with unsuspecting managers and leaders emulating it for years? What if it's the gold standard of all Ponzi schemes, the organizational command-and-control equivalent to Bernie Madoff's fraudulent behavior?

There have been a few scholars, pundits and observers since Taylor first issued his central thesis who have indicated his research was in fact flawed, unethical and just plain wrong. It was in 1898 when Taylor began work at Bethlehem Steel in Pennsylvania. Over the next three years he introduced time and motion studies as ways in which to accurately predict how to improve performance of employees. Some argue he actually fabricated the results.

According to *The New Yorker* magazine,

Whether he was also a shameless fraud is a matter of some debate, but not, it must be said, much: it's difficult to stage a debate when the preponderance of evidence falls to one side. In The Management Myth: Why the Experts Keep Getting It Wrong, *Matthew Stewart points out what Taylor's enemies and even some of his colleagues pointed out nearly a century ago: Taylor fudged his data, lied to his clients, and inflated the record of his success.*[9]

Furthermore, *The Atlantic* magazine provides us the following:

Yet even as Taylor's idea of management began to catch on, a number of flaws in his approach were evident. The first thing many observers noted about scientific management was that there was almost no science to it. The most significant variable in Taylor's pig iron calculation was the 40 percent "adjustment" he made in extrapolating from a fourteen-minute sample to a full workday. Why time a bunch of Hungarians down to the second if you're going to daub the results with such a great blob of fudge? When he was grilled before Congress on the matter, Taylor casually mentioned that in other experiments these "adjustments" ranged from 20 percent to 225 percent. He defended these unsightly "wags" (wild-ass guesses, in M.B.A.-speak) as the product of his "judgment" and "experience"—but, of course, the whole point of scientific management was to eliminate the reliance on such inscrutable variables.[10]

Are you beginning to connect the dots of the Taylorism puzzle?

Part of Taylor's legacy was separating the brain from the brawn, where management was the brain and factory workers the brawn. Decades later, many current managers continue to employ the theory and hierarchical practice from *The Principles of Scientific Management*, but no one really knows that the results he achieved were flawed. Thus, was Taylor's theorem outright command-and-control propaganda? Was the corporate world duped?

Sadly, Taylor might also be the inventor of workplace training. To ensure the job was being done in the most efficient manner, Taylor advocated for very specific education for each employee. It was Taylor's belief that workers, at least those on the shop floors where he performed his tests, needed adequate and mandatory role-based training. He alleged it was the responsibility of management to drive these training programs to each worker so they could perform their roles at the required levels of efficiency. Through the introduction of training requirements, Taylor believed work would then be standardized and the output could be consistently predicted. It still sounds an awful lot like hierarchy to me.

Interestingly, there was a precursor to Taylor's doctrine, entitled *Shop Management*, penned in 1903—some eight years earlier. One quotation sticks out for me as further evidence:

The full possibilities of this system will not have been realized until almost all of the machines in the shop are run by men who are of smaller capabilities and attainments, and who are therefore cheaper than those required under the old system.[11]

The best quotation from his most famous doctrine—*The Principles of Scientific Management*—helps to articulate how command-and-control is now rampant throughout corporations of today:

It is only through enforced standardization of methods, enforced adoption of the best implements and working conditions, and enforced cooperation that this faster work can be assured. And the duty of enforcing the adoption of standards and enforcing this cooperation rests with management.[12]

Therefore, it might be argued that the forefather of today's command-and-control and hierarchically closed organization was our Emperor Palpatine, Frederick Taylor. If Taylor was the father of micro-managing and systems-based work processes, Fayol was the architect of functional and centralized organizational structure. Fayol believed management was solely about planning, organizing, forecasting, coordinating, commanding and controlling. He's our Darth Vader.

For thirty years, Fayol worked as a managing director at Compagnie de Commentry-Fourchambeault-Decazeville, a very large mining shop in France. His claim to fame both in France and at the company was that his management practices resuscitated the company and ultimately turned it into one of France's most successful businesses.

In somewhat stark contrast to Taylor, however, was Fayol's management theorem. If Taylor was about a management approach delineating the worker from the manager, Fayol furthered the top-down approach where the division of management competence was bifurcated into business units, each with its own command-and-control mantra.

There was tension between the two management gurus as well. Take, for instance, what Fayol writes in *General and Industrial Management*, published in 1916:

Taylor's approach differs from the one we have outlined in that he examines the firm from the bottom up. He starts with the most elemental units of activity — the workers' actions — then studies the effects of their actions on productivity, devises new methods for making them more efficient, and applies what he learns at lower levels to the hierarchy.[13]

Fayol really drove the notion there are levels of leadership and production competence in an organization. He felt production workers were simply that. Deviation was not in the definition. If Taylor defined hierarchy through the separation of responsibility between the worker and the manager—with very definitive responsibilities for that same worker—Fayol effectively created the management hierarchy template. It seems like a perfect yin-yang structure for organizations to follow.

ORGANIZATIONAL LEARNED HELPLESSNESS

Did you know that in 1886, the U.S. court system recognized the corporation as a "natural person"? The fourteenth amendment to the U.S. Constitution states that "no state shall deprive any person of life, liberty or property." Perhaps it was used at the time to defend corporations and block any attempt at depriving them of outside or worker interference. To further the argument, President Rutherford B. Hayes said in 1876, "This is a government of the people, by the people, and for the people no longer. It is a government of corporations, by corporations, and for corporations."[14] I wonder if President Hayes was actually against hierarchy and greed, or perhaps he knew something we didn't?

Perhaps the way in which our organizations operate today is a result of something known as "learned helplessness." In 1967, Professor Martin Seligman of the University of Pennsylvania began experimenting on dogs to disprove B.F. Skinner's theory of behaviorism—experiments which were coupled with his interest in depression. So Seligman would experiment by testing the resiliency of a dog. After repeated attempts of administering inescapable pain and suffering—to see whether the dog would succumb to the pain—if given the chance to flee the dog would stay put. The poor dog, even if given the opportunity to leave the situation, would remain in the environment fully expecting that no matter what, the pain would continue at some point.

This condition would later be termed "learned helplessness." It is the act of being unable to remove yourself from a situation that is clearly unpleasant even though there are ample opportunities in which to do so. It's as though you're in the *Millennium Falcon* and being sucked in by the *Death Star*'s tractor beam—there's nothing you can do about it.

Further evidence for learned helplessness suggests depression may actually set in as well. Not surprising, if you're in a situation that seems inescapable and even if you could leave, you feel too paralyzed to do so, I'm pretty sure some form of depression might set in as well.

Which brings me to my point: maybe the concept of learned helplessness has enveloped our organizations. We've *learned* to become helpless. We've become numb to the bosses who don't care. We're ambivalent to leadership that is hierarchical and close-minded. We've become blind to exclusivity and too paralyzed to suggest being included. We won't flee the current situation because we don't believe things will be any better anywhere else.

We are a version of organizational learned helplessness.

Maybe organizations simply *are* tools. Maybe they're simply about making money or providing service or making products in the most efficient manner without regard for its people. Maybe there is no chance for humanity in the organization. Maybe the structure has been there for years because it is the most effective way in which to achieve the goal of dominance. Or perhaps it's the action of getting the most out of the tool that drives today's management practices. Perhaps some form of cognitive inertia or confirmation bias has set in on leaders and managers across many organizations, preventing them from thinking outside the proverbial hierarchal leadership box.

✳ ✳ ✳

My first job as an employee of an *organization* was for a fast-food chain. I was the fry guy.

When I was a 16-year-old, my dad felt it was time for me to learn about the real world. My parents, who emigrated from England when they turned 20 years old, were classic baby boomers. With nothing but a trunk full of clothes and personal items, and just a few dollars to their names, the Pontefracts arrived in Canada. In a few short years they had created a thriving engineering business. Pontefract Controls Limited was built from the ground up, based on the principle of hiring good people and then getting out of the way.

I never did understand why it and other incarnations were so successful when I was just a youth but one thing is for certain: I should have paid more attention. In retrospect, it had a lot to do with empowerment, respect and engagement.

Nevertheless, being a fry guy as a 16-year-old opened my eyes to not only the corporate world but also to my first experience with command and control. Maybe that's why my dad sent me off to that wretched palace of grease, grit and grime.

My first day was an eye-opener.

The manager invited me into the office at the rear of the cooking area for my inaugural performance review. I say "inaugural performance review" because after those first thirty minutes I was made to feel as low as humanly possible, obviously incapable of performing well enough to elevate my role to being the hamburger guy at any point.

The militaristic way in which I was indoctrinated to this management hierarchy was classic command-and-control brainwashing. I was led to believe it was a privilege to be hired. It was a privilege to be employed. It was a privilege to be sitting in that disgusting office redolent with damp mops, cleaning solutions and disinfectants. I was told to follow the training manual as written, to not ask questions, to not deviate from the script, and at all times to be scared for my job. Allegedly, there was always someone waiting to take my spot, so I should have felt lucky to have made it as far as the job itself.

What a way to start.

The manager of this fast-food restaurant was clearly a drone sent from the Capital of Corporate Control. I was not a member of the family. I was part of the system, sucked into the vortex of phantom military rule. Had I fallen out of line, I'd have been punished. Had I been mediocre, a chance for promotion to become the hamburger guy would never have surfaced. Had I obediently listened and done all that was asked of me over and above the pre-established performance expectation, I would have become like the manager. I would have become one of them.

I would simply have become a number.

But I didn't become a number, even at the tender age of 16, because I lasted only a month in that job. Although my dad was initially disappointed when I informed him of my decision, he fully understood why I made the choice that I did. Although successful, he was never a leader who invoked hierarchy for the sake of hierarchy. The good news, as he reiterated to me, was that I had this type of experience and that it would stick with me for the rest of my life.

Indeed, it has.

But what did I learn during my short stint at the fast-food restaurant?

Many for-profit organizations—but not all—are an economic orthodoxy of control, power and profit. People are secondary. The workers actually take away from the profit of the organization itself. I'm not against hierarchy. In fact, situational hierarchy is an absolute must for any organization no matter the size and I discuss this throughout Chapters 4, 5 and 6. What I am against, however, is outright and singular hierarchy cemented by command-and-control tactics with no regard for the employee and with no regard for the customer.

It's prudent to look to current noted management and leadership gurus for insights into corporate hierarchy and operations.

Henry Mintzberg has a brilliant mind, which he exercises in learning and research at McGill University. In his 1979 book *The Structuring of Organisations*, he suggests that an organization structure is "the sum total of the ways in which it divides its labor into distinct tasks and then achieves co-ordination between them. [It's a] framework for order and control, whereby the organisation's activities can be planned, organized, directed and monitored."[15]

Nobel Prize–winning American economist Milton Friedman suggests in his famous 1970 *New York Times* editorial entitled "The Social Responsibility of Business Is to Increase Its Profits" that

[a] corporate executive is an employee of the owners of the business. He has direct responsibility to his employers. That responsibility is to conduct the business in accordance with their desires, which generally will be to make as much money as possible while conforming to the basic rules of the society.[16]

And finally, Charles Handy in his 1993 book *Understanding Organizations* leaves us with this:

There is no logic which says that this horizontal decision sequence needs to be turned into a vertical ladder so that those who take the necessary earlier decisions are higher in the hierarchy than those who implement them. That is where history comes in, for those who got there first obviously set things up this way.[17]

We should all strive for a culture of borderless collegiality, and it is an aim of this book to show you how it can be done. It will leave a much more promising legacy than what our ancestors have passed down to us.

CHAPTER THREE

THE CONNECTED LEADER

Michael Bloomberg became the 108th mayor of New York City, first taking office in 2002. Prior to doing so, he was a successful businessman who founded (and still owns) the eponymously named Bloomberg L.P., a firm with over 15,000 employees in 192 locations that delivers data, news and analytics through technology. In 2012, *Forbes Magazine* estimated his net worth at $22 billion, putting him firmly in the top twenty richest people in the United States.

It's not his innovation, nor his wealth, nor his creative business and political mind that impress me the most (although how can you not be impressed by everything that Bloomberg has accomplished?).

What impresses me most is his instinctive level of sharing and his sense of collaboration.

Firstly, in 2011 alone, Bloomberg donated $311 million to 1,185 non-profit organizations which supported groups from the arts, public affairs and human services, among others. Since 2005, it's estimated that Bloomberg has philanthropically donated over $1 billion dollars to various groups in need. To me, that's an unbelievable amount of sharing. And to embolden the point, in a 2010 *Wall Street Journal* interview, Bloomberg was quoted as saying, "I am a big believer in giving it all away and have always said that the best financial planning ends with bouncing the check to the undertaker."[1] With a net worth of $22 billion, perhaps you might say, "Well, he should be donating to charities."

Perhaps, but it's my belief that Bloomberg was a holistic sharer before he was a philanthropist. He was a natural leader of collaboration before becoming a billionaire. He fully understood that working with people, not people working for him, was the motto that would not only make Bloomberg (and his business ventures) successful, but would also create a more engaged and connected workforce through the process. Incidentally, the word philanthropy is derived from the Greek *philanthropos* which hails from *philein*, which means, "to love" and *anthropos*, which means, "human being." To be a philanthropist, to be a connected leader, perhaps one has to have a love for human beings in the first place.

When Mayor Bloomberg did become the mayor of New York City in 2002, he brought this attitude of sharing, collaborating and loving human beings into the physical office itself.

New York Magazine, in September, 2010, released a photo of Mayor Bloomberg at the helm of City Hall that says a lot. It depicts forty of his lieutenants, direct reports and staff members. The important and magical point of the photo is Mayor Bloomberg himself. In what has to be one of the largest rooms at City Hall, Mayor Bloomberg situates himself in the middle of the room. Yes, this is his office and no, it wasn't done simply for the photo shoot.[2]

Charles Ommanney/Getty Images

Rather than holding court in an elegant and spacious office sequestered away from the hub of activity, where a parade of people would be constantly looking to book time with an executive assistant in order to meet with Mayor Bloomberg, he parks himself in the center of this cavernous room, open to anyone, in an effort to create a collaborative workplace alongside his love for human beings.

This is important to note on several levels:

- The visual cue signaled not only to his City Hall staff but to all citizens of New York is one of openness. There are no walls in his administration.
- The demonstration of approachability is non-hierarchical. One needs only to walk up to the mayor and discuss an idea or an issue or ask for advice.
- His leadership is connected, and his success, and that of the city, is based on being present and available to all.

Mayor Bloomberg has crossed what I call "the Connected Leader Chasm." He embodies openness and solicits it from his team.

But what the heck does being open actually mean?

OPEN SAYS ME

In *Open Leadership: How Social Technology Can Transform the Way You Lead*, author and founder of the Altimeter Group Charlene Li cleverly depicts being an open leader as "having the confidence and humility to give up the need to be in control while inspiring commitment from people to accomplish goals."[3] It's a bit of a paradox, but so too is her overarching point: organizations can be both open and closed. We might argue then that control can be given up but at the same time and in parallel, a level of direct control is applied to inspire people to actually do things. Perhaps it's an "open versus directive" argument. I know every time I open the fridge another voice directs me to close it, so I think we're onto something here.

Luciano Pilotti is currently professor of innovation management and corporate ecology at the University of Milan. Prior to holding this position he was professor of strategic management in the department of economics at the University of Padua in Italy. It's in this role that he studied the industrial districts in northeast Italy and published his findings in 1999.[4] This fascinating research documented the change in leadership and learning styles among local industrial firms (i.e., shoe manufacturers, knifemakers, etc.) in this region of Italy through three discrete eras: 1940–1960, 1970–1990 and 1998–2000. His findings and recommendations seem to pinpoint the first use of the term "open leadership" in a published journal.

Pilotti asserts the local businesses he studied were, between 1940 and 1960, very hierarchical, authoritative and internal-facing, and employed a learning-by-doing approach individualistically. There wasn't a lot of coordination happening between businesses, as the common thread among them was competition. Not out of the norm when you think about it, and certainly akin to how we're still operating today in many parts of the Western business world. Between 1970 and 1990, those same firms began creating alliances among one another codified by informal relationship building and a learning-by-cooperating attitude. Coordination began to increase among these competitors although there was still an element of competition. That is, the firms still competed against one another but they were more successful businesses by virtue of becoming more cooperative. By 1998, Pilotti suggested open networks, codified trust and a multifocal organization began to emerge among businesses in the same region. Coupled with a learning-by-learning-by-innovating mentality, Pilotti—in 1999, don't forget—classified this new evolutionary way in which to manage and operate as an open leadership model.

Through open leadership, the region and thus the economy has evolved into what Pilotti calls a "multilevel neural network," or MNN for short. He writes in the research report the following:

The MNN describes the reality of North East Italy well, particularly the quantity and the quality of the interrelations underlying the area's innovative potential [are] concerned. The system is multi-purpose and multi-centered, oriented to producing through processes of self-coordination and self-learning, through the relationships between agents, systems and institutions coordinated by specific institutions of interaction.[5]

Let us therefore suggest that to be open, to demonstrate open leadership, to act like an open leader, to be like Bloomberg or the

MNN of the industrial district of north-east Italy, one might employ the following definition:

> **Open leadership:** The act of engaging others to influence and execute a coordinated and harmonious conclusion.

An open leader doesn't merely ask for ideas, step aside, and watch things magically happen. She has the gumption to step aside, sure, but it's instilling the behaviors of being open, being coordinated and being harmonious through the process of getting stuff done that defines open leadership. It is she who must create the environment that enables—like Pilotti's industrial region—open leadership to surface inside a team or organization. It is she who must demonstrate humility and vulnerability, and be at the center and visible—as Mayor Bloomberg does.

With our definition of an open leader on the table, there is now a chasm for leaders to cross. Let's explore.

THE CONNECTED LEADER CHASM

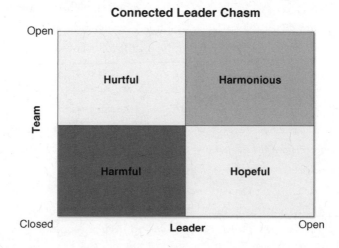

Connected Leader Chasm

Quite simply, through the act of situating himself in the middle of what is colloquially known at City Hall as "the bullpen," Mayor Bloomberg has opened both himself and his team up to a more harmonious way in which to conduct business. That business just happens to be New York City, comprising over 8 million inhabitants. When one is a harmonious, connected leader, one has created a situation whereby both the team and the leader are as open as possible to the execution of business tasks, actions and objectives. In an environment where the mundane day-to-day tasks are also conducted in this open manner, there is harmony between all parties regardless of rank. Openness, both as a quality of the leader and an expectation of the team, fosters a harmonious relationship among all parties. It's arguably a step in the right direction towards higher levels of engagement, productivity and business results. A harmonious leader, ergo, connects with his or her team, parlays the culture as one that can only be successful if both parties are united, equal in nature and convicted to openness. It is this harmonious leader that we are wishing everyone in the organization to become if we agree that leadership is for all.

A.G. Lafley also comes to mind. The name may not ring a bell, but I can assure you, his story of being a harmonious leader is one about openness and collaboration. Between 2000 and 2010, Mr. Lafley was the highly successful president and CEO of Procter & Gamble (P&G)—the personal care, food and cleaning products companies with over $80 billion in revenue and over 125,000 employees worldwide. Through his decade at the helm he helped to double total sales and quadruple profits while increasing P&G's market value by over $100 billion. Furthermore, he helped grow the number of billion-dollar brands at P&G—such as Gillette, Pampers and Tide—from ten to twenty-four. How'd he do it? In his book *The Game Changer: How Every Leader Can Drive Everyday Innovation*, co-written with thought leader Ram Charan, Lafley refers to the unique combination of openness and ideas:

Open architecture is the organizing principle that enables a business and its people to open themselves up to get ideas from anywhere at any time. P&G collaborates with anybody, anywhere, anytime. P&G likes unusual suspects. It will even compete with a company on one side of the street, and cooperate with it on the other. In an open innovation system, anything out there is fair game, even if competitors are sitting on it. And that's fine with both partners because it works.[6]

Does this sound a bit like the example that Luciano Pilotti wrote about?

At P&G, Lafley opened up everything. He wanted his leaders to be more collaborative and, equally importantly, he wanted his employees to be open. When that occurred, magic happened. He branded this open architecture at P&G "Connect and Develop," or C&D for short. It was an open-leadership framework that ran across all employees, regardless of title, and it not only drove revenue and profitability, but also grew employee engagement.

Lafley and Charan further state:

The single characteristic of C&D is the willingness of all people at P&G to be psychologically open and to seriously consider new ideas, whatever the source, thus building a truly open, truly global innovation network that can link up—and be first in line—with the most interesting thinkers and the best products to "reapply with pride."[7]

This is another excellent example of how a CEO crossed the Connected Leader Chasm and inculcated a harmonious environment by instituting a culture of open leaders and employees.

FALLING INTO THE CHASM

On the opposite side of our classic 2 × 2 matrix, we have the story of a leader who created a harmful environment—a leader characterized by being unconnected and closed to any notions of open dialogue, open team meetings, open initiatives, open feedback or generally open settings. As a consequence, the vitriolic nature of such a leader's closed style naturally shuts a team down, closes them off from even wanting to try anymore, and thus the team too becomes closed. Ambivalence swarms over the team like grizzlies to the salmon run; close-mindedness and a sense that *nothing is ever going to change* envelop all members. When both the leader and the team are closed, the situation is dire; it is as harmful as it is mind numbing. It's organizational dysmorphia. If you're in this situation today and you're an employee, find another position in another team or another company quickly.

Our example is the rather short CEO reign of Leo Apotheker at Hewlett Packard (HP). In late 2010, Mr. Apotheker took over as CEO of HP from Mark Hurd after his own somewhat acrimonious departure. Apotheker's work was cut out for him from day one, with employee engagement and trust issues abounding, a stock price that had lost significant value in the previous and current year, and business units operating in alleged isolation from one another. Instead of repairing the culture and the overall engagement of the organization, instead of pushing hard to create a level of openness among leaders and employees to reach the harmonious level of the Connected Leader Chasm from day one, Apotheker's choice of action in his first six months was to make several decisions (with HP board approval mind you) that further rocked the employee population in addition to Wall Street analysts:

- After seven weeks in the market, the HP tablet (TouchPad) was mothballed after millions had been spent on research and development.
- HP announced it was purchasing Autonomy, an enterprise software search company, a business foreign to HP (and which subsequently fell into regulatory issues in late 2012, which HP referred to as "serious accounting improprieties").
- HP announced that it was contemplating spinning off and selling the personal computer business division (a $41-billion component of HP revenues)—the core business that many people believed HP to be actually good at.
- webOS (a popular operating system tied to Palm) was also announced as being discontinued.

Leo's tenure at HP came to a crashing halt ten months later in September 2011, when executive chairman Ray Lane announced via a press release and conference call that Apotheker was being replaced by former eBay CEO Meg Whitman. In the conference call to announce Apotheker's removal and Whitman's arrival, Lane—perhaps unknowingly—provided us with insight into a situation we might deem harmful in terms of the Connected Leader Chasm:

It became increasingly clear that we needed new leadership to focus on operating our business more effectively to meet the challenges of today's environment. Specifically, the board believes that the job of our CEO requires additional attributes to successfully execute in the company's strategic evolution.[8]

Did those challenges include isolation, ambivalence and a lack of collaboration among HP employees? Were HP leaders, including Apotheker, closed off from the rest of the organization? Were those leaders potentially blind to the level of employee disengagement, when employees might have actually helped the company turn things positive if they were being included and open themselves? Was culture being ignored in favor of a close-minded leadership style aimed at introducing big-splash turnarounds?

In the conference call, Lane went deeper to illustrate more of our closed-team and closed-leader harmful example:

This [HP] is a company that requires an executive team to be on the same page. I would spend time here or at board meetings or whatever the occasion was and we didn't see an executive team working on the same page or working together. [Apotheker] lacked the ability to get down deep into the businesses and understand the dynamics that were going on in the businesses, and that could land us on a quarter ahead of expectations.[9]

I don't fault Apotheker completely, but he certainly took the fall for what was a very harmful scenario. A combination of closed leaders and closed team members will never serve you well in the long run.

All is not lost, though. There is an opportunity for raising *eudaimonia*—the flourishing of human spirit—should those in the organization subscribe to it. A leader can change and begin the connected leader quest by moving step-by-step toward open leadership.

One avenue to contemplate, as a reader and a budding connected leader at least, is why a traditional leader might encourage the team members to be open among themselves only to personally embody the traits of being a closed leader. This leader suggests open behavior but does not model this same behavior. Let's label this type of individual a "hurtful leader," someone who allows the team to openly dialogue, converse and ideate among themselves—exhibiting a lack of micro-management—while shutting their office door (physically and virtually) and mandating team members to book an appointment to chat, discuss or vent.

The hurt comes from the fact that there are two sets of rules: the group that is allowed to openly work with one another, and the one that has to deal with the leader who still utilizes command-and-control or, at a minimum, closed-door practices, to conduct the team operations itself. The methods of a hurtful leader are antithetical, ridiculous and, well, hurtful. Things may get done, but the practice may also create a hero complex within the organization akin to Thomas Carlyle's 1840s notion called the "great man theory."[10]

FROM THE HARMFUL TO THE HOPEFUL

An Apple Story

It may seem disrespectful and even wrong given Apple was the most valuable company in history, valued at over $620 billion as of August 2012, but former legendary CEO Steve Jobs might serve as an example of our hurtful leader. Accolades envelop Jobs like snow across the Canadian prairies in January. He was innovative, relentless, futuristic, charismatic and successful. Coupled with his brilliance that was acknowledged by the mainstream, however, was a dark side—a leader extremely closed to mistakes and failures, who would fly into (documented) fits of rage, have tyrannical outbursts, and berate Apple staff in public. He even expressed an arrogant contempt for other people's ideas or celebrated them as his own.

He expected his teams and people to be collaborative, to work together and to execute on the agreed-upon vision no matter the price to pay. But as a leader he was someone who often closed himself off from the rest of the organization through his actions and behaviors. It wasn't a consistent leadership style, either.

In 2010 and 2011, Adam Lashinsky spent time researching, discovering and talking to former Apple employees and those closely associated to Apple, penning an article for *Fortune* magazine entitled "Inside Apple."[11] In the article, he portrays Jobs as rigid and very selective with regards to those he allowed into his inner circle. Lashinsky interviewed a recruiting headhunter who works with Apple, who states, "People join and stay because they believe in the mission of the company, even if they aren't personally happy." Lashinsky also spoke with former designer Andrew Borovsky, who says, "At Apple you work on Apple products. If you're a diehard Apple geek, it's magical. But it's also a really tough place to work." A product management executive who wished to remain anonymous reflects on Jobs and the company by suggesting, "Apple's attitude is, 'You have the privilege of working for the company that's making the fucking coolest products in the world. Shut up and do your job, and you might get to stay.'"

Is Apple successful? Obviously it is. Was Jobs one of the most brilliant minds to lead not just one, but two, successful companies? Yes, if you factor in Pixar, the animation movie studio that brought the world *Cars*, *Wall-E* and *Finding Nemo*. The paradox of course is that attrition is low at Apple, but it is the world's most valuable company, millions of consumers use its products and Jobs is hailed as a leadership icon. It's my humble opinion, however, that Apple might be even greater than it is today if Jobs had employed a more collaborative leadership model not only with those within his inner circle—which he did exquisitely—but also with his entire Apple employee community. Perhaps his successor, Tim Cook, can succeed where Jobs failed, as a defining example of a harmonious leader for all of Apple to benefit from.

The slightly more positive and productive situation occurs when the leader is open but the team hasn't yet caught up to the leader. This leader is our hopeful leader. This state of affairs normally occurs when the leader is new and joining a team that has been shackled by the draconian ways of its former leader, or the leader is driving an open bus but no one wants to get on it because they don't know how. Either way, the leader is in a bit of a conundrum; he may be open, yet the team has no idea of how to get to that level of openness, or (and rather unfortunately) the team is so jaded, perplexed and perhaps scared that they don't have the wherewithal with which to cross the Connected Leader Chasm. Therein lies the opportunity, however. This is the hopeful leader—an individual holding more promise certainly than the hurtful leader, but light-years ahead of the harmful leader. This is a leader who may not yet have the trust, the buy-in or the reciprocity of the team, but a leader who already demonstrates many elements of being a connected leader. But the Holy Grail of being a harmonious leader has yet to be attained.

A JOHNSON & JOHNSON STORY

Johnson & Johnson may teach us something about hopeful leaders. The world-renowned healthcare-products company generating $65 billion in revenue in over sixty countries employs roughly 120,000 employees worldwide and certainly promotes an open environment. For over sixty years, the Johnson & Johnson credo has reflected customer and supplier relationships and promises, involvement with community, the importance of stockholders and of course, the significant connections the company creates for its employees. A snippet off its website outlining the credo specific to Johnson & Johnson employees reads as follows:

We are responsible to our employees, the men and women who work with us throughout the world. Everyone must be considered as an individual. We must respect their dignity and recognize their merit. They must have a sense of security in their jobs. Compensation must be fair and adequate, and working conditions clean, orderly and safe. We must be mindful of ways to help our employees fulfill their family responsibilities. Employees must feel free to make suggestions and complaints. There must be equal opportunity for employment, development and advancement for those qualified. We must provide competent management, and their actions must be just and ethical.[12]

This could be construed as employee-retention-and-attraction poetry.

Upon becoming just the seventh CEO in Johnson & Johnson's 125-year history, Alex Gorsky said, "I am resolute in my determination to keep Our Credo as the foundation of Johnson & Johnson. It will remain at the core of what drives our actions."[13]

According to *Fortune* magazine in 2011, Johnson & Johnson ranked seventeenth among the most-admired global organizations, and it overtly paints employee engagement (through the credo) as an important and critical piece to the success of the company.[14] Its credo acts as a manifesto that ensures current and future employees see the connection between leadership, engagement and business results. It is backed by its CEO, and previous CEOs, and permeates the operational and human capital processes and practices.

But even at a successful company like Johnson & Johnson, which publicly professes such passion with respect to employee engagement, a professional paradox exists. Charles Corace, former director of credo and workplace engagement at Johnson & Johnson, writes, "Our company mirrors the vast majority of corporations today. The relationship of actively engaged to actively disengaged employees is about a three-to-one relationship and that the vast majority of employees are somewhere in the middle."[15]

Whether utilizing Gallup's research, or that of AON Hewitt (another global human capital consulting firm) that states overall employee engagement has slipped to 56 percent, or that of BlessingWhite, which indicates fewer than one in three is engaged and nearly one in five is actively disengaged, the findings at Johnson & Johnson mirror what is actually occurring in most organizations today.[16] There is hope—but not harmony.

A professional paradox is at play. The engaged leader is a rare sighting. Lip service is being provided to the important element of leadership be

it at Johnson & Johnson or countless other workplaces. For any organization, one might argue leaders are being equipped to maintain the
roughly 30 percent that are engaged, but it's possible they don't possess
the right tools in their bag of tricks to help sway the other 70 percent
of the employees in the organization to in fact become engaged. There
is hope—but not harmony.

Corace, who indicates that the middle 50 percent in the organization who are not engaged should be termed the "Quiet Majority," goes
further within his article to state that

*often much of the engagement work focuses on the supervisory issues, because this is often
the path of least resistance and one where tangible progress can be measured. If we are to
make significant gains in winning over the 'Quiet Majority,' then our plans need to include
a short- and long-term strategy for addressing organizational culture.*[17]

I could not agree more. There is a definitive link between employee
engagement and an open culture; but culture is built from within and it
pervades a company through leaders that possess the right mindset and
actions aimed at involving the employee in the health and in the operation
of the organization itself.

What good is being on the most-admired-company list at *Fortune* if
70 percent of your organization isn't engaged? This conundrum is not
a problem that belongs solely to Johnson & Johnson; this is a pervasive
issue affecting organizations globally. The good news is there is hope
across Johnson & Johnson (and similar organizations), and with the right
attitude and execution, many more organizations can join the harmonious
level of the Connected Leader Chasm.

We need leaders of today to be more like the harmonious leadership
example of Mayor Bloomberg in his New York City office setup and less
like Leo Apotheker during his short reign at HP. Once a leader is willing
to demonstrate, if not already demonstrating, harmonious leadership
behavior where both she and the team are prepared to operate in a more
open manner, then graduation day is near and we can shift over to the
Flat Army philosophy and rollout. Drum roll, please.

THE FLAT ARMY PHILOSOPHY

Flat Army Philosophy

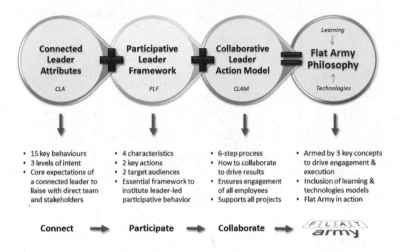

The thesis of this book is based on the graphic above. (I don't recommend you stop reading the book altogether here, but it does provide a nice cheat sheet should you wish to pass the exam.) Leaders invoking Flat Army ideas and aiming to eradicate the shenanigans outlined in Chapter 2, as well as elements of general command-and-control practices found in organizations today, ought to pay particular attention to what this graphic is intended to convey. Let's look at the key elements:

- **Connected Leader Attributes (CLAs):** The fifteen key behaviors that make up a connected leader divided into three key levels: Becoming, Being and Beyond.
- **Participative Leader Framework (PLF):** A handy guide that depicts the collaborative attributes and actions leaders must take with respect to two different target audiences, which ensures leaders know how to collaborate with people in any given situation.

- **Collaborative Leader Action Model (CLAM):** The six collaborative steps a leader should employ every day to ensure their team or organization is connected and working harmoniously—ensuring they have crossed the Connected Leader Chasm.
- **Pervasive Learning and Collaboration Technologies:** We learn each and every day, yet there is a rampant myth embedded in our organizations that we learn solely in a classroom and social tools don't help leaders. Learning is part formal, part informal and part social—as should be our leadership style—and the use of this new model coupled with collaboration technologies will be explored.

Each of the five elements outlined above, has a dedicated chapter (the CLAs are actually broken down into three chapters) and each provides a very thorough definition including examples and how-tos. To whet your appetite, a brief description of the elements appears below. Feel free to skip ahead if you are the competitive sort and need to beat your colleagues to finish the book first.

THE CONNECTED LEADER ATTRIBUTES (CLA)

The Italian town of Pisa is an interesting place full of contrasts. The tower, of course, has been leaning among a sea of straight buildings in the Piazza del Duomo that includes tall Tuscan evergreens as well as columns that have adorned the Duomo, Baptistery and Campo Santo for several hundred years.

Fine art in the various buildings is in stark contrast to a gaggle of locals trying to make a buck by hocking souvenir trinkets of miniature Leaning Tower of Pisa replicas, holy rosaries, fake leather bags and sunglasses. It really is beauty and the beast.

Tourists themselves parade mightily with cameras in hand among the old Romanesque walls gazing at this architectural wonderment, whereas local Italians look rather ambivalently at the surroundings, barely noticing the beatific stone marvels nestled among them.

It's this recognition of contrast in Pisa where we must take pause and articulate a set of leadership attributes that embody contrast. The Connected Leader Attributes necessary to deploy the concepts and ideas of Flat Army across a team and organization must invoke contrast; where there is rigidity there must be flexibility, and where there is give there must be take. Where there is the need to drive business there is the need to understand and work with people.

The Connected Leader Attributes can be thought of as the behaviors that make up an individual wishing to invoke Flat Army ideas in their team or organization. For a leader to be truly connected with his or her team and organization, these fifteen attributes should be worked on over time. It is impossible to become an expert in each within a short period of time. But, in order to reach the level of a harmonious leader, where both the leader and the team are as open as possible and actions are effortlessly worked on in a collaborative manner, time must nonetheless be spent improving those attributes that are at a deficit.

The CLAs are perhaps groundbreaking for a connected leader, but should not be ground *braking*. We've spent far too long putting the brakes on leadership transformation in our organizations. Connected Leaders need to break new ground—not continue to brake on the same ground that has brought us years of hierarchy, hebetude and control. Lowe's chairman and CEO Robert Niblock says in *T+D Magazine*, "To be successful, we must win trust with our customers, and that means enabling and empowering our employees to earn that trust. To make that happen, we must ensure that our management team has every-thing it needs to earn the trust of employees."[18] In other words, or at least in my words, to earn the trust of customers we need to set up a leadership paradigm that ensures employees trust the organization. For employees to trust the organization, and its leaders, the Connected Leader Attributes are the strands of DNA that just might allow that to happen.

They are a set of contrasts like the Piazza del Duomo in Pisa, Italy full of business exactitude and unconditional humanity.

THE THREE BE'S OF GENERAL SHERMAN

Mark Ralston/AFP/Getty Images

Giant sequoias are some of nature's finest gifts. In terms of volume, they are the world's largest trees and the biggest is none other than 2,300-year-old General Sherman, a tree weighing over 5,400 metric tons, spanning 83 meters in height and incorporating 1,486 cubic meters in volume. Its roots reach out some 60 meters, spreading out across roughly four square acres of the Sierra Nevada, California land it inhabits in beautiful Sequoia National Park.

Leaders could learn a lesson from our friend General Sherman. In fact, a connected leader might try to emulate this magnificent natural spectacle: To be such a giving tree, full of life and offering much to those in the vicinity, General Sherman is made up of three key elements: the roots, the trunk and the branches. The roots are the foundation required by General Sherman to grow and to live. Without the roots, it would stagnate, begin to decay, and possibly fall victim to various obstacles. The trunk provides the strength with which to push upwards and outwards. The branches are its real beauty; the green foliage that flows from its trunk provides shade and nutrients, and therefore life, to others.

Let us now try to utilize General Sherman as a model and classify the Connected Leader Attributes (CLAs) into three distinct categories:

- Becoming
- Being
- Beyond

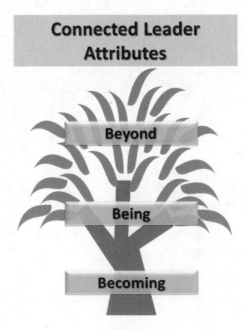

Becoming attributes are the five default leadership behaviors that set the tone for acting as a connected leader. Think of these as the attributes that must be in place before a leader can even begin thinking about leading in a connected and Flat Army manner. They are non-negotiable yet harmonious attributes that ensure a top-down, command-and-control leadership style isn't utilized as the default way in which to lead. The *becoming* attributes drive relationship building and understanding between a leader and her team, regardless of its size. These attributes are the foundation; without them, no leader is ever able to connect with their team or organization. Without them, it is also difficult to nurture either the *being* or *beyond* attributes. The *becoming* attributes provide the nutrients and foundation that help one to grow and to reach new heights. Without these, stunted growth is assured and a mediocre, if not futile, leadership model manifests. *Becoming* attributes are the installation of humanity into a leader.

Therefore, the *becoming* attributes are like the roots of General Sherman.

Becoming a connected leader attributes

- trusting
- involving
- empathizing
- developing
- communicating

Being attributes are the five leadership behaviors that ensure the leader can effectively work with the team to accomplish goals in a manner that is precise yet coupled with collective participation. These behaviors form a way in which the leader can also create a fun and creative environment in which to operate. Through nurturing people (and themselves), as General Sherman does with its core, leaders turn ideas into action. It is the ability to help execute various objectives along the chosen path, and it comes with a responsibility to ensure the leader continues to be open and harmonious yet capable of getting things done. It is the difference between becoming a connected leader in a Flat Army to actually being one.

Being a connected leader attributes

- analyzing
- deciding
- delivering
- cooperating
- clowning

Beyond attributes are the five leadership behaviors that continue a process of transformation in the connected leader, to the point where the leader becomes a rare specimen by today's standards: someone who is capable of not only inclusion (becoming) and open execution (being), but one who is magnanimous and panoptic. Simply put, this final stage ensures a leader is seeing the big picture in his team, goals and objectives, both for today and the future. It is the ability to nurture the team to greater heights coupled with an acknowledgment that we grow through one another's development. The *beyond* attributes are like the branches and foliage of General Sherman. By moving beyond, the connected leader shifts to a third level that drives the entire team or organization to incredible new heights. It is the crown of healthy greenery and foliage that completes the analogy of the connected leader attributes trilogy with General Sherman.

Beyond a connected leader attributes

- coaching
- measuring
- adapting
- exploring
- bettering

These fifteen attributes make up the DNA of a connected leader; without them, it's unlikely that one can be truly collaborative or connected or even successful in one's organization.

THE PARTICIPATIVE LEADER FRAMEWORK

Each and every day, a leader should be interacting with his team. Not for the sake of collaborating, but to drive business results and organizational engagement. Remember, the two go hand in hand and cannot be separated. I liken collaboration and thus the Participative Leader Framework to the Arc de Triomphe in Paris, France.

Commissioned in 1806 and connecting twelve different streets at what is arguably the epicenter of Paris—originally called Place de l'Etoile and now Place Charles de Gaulle—feeding the renowned shopping mecca of les Champs d'Elysse—the Arc de Triomphe is in fact a metaphor for Flat Army and particularly the Participative Leader Framework. The monument itself is situated on a 45-meter by 22-meter block that you can only reach on foot via an underground tunnel. Unless you're a nutty tourist wishing to risk your life through an entertaining real-world demonstration of the classic video game *Frogger*, the tunnel is the only way in which to observe its architectural marvel and historical significance.

To Parisians, the Arc is not only a patriotic jewel, it is the aortic valve of commuting. The City of Light draws its luminescence from its ability to move people across town, and the Arc pumps vehicles through Paris like blood through a body. Cars, buses, trucks, motorcycles and even cyclists act in a harmonious manner, working together to collectively achieve individual goals among the greater and common actions of getting people from point A to point B. As a vehicle or bicycle approaches the world's largest roundabout, it does so with its driver knowing full well that what is about to happen—whether she accomplishes her goal of proceeding successfully in her intended direction—is limited or enhanced by the participative efforts of strangers.

As you can gather from the photo on the next page, there is an onslaught of vehicles and bicycles that eddy and swerve into the manic roundabout at all times of the day and night. Chaos ensues unless collaborative order is also occurring in parallel. Drivers must work together, en masse, in order for the system to work. If one lunatic decides to drive from one intersecting street to

Boris Horvat/AFP/Getty Images

another without so much as looking left or right, or giving way to oncoming traffic, the system breaks down and inevitably a crash takes place. If only one driver becomes paralyzed by fear and maroons his vehicle in the middle of the road, drivers are forced to go around the stalled bucket of metal, further exacerbating a breakdown in the system. If two vehicles compete for the same space without regard for one another's rights, undoubtedly rage erupts and more importantly, an accident occurs, slowing everyone else down who is trying to get to their destination. If that slower, unprotected cyclist isn't allowed into the circle or isn't provided the same equal opportunity to reach her destination, then hierarchy has swallowed intention.

To achieve success, drivers of any vehicle must invoke what is referred to as "priority right." As a vehicle approaches the Arc from one of the feeder streets, it approaches somewhat slowly to ensure a safe passage into the roundabout itself. Somewhat illogically to North Americans, drivers of vehicles already in the giant-sized roundabout pause to allow the new entrant into the circle, who continues on his way towards his exit street. This action seems rather simple, but when factoring in the elements of speed and volume of vehicles, and the fact drivers have no uniformly set direction—remember, there are twelve streets and thus eleven options to exit from the Arc if you've already entered it—you have to begin asking yourself why there are not more accidents. On occasion I simply sit on the edge of the roundabout staring intently to observe the patterns and behaviors. In my roughly six hours over ten years of observing the famed roundabout at the Arc de Triomphe, I've witnessed only one accident.

The Arc de Triomphe is a perfect metaphor for the Participative Leader Framework. It's a circular structure with many moving parts. It contains individual and collective goals. It requires the use of strategy backed with compassion. It is as fast as it is slow. It mixes beauty with heightened anticipation of accomplishment. It is not the hierarchy of closed leadership we see so often in today's organizations. You must consume knowledge and also contribute knowledge back to the grid. You may be with or see people you know, but often you are working with others you don't know to achieve the goal of getting to your destination. There must be care and authenticity when driving, but so too there must be reciprocity and education. There may be accidents and mistakes, but it's how you learn from them (with each other) that allows you to travel again. These are the hallmarks of the Participative Leader Framework. (You can read more about the PLF in Chapter 7.)

THE COLLABORATIVE LEADER ACTION MODEL

Before you begin making fun of me about my use of an acronym that actually spells CLAM, did you know that a clam fished out of the ocean in 2007 has been identified as the oldest extant animal? British scientist Dr. Alan Wanamaker and his team laid claim to a 405-year-old clam they actually named Ming after the Chinese dynasty. It's too bad that our CLAM—Collaborative Leader Action Model—isn't 405 years old, as we might have fewer hierarchical problems in our organizations. But I digress.

The Collaborative Leader Action Model at its root is the default way leaders should be interacting with employees, teams, partners and customers on a daily basis. It aligns heterarchy with situational hierarchy. It embeds the CLA and the PLF into the mix. There are six stages to the CLAM denoted by verbs that start with the letter C. These six Cs are the default yet systematic steps leaders of any ilk or level should employ to ensure stakeholders are involved in any type of action or work flow.

The stages are depicted by the following Cs:

- connect
- consider
- communicate
- create
- confirm
- congratulate

More details on the CLAM are found in Chapter 8. Don't be scared; this clam won't snap shut on your finger.

THE PERVASIVE LEARNING AND COLLABORATION TECHNOLOGIES MODELS

I like to think of myself as both a Socratic learner and a social autodidact. Plain English? I like to learn by challenging myself and the status quo through the act of learning individually and with others. I do it in person and online, through formal, informal or social means. In other words, I don't care how I learn, so long as I am learning.

This brings us to the important element of the Pervasive Learning and Collaboration Technologies models. No matter if you're in a classroom, or if you're with people, or if you're by yourself, or if you're rallying the troops, *technology and learning really have become inseparable.* Purists may scoff at my argument, and there are many more who might clamor for the old days when learning was delivered by a sage on a stage, or leadership was transmitted from an ivory-tower office. Those days are quickly disappearing. Yet the establishment, the regime of education institutions and classic command-and-control organizations, continues its nefarious work, and we fail to recognize what really is going on.

As Internet Time Alliance chair Harold Jarche professes, "Work is learning and learning is the work."[19] Learning is also about leadership.

Leadership, as we're exploring, has to become more open; it has to be a part of the learning process as well. To become more open and thus democratic, the link between learning, leadership and technology must be understood. An engaged organization is one that shares, one that feels part of the process, one that is reciprocal. The final barrier to overcome in our Flat Army model must be defining how learning and technology can assist the connected leader frameworks we have already agreed upon.

Here's something to whet your appetite before you reach Chapters 9 and 10, which focus on pervasive learning and collaboration technologies. Think of a peanut butter and jam sandwich for a moment. One slice of bread can represent the Connected Leader Attributes and the other is the Participative Leader Framework. The peanut butter is analogous to the Connected Leader Action Model—it sticks the entire thing together—but the sweet stuff, the concluding ingredient to complete the sandwich, is the Pervasive Learning and Collaboration Technologies model.

✻   ✻   ✻

Remember, the word philanthropy is derived from the Greek *philanthropos*, which, as we discovered, means "to love." *Anthropos* can be translated as "human being"; thus, our goal through the entirety of this book—to help you become a connected leader and harmonious leader, to be like Mayor Bloomberg in his New York City office—is to prove we all can not only be collaborative, connected and participative, but also that we have a love for humans.

If all else fails, hearken back to these sage words from Pablo Picasso: "I am always doing that which I cannot do, in order that I may learn how to do it."

Let's start learning about something we're not doing in order to do it. Let's next learn about the connected leader through a journey of *becoming, being* and *going beyond*.

CHAPTER FOUR

BECOMING A CONNECTED LEADER

Zenger Folkman, a leadership development consultancy, conducted a study of 2,800 leaders in a very large financial services company.[1] The authors of the study found the commitment level and overall engagement of employees was 92 percent higher when employees were led by leaders judged by employees of the organization to be effective. Employees at the low end of the engagement scale found their leaders at the bottom tenth percentile of leadership effectiveness. The brilliance of the research came from the measure of effectiveness. Colleagues of leaders were responsible for determining— through 360 reviews, focus groups and the like—whether or not leaders were actually being effective as a result of daily interactions, responsibilities and observations. Imagine what the employees would have said for those at the bottom end of the percentile spectrum? I shudder to think.

What did I gather from the research? Leadership is not a whisper. It is not whimsical. To become a connected leader, someone operating in the harmonious zone, there are five attributes in particular that leaders might want to start shouting in unison: build trust, involvement and empathy, and develop and communicate. These attributes are the foundation of our Flat Army concept.

Take, for example the case of Bill Sullivan, CEO of Agilent Technologies, a $5-billion-plus company of close to 20,000 employees. Bill wanted a leadership framework for the organization to ensure clarity and consistency of behaviors. A framework was developed for all employees— and at a level that everyone would understand and be able to embrace, not just the most senior leaders. It was developed to "create a culture of people who thrive in a high performance, results-oriented company based on a foundation of uncompromising integrity, speed and innovation."[2] His is not a leadership style of whispering; it is a demonstrable example of already *becoming* a connected leader. Bill is a CEO of the people, teaching in their internal leadership development business simulation program. Furthermore, to ensure organizational capabilities and to build teams, Bill insists that collaboration be rampant throughout Agilent and that open and transparent communication be applied at all times.

As a result of Bill's leadership, the company has seen the following outcomes:

- 20-percent operating profit (highest in Agilent's history)
- highest employee leadership survey scores ever
- number-one customer satisfaction and loyalty score
- total Shareholder Return now greater than S&P 500 for healthcare, industrial and IT indices

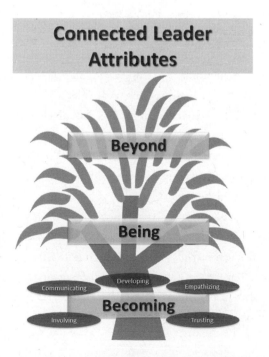

Bill exemplifies these traits, and talking about him is a perfect segue to explore the five *becoming* connected leader attributes. These first five *becoming* attributes are crucial. Far too often I have witnessed leaders skipping past the *becoming* stage only to see it backfire through disengagement, apathy and retention risks. Start here and you are bound to set foot on the right Flat Army path.

TRUSTING

In the book *Start with Why: How Great Leaders Inspire Everyone to Take Action*, author Simon Sinek states, "Leadership is the ability to rally people not for a single event, but for years. Leadership requires people to stick with you through thick and thin."[3] Although I wholeheartedly agree, one might argue the only way that level or type of loyalty can manifest occurs when leaders unilaterally trust their people, their team and their organization to do what's right—and to do what's right always. And when something is not done right, when there is an error in the process or something happens to go sideways such that the goal isn't achieved, a good leader reinforces his trust in his people . Whether a bouquet or a brickbat, whether a high or a low, whether a peak or a valley, whether a success or a mistake, the leader must create an environment that ensures all members of the team (direct or indirect) feel safe not just to do their jobs, but also to break free of them. The members must feel as though they can trust their leader to discuss any part of any process or scenario. The leader must portray herself such that anyone can approach her to ask a question no matter the time and no matter the problem. The act of trusting is table stakes for any leader.

Trust is not about rules. Trust is not about systems. To be trusting is to be mindful of the human condition. We humans have the capacity for good and evil, for right and for wrong. As leaders, we must be able to trust those in our organizations to explore the human condition through the course of regular business practice. Micro-managing, for example, is merely another name for distrust.

JP Rangaswami, chief scientist at the high-tech company Salesforce, said, "More and more, what we need is a more personal experience of trust, one that is tacit, one that is based on interactions and experience."[4]

Trust is not merely saying you trust someone. Trust is about actually acting in a trusting manner. It is about those interactions and experiences a leader creates for any situation. A leader may say he trusts the team, but it could in fact be a scenario unknowingly depicted by his team members through the acronym ATNA: all talk, no action. You might talk a big game about trust, but to be trusting happens when there is action—when there is interaction and experience. Trust is both a noun and a verb. It's when the word becomes a verb that a leader truly demonstrates the attribute of trusting. It's when a leader can allow both the good and the bad to surface mixed with the permission of action. It's allowing the human condition to manifest in a business environment.

Stephen Covey, in *The Speed of Trust*, suggests "trust means confidence. The opposite of trust—distrust—is suspicion."[5] Although trust encompasses confidence, I'd like to suggest trust is actually about belief. Trust is a reciprocal flow of belief between a leader and her team. The team has belief in the leader to do the right thing, to share, to contribute, to be open, to contribute, to defend and to include—and the leader has the belief in the team to innovate, to create, to curate, to ideate, to build, to counter, to execute and to develop.

For a leader to be *trusting*, she must have belief that whatever the scenario, the team will be capable and willing to achieve the objective. For a team to be trusting of the leader, it needs to possess the tacit belief that she is one of the team, not someone camping out behind a closed office door sitting at a marble desk signing expense reports. To be trusting goes beyond being cooperative.

To be trusting is to be able to act with authenticity and moral good. If, for example, a crisis should emerge, there should be palpable trusting actions delivered. When there is triumph, there should be equal levels of trusting behavior. To be trusting may require time, as trust is so often gained only by being earned. It is impossible for anyone in a peer relationship who does not exhibit selfless acts of trust to become a connected leader in our Flat Army.

To allow for failure is to be trusting. To celebrate success is to be trusting. To ride repeated cycles of the mundane and humdrum is to be trusting. Vulnerability begets trust; trust begets loyalty.

How to be *trusting:*

- **You don't know it all:** Listen to the viewpoints of others.
- **People look to you for direction:** Be transparent in your views and actions.
- **In the game of euchre, everyone hates those who renege:** Apply the same thinking to Flat Army.
- **All talk no action is paralyzing:** Less talk and more experience and interaction is fruitful.
- **Mistakes happen, so encourage them:** Harvest and learn for the next suitable scenario.
- **Sporadic, haphazard mannerisms are loathed:** Institute consistency in all of your efforts.

When respondents to the Edelman "Trust Barometer"—an annual survey that asks a variety of questions about consumer levels of trust regarding the corporate world—were asked, "How much do you trust business to do what is right?", only 46 percent said they believed the corporate world was, in fact, trustworthy.[6]

I think this spills over inside the organization itself. Our levels of trust and acts of being trusting inside our organizations are in need of improving. Perhaps what Warren Bennis once said—"hierarchy is a prosthesis for trust"—is the underlying point within the Flat Army thesis.

CEO Darren Entwistle at TELUS encourages team members across all geographies to learn from mistakes. In fact, Darren says, "there is tuition value in mistakes." You can get to that level of organizational learning once trust is pervasive. In the midst of Superstorm Sandy in 2012, a retailer sent out a tweet that might be described as a tasteless and crass attempt to prosper from tragedy by offering online sales discounts to those affected. There is a lesson here. The company trusted their marketing, sales and social media staff to make decisions about what to tweet. That's the good news. The bad news, however, is it was an obvious mistake; no one should be taking advantage in a crisis. The question remains whether there was enough trust inside of this particular company such that all involved could admit such a mistake and learn from making it.

INVOLVING

Have you ever been on a public bus? It's a rhetorical question, but I had to ask to segue to my next point.

Esther Kim of Yale University has been on a lot of them. Over the course of three years, Esther racked up thousands of kilometers of bus trips, criss-crossing the United States studying commuter behavior. What she found, at least in my opinion, contains symptoms of the disengagement found within our organizations.

Esther's research demonstrates that the extent to which strangers on a bus purposefully try to prevent others from sitting near their own occupied space is shocking, if not comical. Furthermore, the single most important observation within her bus travel research—which has led to Esther coining the term "nonsocial transient behavior"—is if you enter a bus, and there are other unoccupied seats available, you don't sit beside someone who has an empty seat adjacent them.[7]

In research published in *Symbolic Interaction*, Esther remarks,

This nonsocial behavior is due to the many frustrations of sharing a small public space together for a lengthy amount of time. Yet this deliberate disengagement is a calculated social action, which is part of a wider culture of social isolation in public spaces.[8]

Let's use the example of the bus and Esther's research to discuss the behavior of *involving* within the Flat Army model. If a situation arises where we need to involve employees in a decision or a discussion or a deliberation, and the default behavior of the employee is to avoid eye contact, pretend they're not paying attention, lie about their level of busyness or flat out ignore the request, what does that say about the state of leadership within the organization? What state is the culture of that organization in?

If the public space in Esther's research maps onto our idea of the organization itself, are leaders exhibiting these types of behaviors because leaders don't know how to properly involve people to contribute and participate? Do members of the organization, in turn, not know how to properly involve themselves in the process due to bad past practice? Do we purposefully look past the open seat on a bus that is adjacent someone because we don't know how to involve?

Being *involving* is being connected, and thus it's a behavior in becoming a connected leader. To involve is to sit next to someone on a public bus, even if there are other seats available elsewhere. To involve is to make eye contact when someone enters the bus, remove any of your bags that impede the seat next to you, and offer up the space. To involve is to be a part of the process leading up to and including action. In the organization, *involving* is calculated social inclusion.

How to be *involving*:
- **You don't own all empty seats on the bus:** Insist others on your team and in your organization to participate, sit beside you and contribute.
- **Discouraging participation is diabolical:** Encourage others to reflect, participate and take ownership.
- **Permitting others to stay on the sidelines of involvement is fraudulent:** To lead is to ensure others are involving themselves.
- **Assisting the creation or continuance of walled gardens is pathetic:** Break down barriers and roadblocks to advance levels of inclusion.
- **Preventing involvement is disengaging:** Openly suggest that everyone has something to contribute.
- **Cutting people off from adding feedback is soul crushing:** Actively seek out people to provide comments, ideas and feedback.

As a leader of people, of teams, and your organization, to enact the behavior of *involving* is to be an open and inclusive bus rider. In doing so, you are building upon the *becoming* attributes of a connected leader.

Although there is much I don't agree with when it comes to Jack Welch, the former CEO of General Electric, and his leadership style (terminating the bottom 10 percent of various sales teams each quarter for not making their quota numbers), one attribute he did demonstrate well was *involving*. His "breakfast with Jack" opportunities were legendary and provided both the employees and Jack an opportunity to learn from one another.

EMPATHIZING

I've always felt that the magnitude of one's ability to lead should be measured by the behavior of empathizing. If you were German and hanging around Robert Vischer in 1873, you would have heard him use this term: *Einfühlung*—the first known use of the term "empathy."

If as a leader you have the capacity to put yourself in the shoes of others and understand what those individuals are going through in any given situation, you are exhibiting empathy. Sadly, this one of the five *becoming* attributes is often the most overlooked, misunderstood and little used. If more leaders were to empathize with their team members, the workplace would be a much happier place.

In 1998, Daniel Goleman published an article in *Harvard Business Review* called "What Makes a Leader?" Goleman labels empathy as one of the five key components of his signature leadership theory, called "emotional intelligence." He defines empathy as "the ability to understand the emotional makeup of other people" and the "skill in treating people according to their emotional reactions."[9] To be connected leaders, we must learn to tap into the feelings of our employees, not on a superficial level but in a deep, caring and compassionate way. If as a connected leader we treat people by their employee number and not by their unique personality, beliefs or distinct disposition, we are treating our team members in carbon-copy format. Equally dismal is that we're acting in an unempathetic manner.

Through empathizing, leaders are being *connecting*. And by being *connecting*, leaders are making an actual connection with the humanity of other people. Goleman insists leaders must have empathy in order to demonstrate emotional intelligence. I further argue leaders must be constantly empathetic in order to connect levels of employee engagement to levels of employee productivity and business results. By tapping into the humanity of an employee, the leader can offer unadulterated and consistent responsiveness. And when a leader is responsive, so is everyone around him, in inspired ways.

One haunting story concerns the Christmas Truce of 1914. German, English, Scottish and French troops managed to broker a spontaneous peace deal on Christmas Eve that led to a short cease-fire among ground troops, despite orders from high command. Particularly on Christmas Eve and Christmas Day 1914, troops stationed along the trenches in Flanders Fields miraculously began discussing their wishes to be back home to celebrate Christmas with family and friends. In a demonstration of empathy, they discussed the situation with one another across the hellish muck and then agreed to stop shooting at each other. Remarkably, the soldiers met in no-man's land—the area of land between the two trenches of each side—to exchange gifts like cigars, cigarettes, alcohol and even uniform buttons. The men also initiated games—football, notably, as the game can be played in the muck in no-man's land. Not to be outdone, those on the sidelines sang Christmas carols.

This amazing scene occurred not because senior leadership dictated it but because a commonality of empathy had been established. Both sides knew the other wanted to be elsewhere—with friends, loved ones and family—and thus this ad hoc respite of fighting ensued. The combatants connected through empathy, and as a result, the unimaginable happened. Sadly, this feat was not to be repeated in subsequent months or at any other Christmas during the war.

How to be *empathizing*:
- **Closing your office door helps no one:** Open it and your heart to the professional and personal lives of your teams.
- **Things don't always go perfectly:** Embrace mistakes and invest time relating with those who have difficulty.

- **Your way or vision will not be understood by all:** Ask for opinions or feedback and determine whether the team understands what is really going on.
- **Work will be there tomorrow:** If someone or a team is struggling, stop to ask why, listen, and provide a comforting shoulder or ear.
- **Employees are not ID numbers:** Get to know their strengths, weaknesses, hobbies, interests and family members.
- **You are not a corporate robot:** Be authentic, transparent and real by admitting mistakes, foibles and dislikes and prove you are an empathizing human just like everyone else on your team.

Dev Patnaik, author of *Wired to Care*, believes that

[a]s sophisticated as our neurological systems for detecting the feelings of others might be, we've created a corporate world that strives to eliminate the most human elements of business. Companies systematically dull the natural power that each of us has to connect with other people. And by dulling our impulse to care, corporations make decisions that look good on paper but do real harm when put into practice in the real world.[10]

Why don't organizations have more attitudes to drive behavior like during the Christmas Truce of 1914? Why have organizations eliminated (or not instituted) the act of empathy, and as Patnaik describes, dulled our ability to connect with other people? Shouldn't we all be playing more empathetic football with one another in no-man's land?

In 2007, the Center for Creative Leadership (CCL) published a research report entitled "Empathy in the Workplace." Analyzing data from 6,371 managers in thirty-eight countries, CCL finds that "empathy is positively related to job performance. Managers who show more empathy toward direct reports are viewed as better performers in their job by their bosses."[11] These are the leaders who are playing football in no-man's land with their team members. These are the ones who connect empathy to engagement to performance and productivity.

Ask yourself how to start every one-on-one meeting with a team member. Do you immediately jump to the current status of in-flight actions or surfacing problems and mistakes you have noticed since the last time you met? That's the opposite of empathy. Why not start your next one-on-one meeting asking about the team member's children or weekend or upcoming vacation? That's a Flat Army leader in action.

DEVELOPING

The 2012 PricewaterhouseCoopers (PwC) "15th Annual Global CEO Survey," where PwC interviews 1,258 CEOs based in sixty countries to gather opinion and insight on various global trends, once again suggests that there are glaring holes in our ability to develop our people for future growth opportunities.[12] Four interesting statistics cement the point:

- Only 50 percent of CEOs are making development changes to improve reputations and rebuild public trust.
- 25 percent of CEOs say they are unable to pursue a market opportunity or had to cancel or delay a strategic initiative because of talent challenges.
- Only 30 percent of CEOs believe they have the talent needed to grow their business during the next three years.
- 67 percent of CEOs plan to develop and promote most of their talent from within the company. (While this may appear to be a point to be celebrated, keep reading.)

In a study conducted by IBM in 2010 with 700 global chief human resource officers (CHROs) entitled *Working beyond Borders: Insights from the Global Chief Human Resource Officer Study*, researchers find the single most critical issue facing organizations in the future is their ability to develop future leaders.[13] Not surprisingly, CHROs also feel workforce skill and capability development is one of the weaker areas that they have not yet cracked.

What does this tell us? CEOs, CHROs and presumably many other C-Suite leaders inherently know that the act of developing people within the organization is the right thing to do, yet, paradoxically, those same leaders are simply not spending enough time, effort or money on the behavior itself to ensure individual-, team-, or organizational-growth success.

There is a breakdown between what we know is right, and what we're actually doing. There is a disconnect between committing to the act of developing team members and exercising the actual behaviors to do so. Ralph Waldo Emerson once said, "What I need is someone who will make me do what I can," and that statement, in a nutshell, is what leaders need to be thinking about when it comes to the attribute of *developing*.[14]

At its core, the *developing* connected leadership attribute is about recognizing the talent that exists within your team. What are the strengths in your individuals and your team? It is also the ability to assess the talent delta gap in individuals and the team, to ensure you are proactively plugging the capability holes. It is, therefore, about taking action. This must be done for both short- and long-term purposes and it must be done individually and at a team or project level. How you as a leader are successfully adjudicating your talent level and subsequently taking the necessary steps to develop your people is a critical piece to the *becoming* attributes of a connected leader.

To be a *developing* leader, one must be thinking continuously about opportunities for improving the team. These ways of fostering improvement certainly do not come solely in the form of formal instructor-led courses found in a classroom or on the web. The leader should be thinking about developing opportunities for employees such as job rotations or job swaps, job shadowing, short-term stretch assignments on other teams, coaching or mentoring, or even off-site unrelated examples like excursions to assist not-for-profit organizations.

It is the responsibility of the leader to ensure employees understand they have an equal responsibility to participate in the developing process. The leader that abdicates such responsibility and expects that the employee will go through some kind of magical self-development process is as naive as those who expect clear sailing on Interstate 101 between San Jose and San Francisco on any given Friday afternoon.

In 2007, Marjolein Lips-Wiersma of the University of Canterbury and Douglas Hall of Boston University studied a public organization in New Zealand with 2,400 employees to determine if employee development was a source of concern in the organization. Did the responsibility for employee development lie with Human Resources, the individual, the leader, all three, or other parties? Their research, published as "Organizational Career Development Is Not Dead: A Case Study on Managing the New Career During Organizational Change" in the *Journal of Organizational Behavior* provides three key points about the attribute of *developing*:

- HR is not unilaterally in charge of developing employees, but the responsibility should be moving down the organizational structure, while supported by HR or the corporate learning team itself.
- Immediate supervisors or leaders don't always have the skills to provide such development support to employees.
- Employees are therefore confused and often struggle to find the right level of support to address their development needs. They too don't know where ownership lies.

Specifically, Lips-Wiersma and Hall recognize that

"bureaucracy needed to get out of the way" to provide flexible career opportunities and achieve a flexible organizational climate. One way in which it attempted to do this was by putting responsibility for career planning and feedback further down the organizational structure. We saw that this had variable results, as some team-leaders took on this role whereas others did not. This example of "bureaucracy getting out of the way" shows that career development still requires careful planning so that not only responsibility, but also accountability is systematically integrated.[15]

How to be *developing*:
- **Assuming your employees are developing themselves on their own is foolish:** Be proactive and identify with them their strengths and weaknesses, related to both their own self-development and the needs of the team or project at hand.

- **Presuming that development actions are naturally occurring is naive:** Establish regular conversations and review check-in points with your team to assess progress on both short- and long-term developing goals—be accountable.
- **Agreeing to a development action plan and either not investing the time or money, or, worse, ignoring it outright, is leadership suicide:** When the plan is mutually agreed to, stick to it.
- **An all-formal-classroom learning strategy is anachronistic:** Read Chapter 9 and ensure you are utilizing all facets of the learning spectrum.
- **Micro-managing all aspects of the developing attribute runs counter to the connected leader framework:** Ensure there is equal responsibility between all parties.
- **Developing your people is mission critical:** Relying solely on HR, the corporate learning team or the employee to do so runs counter to being a connected leader.

The *developing* attribute is not merely for the chosen few; a leader must be able to scan all pockets of her team and ensure the behavior is being applied to all members. Whether it is during times of prosperity or times of economic turmoil, the leader who stays abreast of her talent scorecard and who—more importantly—takes action to develop her people truly becomes a connected leader. It is the responsibility of the leader to ensure members of her team are being challenged and progressing with talent, skill and competence upgrades. This is the leadership attribute of *developing*.

By developing their people, Shell Jiffy Lube has witnessed a dramatic increase across many metrics. Using the adage "employees first," this company of 38,000 employees across 185 franchise stores in the U.S. and Canada invested in new development models for their people and it paid off in a big way. For example, from 2010 through 2012, franchises have seen a 38.5-percent increase in revenue, a 33-percent decrease in attrition, and a customer loyalty score that is up to 90.6 percent. By rethinking how they should be developing their people, Shell Jiffy Lube saved roughly $20 million in only a few short years.

COMMUNICATING

Most CEOs are peripatetic—always in motion. They travel from function to function, from meeting to meeting, from stakeholder to stakeholder, to fulfill CEO responsibilities. There is one common behavior the CEO exhibits throughout her travels and that is the act of communicating. How well she is communicating illustrates whether she is a connected leader or not.

Apollo 13—the infamous story of an attempted moon landing that went awry in 1970 due to a technical malfunction—contains an excellent example of a CEO who knew that the behavior of *communicating* would make or break a situation. Gene Kranz, the flight commander (CEO) at NASA mission control in Houston, during an interview in 2010 with NBC's "Dateline," which was commemorating the fortieth anniversary of the incident, suggests that he hadn't been worried that a human error either in space or on the ground might have thwarted plans to bring astronauts James Lovell, Jack Swigert and Fred Haise safely back to Earth. Quite simply, Kranz indicates, there was such a high level of communicative behavior between him and the team on the ground and the astronauts in orbit (and vice versa) that it never dawned on him (or the teams) that they could have failed.[16] The degree to which all affected personnel were communicating among one another evokes our Flat Army concept, but more importantly, in this case it saved the lives of three men.

In what was literally a life-or-death situation, it was the communicating behaviors among all parties that drove the successful outcome of Apollo 13. There were no egos; there was only communicative problem solving. There were no hierarchies of knowledge; only communicative levels of sharing. There was no close-minded thinking; only communicative, open conversations.

During the crisis, after realizing he had to rally his team, Kranz gathered everyone together and said,

Okay, listen up. When you leave this room, you must leave believing that this crew is coming home. I don't give a damn about the odds and I don't give a damn that we've never done anything like this before. Flight control will never lose an American in space.

You've got to believe, your people have got to believe, that this crew is coming home. Now, let's get going![17]

Once Apollo 13 landed safely into the Pacific Ocean, Kranz openly wept.

Too many leadership and business book authors predicate the behavior of communicating on being open, transparent, clear and consistent. While these traits are critically important when being communicative, a CEO, leader or anyone in charge of something must also be persuasive, emotional, direct and a true listener. Gene Kranz is known in mainstream public society as the flight director who helped save the men from Apollo 13. His NASA career, however, spanned decades until his eventual retirement in 1994. Throughout those decades Kranz utilized a style that was both blunt and compassionate; he serves as an excellent example of a communicative leader.

The Apollo program itself got off to an ominous start with the deaths of astronauts Gus Grissom, Ed White and Roger Chaffee. During what was regarded as routine ground testing of Apollo 1 on January 27, 1967, a fire engulfed the astronauts, who were locked in the spacecraft. They did not have time to unlock the hatch door and escape. All three astronauts died on the scene. Although not on-site during the incident, upon hearing the news Gene Kranz raced back to the office from his home to help. Several hours after assessing the situation, Kranz gathered his flight control team into the NASA auditorium and he uttered these words:

From this day forward, Flight Control will be known by two words: "Tough" and "Competent." Tough means that we are forever accountable for what we do or what we fail to do. We will never again compromise our responsibilities. Every time we walk into Mission Control we will know what we stand for. Competent means we will never take anything for granted. We will never be found short in our knowledge and in our skills.[18]

It's amazing to read those words and realize he said them three years prior to the Apollo 13 crisis. It further demonstrates my point and the importance of being a *communicating* leader at the *becoming* level.

How to be *communicating:*

- **If you beat around the bush or are too vague, your people will question everything:** Be direct and clear in your verbal and written communication.
- **A verbose or overly wordy communicating style is equally appalling:** Work towards finding the appropriate volume in your messaging
- **Don't dumb down or water down your content:** Straight talk is the preferred method.
- **If you aren't listening to your team, you aren't communicating:** Pay as much attention to what others have to say as to what you have to say.
- **A singular medium is as useful as a flashlight mid-day:** Expand your modalities to include blogging, micro-blogging and video-casting, among others (see Chapter 10).
- **Content isn't king—context is king:** Communicate with context by connecting dots within the team or organization's priorities and objectives. Make it make sense.

To be a *communicating* leader, we should remind ourselves of Gene Kranz; be smart enough to listen, to display compassion and to emote while being brash enough to persuade, to be clear and to clarify. By way of his communicating behavior, Kranz was a connected leader and a worthy example of our Flat Army mission.

※　※　※

I don't believe in the superhero leader—at least, I don't believe in that concept in an organization. Does any one person own the vision of a company? Can any one person drive revenues and profitability? Is it the responsibility of one person to improve employee engagement? Perspective is as diverse as it is experiential. The strengths of an organization lie not in the superhero, but in the people that comprise its employee database. Those people yearn for inclusion, for engagement, for happiness in their place of work. They need not be reminded of hierarchical decision making or white ivory towers—anachronisms they are already used to.

Hitachi Data Systems knows exactly what this means. Theirs is a culture enshrined in something they refer to as the "Hitachi Spirit." It is broken down into three key components:

- *Wa* (harmony, trust and respect)
- *Makoto* (sincerity, fairness, honesty and integrity)
- *Kaitakusha-Seishin* (pioneering spirit and challenge)[19]

There are no superheroes at Hitachi Data Systems. Whether rolling out technology options or new leadership development initiatives, *Wa*, *Makoto* and *Kaitakusha-Seishin* are adhered to by all regardless of title or level.

In becoming a connected leader in the Flat Army model, supposed superhero leaders might want to drop the cape and instead grab a cup. Actually, make that two cups—and with them, take an employee out for a coffee to start building up some trust. Communicate with them, empathize with them about their environment, their family, and their hobbies and begin developing—with them—some of the skills they may wish to enhance. Over the course of the coffee conversation, involve them, ask for feedback and ask them to contribute their knowledge back to the grid. These are the traits of becoming a connected leader, of becoming a catalyst for disrobing from the superhero costume that has dominated leadership for decades. Go ahead, try it on for size. You're on your way to becoming a harmonious leader.

CHAPTER FIVE

BEING A CONNECTED LEADER

I'd like to open this chapter with a reference to "Management Practice & Productivity: Why They Matter," a report produced by Nicholas Bloom of Stanford University and a few of his colleagues that researched the performance of more than 4,000 manufacturing operations in the U.S., Asia and Europe. In this landmark study, the researchers found that

[i]mproving management practice is associated with large increases in productivity and output. Across all the firms in the research, a single point improvement in management practice score is associated with the same increase in output as a 25 per cent increase in the labour force or a 65 per cent increase in invested capital.[1]

That is, if leaders do a better job of *being* leaders, every single percentage point of improvement is equal to vast amounts of other operating or capital expenditure investments. The authors of the report went on to further assert that

the majority of firms are making no attempt to compare their own management behavior with accepted practices or even with that of other firms in their sector. As a consequence, many organizations are probably missing out on an opportunity for significant improvement because they simply do not recognize that their own management practices are so poor.[2]

Talk about the blind leading the blind.

If a leader within the Flat Army is paying attention, the next level to aim for and achieve is *being* a connected leader. Being a connected leader is about paying attention to the business of leading, getting things done, while having a little fun. At this level I see vast opportunity for improvement, and it's at this level where I believe leaders can turn the disengaged right around and bring the nearly engaged closer to being engaged. It is a level that consists of inclusive action and execution mixed with humanity. If *becoming* a connected leader is about nurturing and creating an open environment of communication and development, being a connected leader is about accomplishing actions in a comprehensive yet lighthearted manner. It's about analyzing, deciding, delivering, cooperating and clowning around with your people. Let's ensure your management practices aren't poor. Let's dispel the research from Nick Bloom et al.

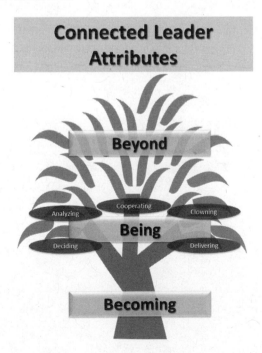

ANALYZING

For centuries, war has epitomized hierarchy. In March 1945, Germany was on its heels as Allied troops pushed forward to free the people of Europe. Adolf Hitler's orders to the German military were to fight to the end no matter the cost or the number of casualties. Similarly, as the Allies entered Germany to hunt down the Third Reich, orders were issued from Allied high command to obliterate everything in sight regardless of consequence and historical significance. Now, that's hierarchy, on both sides of the war.

Perched on a hillside plateau picturesquely overlooking the Tauber River is the German town of Rothenburg ob der Tauber, or Rothenburg for short. Throughout the Middle Ages, the imperial and Protestant city of Rothenburg, located on a trade route between the north and south of Europe, was a hub of activity. But after a Catholic sect took the town over through an orchestrated siege, the weakened townspeople were then exposed to the plague; the city was devastated and remained nearly deserted until the end of the nineteenth century. While Romanticism began finding a home throughout Europe in the late 1880s, Rothenburg was rediscovered, and, since then, the town and its inhabitants have worked tirelessly to preserve its medieval and Bavarian charm. In the present day, tourism—not surprisingly—provides the largest percentage of the local economy.

Rothenburg might not be the perfectly preserved medieval walled town within the Bavaria region it is today, had it not been for two individuals sporting critical analyzing abilities during World War II. These *being* leadership attributes helped preserve a city, allowing it to prosper and be enjoyed for many generations.

Allied troops had pushed forward towards Rothenburg after conquering Nuremburg and were poised to wreak a firestorm upon it. In fact, the Allies had conducted an air raid in late March of 1945, killing hundreds and destroying a few of the buildings in Rothenburg, including nine of its historic watchtowers.

John McCloy, an American, served as the Assistant Secretary of War for the Allies at the time. Major Thömmes was the high commanding

German officer responsible for carrying out Hitler's orders of fighting to the death. These two unlikely heroes of Rothenburg never met, but they both were analytical leaders in their own right demonstrating qualities that embody our definition of a connected leader.

As the Allies began their normal routine of planning for heavy artillery, bombs and shelling to overtake the Third Reich in another German town, McCloy understood the historical importance of Rothenburg and immediately ordered a different tack. The story goes that there was a painting of Rothenburg in his home, and his mother used to recount stories about its significance, and thus McCloy wanted no part in obliterating the town. His orders, counter to what was happening throughout Germany at the time, was to preserve the city at all costs and negotiate with local German military leaders a less destructive overtaking.

When presented the offer, Major Thömmes had to analyze the situation. Should he stay the course, follow the hierarchy, and watch another town be destroyed by the Allies? Or, should he deviate from orders and preserve the city for generations to come?

In the end, we can see two acts of courage and two examples of men who had to analyze a situation and recommend a course of action that deviated from the norm. Assistant Secretary McCloy easily could have ignored his instincts and simply let the town burn. Major Thömmes could have opened fire on the Allies, ignoring the peace offer, and a retaliation of colossal proportions would have ensued. Instead, these two men analyzed the situation and displayed *analyzing* attributes that resulted in millions of tourists still being able to enjoy the thrills and history of Rothenburg.

This story encapsulates another key ingredient of being a connected leader. Leadership is about being able to analyze situations, not only in terms of profit and loss or goals and objectives, but in terms of the human condition. A leader who is conscious of team culture and levels of engagement is one who analyzes situations with people in mind, who observes the pros and cons of various situations before actually making decisions. It is deleterious to the health of a team or organization to do otherwise.

How to be *analyzing*:

- **If it looks good on paper, it might not look good on skin:** Analyze through empathy (a *becoming* attribute).
- **Situations are not always as they seem:** Connect with people directly to conduct a proper and thorough analysis before executing.
- **Close-minded analysis is for those who love hierarchy:** Open your analysis to multiple possibilities before acting.
- **Doctors don't normally operate on the spot:** Analyzing requires time as well as assessment, diagnosis and investigative skills—patience in analyzing serves you well.
- **Analysis is flawed if it's used flippantly:** Devise personal methods that can be repeated with which to analyze.
- **Myopic evaluation of options and opportunities forfeits any chance of success:** Become a specialist in the holistic big picture with your analyzing skills.

Both McCloy and Thömmes demonstrated the behavior of *analyzing* sublimely. In particular, their abilities helped saves lives during the moment, and also had long-lasting positive benefits for other humans thereafter. It behooves connected leaders to effectively analyze situations with humans in mind, moving from binary-only scenarios to ones with vivid representations of color and depth. To involve members of your team or organization in the behavior of *analyzing* ensures you are in fact being a connected leader.

One action I like to take every year around the beginning of October is to ask my team to reflect back on the year—to analyze—and to come prepared to discuss what's going right and what's going not so well as it relates to our goals, actions and objectives. Why? In preparation for the next year. It takes patience and time to get people thinking about the past in order to improve the future. Starting the analysis early on allows the team to feel part of the process and permits enough time to incorporate the feedback for the next year. It's looking at the big picture while critically analyzing the good, the bad and the ugly. It's the attribute of *analyzing*.

DECIDING

The Latin root of the word "decision"—*cis*—literally means to cut. I believe there are too many negative connotations to the word "cut." For example, I once was cut from a national-soccer-team roster, but the way it was handled impacted me so much I haven't played on an organized club since that day. I once cut my finger while chopping vegetables for dinner and woke up with two of the children hovering over me on the floor asking if I was dead. I once received a haircut that was so unimaginably bad I had to continue cutting until there was no hair left. Some argue the improvements were minimal.

To make a decision is to decide. To decide is to cut. Seems simple enough. We shouldn't think of the act as negative, though; we should embrace it and ensure it's an appropriate piece to the Connected Leader Attributes mix. Deciding is a process rather than a one-time action. The examples I cite above lend themselves to seeing deciding as a one-time act. It's not. By defining it as a process we take away the illogical thinking that it's an absolute. It really is about *being* a connected leader. Those leaders who are, in fact, connected utilize the *deciding* attribute as a basis to collaborate with their team and the organization. Deciding, as a process and in the context of a team or organization, should involve others. Deciding is not about consensus but it is about inclusion. Deciding is an action that takes place in the present. Once you make a decision, it's in the past. Connected leaders must shift the focus from the weight of making a decision to involving others in the process.

In the book *Judgment: How Winning Leaders Make Great Calls*, authors Noel M. Tichy and Warren G. Bennis suggest that "the judgment calls that leaders make cannot be viewed as single, point-in-time events." They go on to describe a three-stage process that proved successful in the myriad leaders and companies they studied:

- *Time—the period before, during and after deciding what to do*
- *Domain—deciding about people, strategy and time of crisis*
- *Constituencies—the relationships needed to make knowledge decisions*[3]

Here I further the work of Tichy and Bennis by suggesting the following *deciding* model:

- **Area:** Outline who the decision affects and any potential ramifications.
- **Ask:** Consult others as appropriate regarding who should be involved to help decide which way to proceed.
- **Alternatives:** What options present themselves through the deciding process.
- **Accountable Action:** Someone holds the ultimate yay or nay; hold them accountable for timely action.

Tichy and Bennis' decision model reminds me of an example at TELUS. In mid-2010, an internal program was born, entitled Customers First. The overarching goal of the program was to improve the likelihood-to-recommend scores of TELUS customers, be they consumers, small-to-medium-sized companies, enterprise organizations, international clients or even members of the health solutions practice. The program quickly turned into a mission, finding its way into the corporate scorecard and truly becoming a way of *being* for all 40,000-plus team members. As the mission began to gain traction, another idea surfaced: to create something known as "Customer Commitments." Think of the Customer Commitments as promises to the customer—specific actions that any TELUS team member should carry out to help a customer, regardless of her own role.

Ritz-Carlton had a similar idea years back when it created its "Three Steps of Service" promises that are upheld by everyone across the hotel chain:

- *A warm and sincere greeting. Use the guest's name.*
- *Anticipation and fulfillment of each guest's needs.*
- *Fond farewell. Give a warm good-bye and use the guest's name.*[4]

Back to TELUS. What the company could have done was locked its most senior executives in a room and decided what the Customer Commitments were going to be for the organization. Or those same

Commitments could have been decided by CEO Darren Entwistle unilaterally, without anyone else being involved. Instead, the organization went through a deciding process that involved anyone wanting to participate right across the entire organization. The *area* was defined as the organization and the ramifications were that if team members didn't participate, they weren't being involved in the deciding process. Quite simple, really. The *ask* was of the team members; they were asked to help the organization decide what the Customer Commitments were going to be. Over 1,000 different examples surfaced over a two-month period. An amazing level of involvement was demonstrated and the deciding process was well in motion. The *alternatives* weren't simply the 1,000 user-generated Customer Commitment responses. The options that manifested thereafter came as a result of further deciding through focus groups, interactive online polling and voting to ultimately get the one thousand down to ten. From there, the deciding process homed in on a top four, and once they were decided, *accountable action* continued as the Customers First team and other colleagues embarked (and held the responsibility) to implant the new Commitments into a variety of actions and opportunities. That same team held the accountable action responsibility throughout the deciding process.

From over 1,000 ideas down to four, involving hundreds of team members across the organization in the deciding process. That's how the act of deciding should be employed by connected leaders in Flat Army. The TELUS Customer Commitments, decided by the organization, are as follows:

- *We take ownership of every customer experience.*
- *We work as a team to deliver on our promises.*
- *We learn from customer feedback and take action to get better, every day.*
- *We are friendly, helpful and thoughtful.*[5]

How to be *deciding*:
- **The decision tree of one is yesterday's way of thinking:** Demonstrate the confidence to include others in the deciding process.

- **It's not about power in the decision:** It's about empowering your team in deciding the path and outcome.
- **The inability to start or conclude the deciding process is gutless:** Define the schedule and stick to it
- **Consensus is nice but not a necessity in the deciding process:** Inclusion in the process is fair, but the outcome doesn't have to be.
- **Small-minded, myopic thinking in the deciding process is foolish:** Be holistic and look at the overall impact to the organization.
- **Hoarding details, facts and information helps no one:** Open up all of the data to improve the deciding process.

"Cut!" When making a movie, a band of actors and a cadre of crew await word from the director as to when a scene is to conclude. There is a lot of involvement going on beforehand in which the team unites through the *deciding* process to get to the point where the "Cut!" call is made. To cut is not a pejorative term. If we utilize unilateral command-and-control decision making and refuse to think about the area, the ask, the *alternatives* and the *accountable action*, then yes, things remain bloody for team members in the organization. Try to be a cut above the rest and employ the deciding process as opposed to absolute decision making.

DELIVERING

A research study entitled "Return on Leadership: Competencies that Generate Growth," produced in partnership between Egon Zehnder International and McKinsey & Company in 2011 investigates the relationship between "managerial quality and revenue growth" through more than 5,000 leaders working in forty-seven different companies across the globe.[6] I'm not a fan of the word "competencies," but what the authors brought to the surface helps us label the Connected Leader Attribute known as *delivering*.

One of the main points in the study indicates that good leadership is fine, but it is not nearly enough to actually drive improvement in business results. In fact, the authors suggest "only excellence makes the difference."[7] One form of excellence comes from leaders who have the attribute of *delivering*. Their research demonstrates that the critical competency that all leaders require to drive strategy and organizational growth—and where the most gaps exist—is in what they term "results orientation." Be it the top team, senior executives or talent that resides elsewhere in various business units, a "results orientation" competency is "driving improvement of business results" or, in other words, it's about *delivering*.

Sir Richard Branson, chairman of Virgin Group, can help illustrate the example of being a connected leader who knows how to act on the attribute of *delivering*.

Business life started for Branson on January 26, 1968, with the launch of a magazine called *Student*. He quickly began to realize that profit begot growth and being able to deliver as a leader permitted innovation. Thus the birth of a mail-order operation in 1970 was followed in 1971 by the first Virgin record shop, which then led to the opening of the first Virgin recording studio in 1972. Today, the Virgin Group consists of roughly 400 companies in areas ranging from airlines, to games, to hot air balloons, to space travel to mobile phones.

Along the way, Branson employed a strategic competitive advantage—its corporate culture of delivering. Virgin employees across the globe are continually asked—perhaps strategically pushed—to innovate, look outside the box, and to deliver as a high-performing and unified team. Branson gained loyalty not by command and control but through the successful delivery of initiative after initiative. He set the tone by immersing himself in a new business venture, including and hiring smart(er) people to be around him, sticking to timelines while driving forward in a clearly organized fashion. He knew that if he or the team couldn't deliver, other innovative initiatives wouldn't surface, and growth in the overall Virgin conglomerate would stagnate. He used separate initiatives to fund other initiatives within the Virgin empire. Branson figured it out early on: instill a results-focused yet passionate culture, and ensure everyone both knows how to deliver and is empowered to do so.

In his quirky and fascinating official autobiography, *Losing My Virginity: How I Survived, Had Fun, and Made a Fortune Doing Business My Way*, Branson writes:

My vision for Virgin has never been rigid and changes constantly, like the company itself. I have always lived my life by making lists: lists of people to call, lists of ideas, lists of companies to set up, lists of people who can make things happen. Each day I work through these lists, and it is that sequence of calls that propels me forward.[8]

Doesn't that sound to you like a leader who is *delivering?* He's a leader who knows all too well that in order to achieve strategic growth and business results, specific order is required—but coupled with an eye towards the human condition. It's no wonder he is personally worth over $4 billion and revenues earned at Virgin Group exceed $20 billion.

How to be *delivering*:

- **Unclear, wishy-washy objectives help no one:** Use SMART objectives to ensure clarity.
- **Rushing to deliver may impede a positive outcome:** Adjust as necessary and remain malleable.
- **Ignoring problems and underperformers is disengaging:** Address issues as soon as possible.
- **Being oblivious to time, people and budget constraints ends badly:** Build in proper resource-management, evaluation and priority processes.
- **Unaccountable leadership is confusing to all:** Ensure roles and responsibilities that pertain to you and to the team are clearly articulated.
- **Forgetting to celebrate and reward the team is foolish:** Inspire and fête the team throughout delivery of the action or project.

Once the act of *delivering* becomes ingrained in your own leadership style, work on coaching members of your team. Over time, it just might spill over to the entire organization. Take, for example, perennial powerhouse IBM. Revenues at the company over the past seventy years were reported as follows: [9]

- 1939—$40 million
- 1955—$564 million
- 1965—$3.7 billion
- 1981—$5.5 billion
- 1990—$69 billion
- 2000—$95 billion
- 2011—$106 billion

Do you think this impressive track record came as a result of corporate luck? Growth can come in the form of organic sales increases (units sold or price increases), new products or acquisitions. IBM has made more than one hundred acquisitions over the past decade alone. To acquire and integrate a company into IBM requires an exemplary level of *delivering* that clearly is working. And from an innovation perspective, according to the U.S. Patent and Trademark Office database, IBM has 70,715 patents on record, including more than 6,800 that were filed in 2011.[10] Patents aren't easy to create or file and require leaders at any level to demonstrate the act of *delivering*.

It might be argued that both IBM and Sir Richard Branson are demonstrating the skills outlined in the Egon Zehnder International and McKinsey & Company study cited above, *Return on Leadership: Competencies that Generate Growth*. In the case of IBM and in the case of Branson, they are exhibiting the behavior of delivering. Their focus on "results orientation" accelerates the business strategy in each case and it also produces revenue and profit growth. It's something to think about as you build out your plan for Flat Army.

COOPERATING

"To work with"—that's really what cooperating means. Sounds easy, doesn't it?

At the level of *being* a connected leader, *cooperating* is arguably the Connected Leader Attribute that drives home whether members of your team are with you or against you. It determines whether you're with the team or not. Up until this point, you have demonstrated being trusting with them, you're involving them, communicating with them and developing them, and you are empathizing with their concerns and work issues. At the *being* level, you've so far recognized that a connected leader has to get things done *with* the team. This leads to the attributes that demonstrate you are analyzing, deciding and delivering on the results of the team, business unit and organization.

But cooperating puts things into a whole new perspective. Recall from Chapter 3 how leaders need to cross the Connected Leader Chasm. The harmonious state of leadership occurs when both the leader and the team are open. To achieve harmony in the team or organization is also to act by cooperating with one another. There must be cooperation between leader and team; harmony is the end destination. Thus, all parties must cooperate to enable Flat Army.

In research conducted for her book *Hot Spots: Why Some Teams, Workplaces, and Organizations Buzz with Energy and Others Don't*, Lynda Gratton summarizes a team environment that is effectively cooperative as follows:

> [T]he energy of the cooperative mindset comes not from a mindset of competition but rather from a mindset of excellence. The focus is on the excellence toward which people are striving together rather than the competition of beating everyone else to the goal."[11]

A leader may work tirelessly in the *being* level of connected leadership to analyze, decide and deliver, but if these activities are being undertaken in a competitive environment and if the team feels as though its members are being less than cooperative it is unlikely to produce the results or objectives it has been tasked to do. As a leader, this outcome may stall your efforts to improve employee engagement, which will ultimately stall levels of productivity and business improvements. Instead of having a Flat Army at hand, you've got a group of competing units to referee.

Speaking of refereeing, let's examine the game known as "the prisoner's dilemma" to extend our argument about cooperating versus competing, as well as being open and harmonious versus closed and hurtful. Invented under another name in 1950 by Merrill Flood and Melvin Dresher at the RAND Corporation, the actual title "the prisoner's dilemma" originated with Albert Tucker, when he added specific prisoner sentences to the game. The prisoner's dilemma, at its root, is a game about cooperation versus competition. The intent of the game is to test how cooperative people really are against the backdrop of pressure, stress and options. Imagine you're a criminal and you and your associates (the game is played with several players) were recently caught by law enforcement. You've been summoned in front of a judge who has issued a sentence to be served immediately. Due to unforeseen circumstances, there are no witnesses and no evidence, so the sentence issued is minimal; however, government prosecutors want to ensure someone pays dearly for the alleged misdemeanor.

You've been offered a plea bargain: rat out your colleagues and your sentence is reduced, but your colleagues have their own sentences multiplied by a factor of five. Of course, unbeknownst to you, the same offer is issued to each of your accomplices. Hence, the "prisoner's dilemma": do you cooperate and together as a team each receive the original sentence, or do you take an easier way out, leaving your colleagues to suffer?

In the context of being a *cooperating* connected leader, what would you do? Dilemmas surface all the time within the work environment for leaders. The prisoner's dilemma is a fictitious scenario, but when pressed to hit a deadline, to cut costs, to increase production or to mitigate a negative business result, do you as a connected leader demonstrate a *cooperating* attitude with the team or, conversely, do you compete, throw team members under the proverbial bus, and take the plea bargain? When the stresses of work pile up, do you cooperate or compete? Will your harmonious and open environment be destroyed by acts of fear driven by pressure, resulting in a more competitive environment within your team than reflected in the intended way of being, which is to be *cooperating?*

I recall a situation that occurred in one of the high-tech companies I once worked for. For about a ten- to fifteen-year period, software companies killed several thousand trees and shipped user and help guides in each box to accompany the software CDs. Under research and development was a team that was tasked to develop said guides. In another part of the company sat a team that also killed several thousand trees through the creation of printed classroom training guides. When it comes to software, and particularly when there are end users in mind, the overlap of content between user guides and training guides is quite high. Both teams, however, had independent content management systems and processes. Repeated attempts to cooperate were made at various leadership levels, from content developers, to graphic designers, to vice presidents. In the end, the teams remained competitive as opposed to cooperative. Sure, they liked each other, but not enough to consolidate systems and develop content—through shared processes—cooperatively and in unison. They chose to punish each other rather than assist. Were the leaders being harmonious or hurtful?

How to be *cooperating*:
- **Green thoughts are good and red thoughts are bad:** Be cooperative, not competitive.
- **Singularity is hierarchical:** Work with your team through both good times and bad.
- **Your team is not the competition:** The competition is the competition. Use your team cooperatively to defeat the competition.
- **Pressure will surface, but don't go rogue:** A cooperating leader involves others along the way.
- **Don't be petty, as your team will see through it:** Act magnanimously; be above the pressure.
- **Trees get in the way of light:** See through them to better your openness and your team.

Cooperating means "to work with." As you work with your team, as you create a community among the team, you are bound to achieve excellence. More importantly, it sets you up accordingly to continue the demonstration of being a connected leader at the harmonious level. Anything less than being *cooperating* is a failure in our Flat Army model.

CLOWNING

On average, Americans aged between 25 and 54 spend 26 percent of their time working, 33 percent of their time sleeping and the rest—roughly 41 percent of their time—doing anything but sleeping or working. This is according to the U.S. Bureau of Labor Statistics.[12] By comparison, the Organisation for Economic Co-operation and Development (OECD) estimates in their Better-Life Index that member countries spanning the globe spend on average 20 percent of their time working and the rest on leisure, sleeping, personal care, etc.[13] So, depending on where you live and how researchers arrive at the data points, workers are spending somewhere between one-fifth and one-quarter of their total available time working and earning a wage to help fund those leisurely activities, life-long planning, trips to Old Trafford to watch Manchester United and so on.

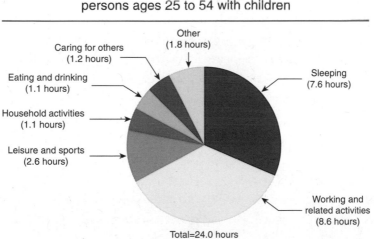

Time use on an average work day for employed persons ages 25 to 54 with children

Other (1.8 hours)
Caring for others (1.2 hours)
Eating and drinking (1.1 hours)
Household activities (1.1 hours)
Leisure and sports (2.6 hours)
Sleeping (7.6 hours)
Working and related activities (8.6 hours)
Total=24.0 hours

NOTE: Data include employed persons on days they worked, ages 25 to 54, who lived in households with children under 18. Data include non-holiday weekdays and are annual averages for 2010.

SOURCE: Bureau of Labor Statistics, American Time Use Survey

But when you cut the data a little differently and focus on total available waking time versus total time, it looks somewhat different. Based on the U.S. Bureau of Labor Statistics data, 33 percent of time is spent sleeping. Each year, we all get 8,760 hours to use as we see fit. If 33 percent of the time is spent sleeping, it leaves us with 5,869 available waking hours. Americans work on average 2,278 hours per annum, which now correlates to a hair shy of 40 percent of waking time being spent on work. Said differently, Americans spend 60 percent of their waking hours with family and leisure, household or other activities while 40 percent is spent with work colleagues, wherever that employment takes place.

Now that we're looking at data that suggests 40 percent of our waking hours are spent with work colleagues, don't you think leaders should be spending a portion of their time clowning around? I do—it's an important part of being a connected leader. In a world of quarterly targets, profit margin quests and cost constraints, a little levity can go a long way.

Take for example Taco Bell, an American fast-food chain. In 1996, Jonathan Blum, then vice president of public affairs for the company, gathered his team together and suggested they have a little fun with an advertising campaign. Together they plotted to devise an advertising piece that announced Taco Bell had purchased the sacred Liberty Bell and that it was renaming it the Taco Liberty Bell. The actual advertisement ran as a full-page ad and it appeared in six American newspapers including *The New York Times*, *USA Today*, *The Philadelphia Inquirer*, *The Washington Post*, *Chicago Tribune* and *The Dallas Morning News*.

Accompanied only by a picture of the Liberty Bell and the Taco Bell logo, the text of the advertisement read as follows:

Taco Bell Buys the Liberty Bell

In an effort to help the national debt, Taco Bell is pleased to announce that we have agreed to purchase the Liberty Bell, one of our country's most historic treasures. It will now be called the "Taco Liberty Bell" and will still be accessible to the American public for viewing. While some may find this controversial, we hope our move will prompt other corporations to take similar action to do their part to reduce the country's debt.

Despite the public outcry and thousands not understanding the joke, imagine if you were a member of Blum's team. How great would it be to know you had the latitude to pull something off like this? Moreover, imagine the type of *clowning* culture that already existed on this team to even allow for such zaniness. That's the type of levity I'm referring to.

One of the fourteen characteristics Etienne Wenger suggests that makes up a true community of practice is "local lore, shared stories, inside jokes, knowing laughter."[14] Several researchers including Sigmund Freud himself have also emphasized the function of humor in the organization as a relief trait. They suggest humor offers a safe release for feelings at work which ultimately prevent anti-social behavior while fostering organizational harmony.

Before SAP acquired Business Objects in 2007, I worked at a different high-tech company called Crystal Decisions which was in fact acquired by Business Objects in 2003. Bill Gibson was the chief operating officer at Crystal Decisions, a gregarious man from Georgia. Throughout his tenure Bill knew the importance of clowning around. During the sales kickoff conference in 2002, Bill spent most of the time in a boxer's outfit playing on the tagline "We're going to knock the BO out of BO"—Business Objects being a competitor to Crystal Decisions at the time. Throughout the office, Bill was known to kid around with anyone who he came into contact with. He knew what it meant to get down to business, but through his humor and down-to-earth, humble and *clowning* attitude, Bill was a legend. People wanted to be around him; people would go the extra mile because he made things fun. Bill knew the link between people and emotional intelligence. As COO, he didn't have to employ such an attitude, but everyone throughout the organization wanted to be a part of his environment. He was king of the clowns at Crystal Decisions, and this was a very positive thing for employee engagement and productivity.

How to be *clowning*:
- **Business is serious but you don't have to be all the time;** ease up and smile for starters.

- **Lighten the mood;** encourage those on your team to poke a little fun at you once in a while.
- **Don't work till you drop;** clowning can come in the form of coffees, lunches and outings.
- **Gaming isn't just for kids;** participate in online games or outings like bowling with your team.
- **April Fool's is just one day of the year;** clowning should become part of your regular leadership style.
- **Jokes aren't taboo;** learn how to tell them and, even better, encourage your team to do so as well.

In a 1985 paper the communication department of the University of Delaware explores patterns of humorous communication against the context of organizational culture. The research indicates humor can:

- *manage the tension between hierarchy and egalitarianism that emerges from the group's enactment of power structure;*
- *regulate interdependence among group members; and*
- *balance the forces of differentiation and integration in the group's communicative enactment of cultural identity.*[15]

I'm not suggesting you join the circus, but start by adding a little humor to your leadership style. Clowning around is an excellent attribute to add to your connected-leader-*being* repertoire. You don't need a giant red nose or purple hair to prove it.

✵   ✵   ✵

In Chapter 3 we discuss A.G. Lafley and the spectacular results at Procter & Gamble. In the seven years that Hay Group has been conducting its influential "Best Companies for Leadership" study, this organization has been ranked number one or number two in six of the seven years. Why do you think that is? One aspect has to do with their leadership framework and the concept we introduced earlier called "C&D," which stands for "Connect and Develop." Only 54 percent of P&G's global peers let their employees behave like actual leaders, yet Mr. Lafley instituted a culture of being leaders through C&D to analyze, decide, deliver and cooperate.

Larry Bossidy and Ram Charan authored *Execution: The Discipline of Getting Things Done* in 2002, in which they say, "Execution is the great unaddressed issue in the business world today. Its absence is the single biggest obstacle to success and the cause of most of the disappointments that are mistakenly attributed to other causes."[16]

Being a connected leader is having the ability to drive results while inspiring and motivating your people to act as one. It builds off the *becoming* attributes to hone in on the business of execution. By employing the five *being* attributes in your leadership style, you are well on your way to implementing Flat Army.

CHAPTER SIX

BEYOND THE CONNECTED LEADER

Compassion leaves an indelible blueprint of the recognition that life so sorely needs between one individual and another; one nation and another; one culture and another. It is also valid for the road which our spirit should be building now for crossing the historical abyss that still separates us from a truly contemporary vision of life, and the increase of life and meaning that awaits us in the future.

—Laurens van der Post[1]

Let's take a trip down memory lane. When I was working in higher education at the British Columbia Institute of Technology, the team and I were doing our best to rewire how people thought businesses should be operating through the career-changing programs we offered. For many of the programs, significant work experience was a requirement to being admitted. Rest assured that those who had work experience brought with them attitudes about ingrained hierarchy, fiefdoms and hoarding.

For one activity, we would take certain student cohorts ice skating. Needless to say, the activity was a surprise to all. The only instructions issued beforehand were to dress warmly and keep an open mind. Potential lawsuits aside, why would we have thirty full-grown adults—average age of 32 years—head off for an afternoon of ice skating as part of the program?

The composition of each cohort was intentionally similar: three to five skating wizards and ten to fifteen others who were quite good skaters, but not in the wizard ranks. We'd call these folks the "A/B" group. There also were six to eight who struggled much like Bambi on ice, and one to four who had never been on skates before. We'd label these students as "C/D." For this latter group I coined the term "the-end-of-Dan's-career crazies." Luckily no one took a serious fall, but we did have a few bruised knees over the years.

There were no instructions given once everyone convened at the rink. It was a simple free skate for ninety minutes—at least that's what I would tell each group before they stepped onto the ice. Can you imagine what happened? Did the wizards start pointing fingers at the skating misfits as they lapped them once a minute? Did the good skaters mock those imitating Bambi, who unfortunately had their ankles hugging the ice with their knees trembling?

Absolutely not. Any time I conducted the experiment—sorry, the activity—the A/B skaters looked around and realized they were skating much better than their C/D colleagues. Instead of showboating, these *beyond* leaders stopped and observed, and ultimately helped their colleagues in their time of need. It was a wonderful demonstration of heterarchy, let alone the human condition. And what really was happening throughout the ninety minutes? Those A/B skater-leaders were being thought of in a different light by the C/D skaters. The opposite occurred as well. Some of the C/D skaters, who were leaders in the classroom, were regarded in a different light while on skates. Once all groups figured out what was happening—after the first ten minutes or so—true harmony began to occur between all groups on the ice.

At around the sixty-minute mark I would always call the students into the center of the ice rink, and we'd conduct a mini-debrief lasting no more than five minutes. Each time, no matter the cohort, the conversation was the same. "Never judge a book by its cover" was a recurring theme that usually came up near the beginning of the debrief. I can assure you that previous to this day the students weren't discussing who could skate and who couldn't. But when we dug a little deeper into what was occurring during the mini-debrief, the students then began to connect the dots. They were no longer transacting—they were transforming. They were no longer worried about egos. They were becoming flat. They no longer cared about A/B or C/D titles—it was about chipping in to get things done. Both groups measured themselves against the other but, in doing so, they were sorting out how to demonstrate a better way in which to interact with each other. Both groups were learning how to be *spacing*; that is, understanding what is the appropriate amount of give-and-take.

These students, perhaps unbeknownst to themselves, were demonstrating a higher level of leadership; they were going *beyond the connected leader*.

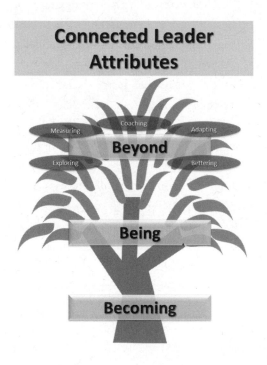

COACHING

The most overused yet inappropriately applied term in an organization is "coaching."

There are organizational coaching models, executive coaching programs, external executive coaches, company-defined coaching steps, coaching interventions and in-house coaches too. Group coaching? Sure. Speed coaching? Why not. Virtual coaching? But of course. We see requests aplenty from keynote speakers who are so-called coaches. Not to fear, you can become a coach yourself by enrolling in an executive education program at a university that offers executive coaching certificates as well. And now, coaches are getting coaches for themselves too. Wow, I think I need a couch . . . er, coach.

To be clear, it is an expectation of mine that if you want to become a connected leader, to demonstrate you are going beyond the call of leadership duty you must agree that coaching your team and others in the organization is mission critical. But what is *coaching* in the Flat Army paradigm? Let's first dish up what it's not. *Coaching* is not a formulaic process when demonstrating the connected leader attributes. It is not the act of hiring an external executive or otherwise coach to assist you with your team. It isn't an intervention and should never be used as a means to solve some form of employee crisis or singular performance issue. Any of these acts runs up against our view of *coaching*.

In a study of approximately 285,000 employees and leaders across U.K. firms, the Chartered Institute of Personnel and Development finds that 30 percent of leaders, with reference to whenever they meet for a one-on-one meeting with their direct reports, suggest they are—in their minds—coaching their people first and foremost.[2] Sixty-four percent of leaders feel they are actively coaching only part of the time in one-on-one meetings. Not too shabby when you think about it: a total of 94 percent of leaders believe they are coaching their team members in one-on-one meetings.

Now, the flip side. Employees report that in their minds coaching only occurs 6 percent of the time at those meetings where leaders feel they are actually coaching. Where employees experience partial coaching, a measly 34 percent indicate they believe some coaching takes place. My hypothesis is that the definition of coaching is misconstrued by both sides of the equation. Leaders think they are doing it and employees think they aren't receiving it.

Ian Chisholm, Bradley Chisholm and Mark Bell penned the article "Coach vs. Mentor: Designing the Finest Meaning of Words" and it's within this piece that a paragraph caught my attention:

Coaching is the intentional positioning of others to perform at incrementally higher standards, to learn more from their experience as it emerges, and to be increasingly engaged in their endeavours. It is an approach to leadership that invites more leaders from all levels in our organizations, communities and families.[3]

I like to think that the phrase "intentional positioning" can be reflected by the terms "counsel," "feedback" and "advice." That makes sense to me. And I love how they determine the stakeholder audience as including "organizations, communities and families." Leadership isn't a nine-to-five job; it's communal, holistic and accretive.

Coaching—in the context of Flat Army and thus going *beyond* a connected leader—is an ongoing informal conversation with the employee who focuses on providing the following:

- counsel on current objectives and actions to categorically improve the result
- feedback concerning their progress or improvements on Flat Army habits
- advice on personal or career advancement or opportunities

In summary, to demonstrate the attribute of *coaching* is to assist your team member—and to help them improve—with issues going on at work, on the personal development front and with respect to career development. That's it! It's an ongoing and informal discussion with your team members, albeit individually, to help them get better. Seems simple, doesn't it? The problem is, too many human resources professionals, consulting shops and accrediting institutions have whipped organizations into frenzies just by the mention of coaching. We must demystify the term in order to bring some sanity back into the definition of leadership and to the definition of coaching.

How to be *coaching:*
- **Binary is not an option:** Relate to your people through a spectrum of colors, not simply black and white.
- **It's not a contract with your team member; it's a relationship:** Nurture it at all times and pervasively.
- **Every minute matters:** For any situation, treat it as an opportunity to counsel, advise or provide feedback that aims to improve.
- **The ignorant and reckless command before listening:** Instead, lend an ear and help bring the story to the surface before advising on anything.
- **Your brain is not a contingency backup:** Create a system in which you're recording conversations, thoughts and ideas for each of your team members. Review these regularly.
- **Don't be purposeless:** There should be purpose in each coaching situation, always intending to improve the employee's overall capabilities on actions, habits or personal quests.

Between 1993 and 2003, David Galloway was the vice president of customer care at Crystal Decisions—the original makers of Crystal Reports software—a company I used to work at until it was acquired by Business Objects in 2003. He continued on in his role until 2006. When I joined the company in 2002, I joined the services arm, not even in Dave's bailiwick. But he took me under his wing, and through a series of coaching conversations over an eighteen-month period, Dave helped me in my adjustment to the new company, navigating my actions and objectives, and helped me become a better leader at the company. He was an incredible listener and an idea factory, and had at all times a genuine interest in my well-being and my success. He was (and still is) the example connected leaders should be striving for. Any time we talked, it was a coaching conversation. It's always been there in the back of my mind as I strive to be a better leader: "Am I being like Dave?"

> *Coaching* should be an expectation of all connected leaders. That is, if the guidelines and definition above are adhered to. If all else fails, just be like Dave.

MEASURING

A passage from David Halberstam's *The Best and the Brightest* sat on the desk of Citigroup's ex-CEO John Reed for many years to remind him that in the act of *measuring*, judgment just might be more important than facts:

The first step is to measure whatever can be easily measured. This is O.K. as far as it goes. The second step is to disregard that which can't be measured or give it an arbitrary quantitative value. This is artificial and misleading. The third step is to presume that what can't be measured easily really isn't very important. This is blindness. The fourth step is to say that what can't be easily measured really doesn't exist. This is suicide.[4]

The moral of the story? Connected leaders are wise to begin measuring their various actions (personal, team, unit, and organization) if they want to go beyond a standard level of leadership. It is not simply about quantity but also about quality. But how?

In New Zealand, researchers investigated human resources practices seeking a relevant link between measurement and performance. They conclude:

It appears from our research that the HR profession as a whole needs to move towards expressing value in both human and numeric terms, and be able to justify their decisions where possible in dollar terms. Results suggest that HR metrics as the Holy Grail of human resources management remain elusive.[5]

Not a great start if you're in HR, I agree. But the underlying point I'd like to raise is the link between human and business metrics. Perhaps it's why John Reed kept Halberstam's passage firmly planted on his desk.

Quantitative and qualitative. Quantitative can be viewed as the effort of measuring business results, team goals, etc. Qualitative can be thought of as measuring the interpersonal factors and criteria that—for far too long—have been overlooked by leaders.

Connected Leader Measuring Matrix

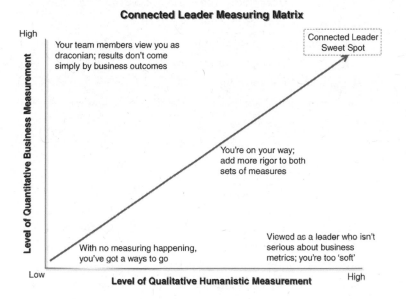

By introducing the Connected Leader Measuring Matrix, we argue that connected leaders must invoke the act of *measuring* by paying equal parts attention to quantitative business metrics as they do to qualitative humanistic metrics in order to truly summon a Flat Army organization.

Quantitative business metrics, ideally, are already ingrained in leaders. Financial targets, sales quotas, traffic volume, profitability increases, shareholder return, operating expenditures, capital objectives and the like are all quantitative business metrics. There are others, but the intent of this attribute (and book) is not to go into deep detail regarding what has already been discussed by authors such as Martin Klubeck in *Metrics: How to Improve Key Business Results* or Dean Spitzer in *Transforming Performance Measurement: Rethinking the Way We Measure and Drive Organizational Success*. It is rather to acknowledge that quantitative business measures must continue to be deployed.

But we must add another component to the attribute of *measuring*, and that is to see that qualitative measurement is on an equal footing with quantitative business metrics. So:

- Are people in your organization working more collaboratively, communicating more efficiently and feeling as though more cooperation is happening as a result of implementing Flat Army? These are qualitative measuring actions to consider.
- Are your employees satisfied with senior leadership, company direction and strategy, corporate social responsibility and community efforts? These are qualitative measuring actions to consider.
- Are team members asked about concepts like life-work balance, career development opportunities, their feelings on the state of compensation, work processes or organizational learning opportunities? These are qualitative measuring actions to consider.

An organization will not be successful unless its people are fully engaged. Recall our original thesis from Chapter I. Disengagement is at alarming levels in our organizations. Thus, in order to go *beyond*, a connected leader treats both the quantitative business metrics equal with the qualitative humanistic metrics and ensures action is taken on both.

How to be *measuring:*
- **Number cruncher? Evolve:** Numbers are good, but take into consideration both the business and humanistic side of your team or organization
- **Don't kowtow to the financials:** Yes, it's important to be in the black, but dismissing or forgetting the humanistic side will only bite you in the end.
- **Constraints are bound to occur:** Recall there are two sides to our equation and work with the team to help make those adjustments.
- **Establish qualitative humanistic targets as you would the quantitative business ones:** Parity is important in Flat Army—consider SMART goals.

- **Don't be clueless or forgetful:** Monitor progress, focus on improvement areas, and readjust tasks or actions as necessary to achieve targets.
- **Scorecards aren't simply for baseball managers:** Consider employing one to identify your qualitative and quantitative metrics in a unified statement to the organization.

Measuring is not new, but the equal weighting of both quantitative business metrics and qualitative humanistic metrics might be for aspiring connected leaders. In describing the African humanist philosophy known as Ubuntu—a philosophy focusing on people's allegiances and relations with each other—Nelson Mandela said, "[Ubuntu is] the profound sense that we are human only through the humanity of others; that if we are to accomplish anything in this world it will in equal measure be due to the work and achievements of others."[6]

I like the message in that. Let's start measuring it.

EXPLORING

Connected leaders can be individual contributors too. Leadership is not about your number of direct reports; it is the behavior one brings to their job that depicts whether they are a connected leader or not. That's hopefully why you're reading this book.

The attribute of *exploring* demonstrates this argument well. First off, *exploring* denotes the ability of an individual to deviate from the norm, to look outside the box and to play devil's advocate in any given situation. It's to be a well-rounded leader, thinker and person. *Exploring* encourages connected leaders to be contrarian. If looking at situations or problems the same way, time and time again, you're simply not exploring the options from different angles well enough to make a discernible difference for anyone.

Kelly Martin is a senior business analyst working in the TELUS Customer Solutions business unit. She is a quintessential example of why it's so important to look at situations differently from time to time.

Kelly was a part of an enterprise-wide program launched at TELUS called "Closer to the Customer." Twice a year, leaders in the company (with direct reports or not) venture out for a full day of job shadowing with front-line team members. These could be agents in call center roles, escalation positions, or sales—be it enterprise, health, small-to-medium size business—or in the case of Kelly, field technicians driving from house to condo to house to condo solving home-related issues or installing new consumer services.

At the time, Kelly was new to TELUS and admittedly was feeling like "a small cog in a big machine."[7] When she spent time exploring her role in a different light while being part of a one-day ride-along with a field technician, she said, "It had a huge impact on my view of the company, its employees, and my role." Throughout that day, Kelly was *exploring*. She was thinking about her role differently, and it had a tremendous impact on her. She finished an interview with me by saying,

Not only do I have a much better understanding of the work process, but more importantly, I witnessed the impact a technician can have on so many other people's daily lives. Sukh was inspirational in his ability to turn a frustrated customer into a smiling, delighted customer. Spending time outside of my area helped me to look at the data differently and makes me feel more connected to the technicians, our customers and the company.

Notice the last line? By exploring the role, situation and experiences of a field technician, Kelly not only felt more engaged with the organization, but she was also absolutely pumped up to explore her role differently. This will have a significant impact on Kelly, her leadership and engagement, as well as what she can accomplish in terms of her objectives. But you have to have the *exploring* attribute in your bag of tricks as a connected leader in order for this to happen in the first place.

Henry Mintzberg—iconoclastic professor from my alma mater McGill University—uses the expression "Worldly Mindset" to depict a leader who takes advantage of external environments to further one's leadership competence. In his book *Managers not MBAs: A Hard Look at the Soft Practice of Managing and Management Development*, Mintzberg states,

Should we not, therefore, be encouraging our managers to become more worldly, defined earlier as experienced in life, in both a sophisticated and practical way? Managers need to get into worlds beyond their own—other people's worlds, their habits and cultures—so that they can better know their own world. To paraphrase T.S. Eliot's famous words, they should be exploring ceaselessly in order to return home and know the place for the first time. That is the worldly mindset.[8]

Of course Mintzberg is advocating for leaders to spend time abroad, to learn from the habits and cultures of others in order to return home and be more effective, if not holistic, leaders. But the same analogy can be applied inside the organization. Our friend Kelly from above already demonstrated this. The term "job shadowing" has very unfortunate and negative connotations inside an organization. It sounds as if the term was coined by an HR professional in 1965. That is, it sounds old. It also implies you have to be quiet and on the tail of someone for a longer period of time without true interaction. Exploring is the exact opposite. It isn't about shadowing, it's about exploring with the employee what's going on in his or her role, in an effort to help both sides of the newly formed relationship. By exploring, you are imparting your wisdom, understanding and insight with respect to your role and how it impacts their role. And conversely, you are there to explore the intricacies of their role so as to learn and bring back that value to your own role and responsibilities. It's a way in which to break down the organizational silos while simultaneously building culture, engagement and competence. How is this a bad thing?

How to be *exploring:*
- **You are but one fish in an ocean of many:** Get your trunks on and dive in. Relate to others in different parts of the organization as well as outside of it.
- **Being an organizational *advocatus diaboli* is not a bad thing:** Examine situations from different angles to better your overall IQ and EQ.
- **Offices are horrible:** Get out regularly to explore what's going on elsewhere.

- **Front-line is not the enemy:** Bridge gaps and reach out to observe and understand how their roles impact yours.
- **Shame on you if you don't reciprocate:** Allow others to explore you, your role and what ticks you off and makes you tick.
- **Don't believe for a minute that the organization is like a puzzle— it's not:** The pieces will never fit together nicely, so explore options regularly and think outside the box always.

Exploring is a key attribute in going *beyond* connected leadership. Alternative solutions that may seem incongruent or deviating from the norm should at least be considered if not celebrated. The organization will always be in flux; it is the responsibility of the connected leader to think through different possibilities and scenarios. In particular, seeing things in the different light of other organizational roles is key to becoming a truly *exploring* connected leader.

ADAPTING

When I think of IBM and Xerox I tend to think of paradoxical leadership. In the blue corner we have a company—and a leadership model—that enacted the attribute of *adapting* superbly. In the red corner we have a company that was highly innovative and thought-leading, yet for a period of time didn't possess the *adapting* attribute and as a result suffered for years thereafter.

Back in 1993, newly appointed IBM CEO Lou Gerstner had been parachuted in to salvage a beleaguered, if not bankruptcy-destined, organization from the verge of collapse. The instructions given to him by the board of IBM were clear: "Help us adapt to the new world of business." Gerstner wasn't an engineer, nor was he a technology expert; at his core, he was an *adapting* change agent who could help Big Blue with its transformation needs. Drawing on similar experiences from his days at Nabisco, American Express and McKinsey, Gerstner successfully brought in an *adapting* leadership attribute to the organization. It permeated throughout all facets of the company. Through his leadership and a willingness and perseverance to push the company into a new way of thinking—a more adaptive way of operating—IBM trimmed anything that wasn't working and evolved into the technology idea factory it is known for being today. Through Gertsner's nine-year reign IBM's value and revenues grew by more than 40 percent, and it radically transformed from a monolithic, rigid giant to a flexible and *adapting* organism. As he left his post, to underline the point of his belief in *adapting* and in people in general, Gerstner said, "In the end, an organization is nothing more than the collective capacity of its people to create value."[9] By instilling the behavior of adapting, IBM has gone on to be a role model organization.

In the 1970s things were as positive and rosy as can be if you were a member of the Xerox team. The world was gobbling up Xerox technologies everywhere, from photocopiers to highly sophisticated laser printers. Today we take these technologies for granted, but it's Xerox and its innovative culture we have to thank. It's this innovative mindset throughout the organization that also saw the launch of Xerox PARC—Xerox Palo Alto Research Center—a facility instituted by CEO Charles McColough to cook up even more cool gadgets. But this is where our *adapting* attribute story takes an unfortunate twist. Imagine a research center that developed technology we use today like the mouse or electronic file folders or the graphical user interface or what-you-see-is-what-you-get (WYSIWYG) software. Yes, all of these were born at Xerox PARC. But due to a culture that was very territorial, less entrepreneurial than Silicon Valley counterparts and absolutely lacking the *adapting* gene, Xerox squandered the opportunity to bring these magnificent inventions to mass market. Instead, because it was lacking the *adapting* gene, the innovations they developed were sold to budding (and *adapting*) leaders like Steve Jobs, who ran wild with their functionality. Why didn't McColough or his successor, David Kearns, see the inherent opportunity in PARC-related technologies? Why didn't they adapt to the changing societal and business needs? My bet is because they did not have the adapting attribute like Lou Gerstner did. And we know full well what Jobs did with the technology afterwards, don't we.

Which brings us to the definition of *adapting* as a connected leader. What is evident in the business world is steadfastly simple to some and eerily overlooked by others. A failure to adapt, to anticipate or to possess continual flexibility in previous decisions will be the unnerving undoing of an organization. The company Research in Motion (RIM), makers of the iconic BlackBerry smartphone line, is a classic example. Former co-CEOs Jim Balsillie and Mike Lazaridis were innovation machines, producing technology products that were snapped up in droves by their customers. But an unwillingness to adapt or to look ahead and predict what was going to happen in the smartphone market ultimately led to their resignations in early 2012. RIM's board and the company (with new CEO Thorsten Heins) are currently attempting to play catch-up to the likes of Apple and Samsung. It's a desperate quest to adapt. Only time will tell if it's too late for the company.

What of Digital Equipment Corporation (DEC) as well? In 1977, founder Ken Olsen quite famously said, "There is no reason for any individual to have a computer in his home."[10] This oft-used quote illustrates the *adapting* attribute nicely. DEC was a market leader in technologies such as the minicomputer, data processors, mainframe computers and networking, yet didn't see the benefit of personal computers until it was far too late and others had flanked, outwitted and adapted much earlier. Unsurprisingly, the company was pared back, bit parts were sold off until eventually what remained was sold to Compaq. If only DEC had a better adapting attribute, perhaps it would be the world's most valuable company and not Apple as it is today.

How to be *adapting*:
- **The future happens every day; get used to it:** Leaders need to be continually uncomfortable with the status quo.
- **No road is ever smooth:** Anticipate bumps and barriers so others can succeed in changing business conditions.
- **Uncertainty is not a negative:** Explore options, dig into possibilities, get creative and be relentless to improve.

- **Do not stay on the white line:** Shift priorities or approaches to address needs of today and the future.
- **Perfection is not the goal:** Adapting to change and progressing forward is how to be perfect.
- **Others don't own the future:** Be accountable to yourself. No one will adapt for you.

The words of Alexander Graham Bell nicely summarize the *adapting* attribute for a connected leader: "Don't keep forever on the public road, going only where others have gone."[11]

BETTERING

In the 2012 Democratic National Convention held in Charlotte, North Carolina, First Lady Michelle Obama gave a rousing speech (some argue) for the ages. It poetically painted her husband, President Barack Obama, not as the President of the United States, but as a true connected leader of the people. She depicted a graceful, loving and empathetic man who clearly possessed the attributes of becoming, being and beyond a connected leader. One line in particular stuck with me: "Success isn't about how much money you make; it's about the difference you make in people's lives."[12]

We might take some creative license with her words and suggest the attribute of bettering in our connected leader attributes framework is as follows: "Success isn't about how many direct reports you have; it's about how well you are bettering your team and the organization whatever the situation."

Who cares how big your team is or what your organizational girth is. The goal is not a larger team; it is making that team—whatever the size—the best it can be. It is the leader's responsibility to assist team members to hit their professional or career goals. And the truly connected leader takes interest and provides counsel on personal endeavors as well, as discussed in the *coaching* attribute. Likewise, it is incumbent upon connected leaders to refrain from invoking a culture of status quo. Jim Collins, author of *Good to Great: Why Some Companies Make the*

Leap—and Others Don't, said, "Good is the enemy of great," and it is this phrase leaders should tattoo onto their foreheads.[13]

Bettering is improving. This is the essence of moving beyond status quo leadership.

Euan Semple quite simply is one of the brightest organizational intelligence minds out there. With one eye on the humanity of an organization and the other firmly on its use of the social web, Euan can speak from experience as to why organizations and their leaders have difficulties as well as successes. He knows how they can be better. A speaker, consultant and the author of a book I highly recommend, *Organizations Don't Tweet, People Do,* the former director of knowledge management at the BBC can also pinpoint with sublime precision the various cultural stumbling blocks leaders have encountered with their teams. When I asked Euan in an interview what three actions he recommended leaders employ in their organizations, he suggested the following:

- Do whatever you can to make it easy for people to say what they think and connect with each other in your online environments.
- Encourage a shared sense of ownership of these environments and allow effective behaviors to be learned and shared.
- Keep adapting and be willing to allow an effective ecology to flourish rather than over-plan.[14]

Do these not sound like the behaviors of bettering your people and the organization? Does that not sound like the Flat Army concept in action? Euan states that you should "do whatever you can" and "encourage a shared sense of ownership" and "keep adapting and be willing," which all help us understand the importance of consistently demonstrating the behavior of bettering your people and the organization.

I personally believe *bettering* is much like good parenting. The term "helicopter parenting"—coined by Foster Cline and Jim Fay in 1990—is the act of over-parenting or child smothering and it's an awful way to raise children.[15] Of course, the same can be said of leadership. When you are helicopter leading, you are micro-managing, which no one cares for in this day and age. The other end of the spectrum is absent parenting, those moms and dads who have checked out of the process, leaving the child to fend for his or her own well-being through life's crucial decisions and actions. The latter can be thought of as those leaders who just don't care about the growth of their team and who simply fill in the performance review once a year. That is as ugly as it gets. But when a parent gets it right, when he or she knows the fine balance between assisting and letting go, it is in fact the act of bettering the child. In the workplace, why can't leaders find the right balance too?

Bettering the team helps in so many different ways. For example, when I joined TELUS in December 2008, it was evident to me a number of individuals on the team were in need of some bettering action. And to be clear, bettering isn't about sending people off to a training course. It is improving the situation of the employee with the employee, team and organization all equally in mind. Two individuals in particular, Rob Sharpe and Marguerite Behringer, were learning and collaboration consultants working on various projects. They were rock stars and the company was lucky to have them. When I approached them separately about their portfolios, ambitions, likes, dislikes and traits, it became evident they were in need of some bettering action. Rob and I, for example, had numerous conversations about his passion and ways we could tap into that, outside of our team, to better his skills and experiences. We found a three-month job-shadowing opportunity in a completely different part of the organization—fully paid for by his current role—which then led to other bettering opportunities outside of our team. Rob is still a highly contributing member at TELUS—on a different team—and now has a team of his own that he is leading. I like to think the act of bettering helped Rob in his career at TELUS, and more importantly, it kept him at the company as well. Through many conversations with Marguerite, focusing on bettering her skills, career options and talents, we shifted her portfolio on the team from one that focused on a single deliverable to one that supported an entire business unit. From there, we continued our bettering dialogue and she happily graduated from our team to go on and become a highly successful HR Business Partner for the TELUS Enterprise Sales team. It's another example of how the act of bettering can help both the employee and the organization as a whole.

How to be *bettering*:

- **Marking your territory by pissing on posts is akin to hoarding your employees**: Look out for the betterment of the organization and stop thinking you own your team.
- **Being close-minded only punishes the employees and the organization**: Start an open dialogue with team members about wants, needs, wishes and expectations.
- **You are a member of the organization**: Openly encourage your team to better themselves by being open to other career opportunities in the organization.
- **Performance reviews are a formality**: By *bettering*, you should be conducting a running conversation with team members about their development and goals.
- **The ostrich effect (head in the sand) doesn't work either**: Get out in front and initiate the *bettering* actions with your team members.
- **No one is irreplaceable**: Holding on to talent for selfish reasons is the antithesis of *bettering*—be brave and think holistically for the sake of the employee and the organization.
- **Read *30 Reasons Employees Hate Their Managers: What Your People May Be Thinking and What You Can Do About It* by Bruce Katcher and Adam Snyder.**

Such support for employees is not merely altruistic; it furthers the goals of the organization by keeping a cadre of highly motivated, accomplished and upwardly mobile employees who refuse to become complacent slaves. It is also attractive to potential new employees to know that the organization supports employee growth and development.

✻ ✻ ✻

How best to summarize a leader that knows how to go *beyond*? By introducing you to Stan Garfield—that's how. Stan is the community evangelist at Deloitte Consulting LLP, one of *Fortune*'s 100 Best Companies to Work For, among other accolades. Be it technology, strategy and operations, or human capital, Deloitte Consulting serves clients in myriad industries through its 184,000 employees that garner $28 billion in revenue.

Stan is that rare breed of a leader who can connect the dots. He can see the link between technology, humanity and culture and has been an impeccable force at Deloitte, helping to drive its ranking as one of the best places to work.

When a connected leader has gone *beyond*, it implies he or she already has mastered the becoming and being stages described in Chapters 4 and 5. Stan is a quintessential representation of the full package. He is *becoming, being* and *beyond*—a perfect specimen of the connected leader. When I asked him what attributes makes up a connected leader and thus a collaborative culture, his reply was the following:

Caring, cooperative, networked, decisive, egalitarian, supportive, open, sharing, trusting, transparent, fair, inclusive, willing to try new ways, giving credit, adopting good ideas; volunteering, communicative, bold, respectful, honest, responsive, thorough, nurturing, generous, helpful, altruistic, appreciative, pleasant, accepting responsibility, and optimistic.[16]

He wasn't done, because he wanted to ensure I knew there were negative aspects as well. Those traits that should not be part of a leader or culture, according to Stan, included these:

Fearful, insensitive, selfish, undermining, having not-invented-here syndrome, covering your rear, perpetuating an old boys' network, reticent, secretive, closed, dictatorial, waffling, uncooperative, isolated, manipulative, exclusive, blaming, ridiculing, usurping credit, hierarchical, controlling, resistant to change, hoarding, siloed, passive-aggressive, critical, making excuses, backstabbing, complaining, and pessimistic.

Do you see a pattern emerging here? We are at Chapter 6 of our Flat Army construct, and thus far we've ventured into a world full of employee engagement questions and explored the history of hierarchy and rigidity, and spent the past four chapters outlining what it means to be a connected leader. Do you recognize the positive words above that Stan uses at Deloitte? Did your face cringe into the shape of a raisin when you read the negative ones? If you need more proof, analyze for a second the leadership credo that he instilled:

- *I will practice and reward caring, sharing, and daring—caring for others, sharing what I know and daring to try new ideas.*
- *I will insist on trust, truth and transparency in all dealings—earning and respecting the trust of others, communicating truthfully and openly, and demonstrating and expecting accountability.*
- *I will look for opportunities to help, thank and praise others.*
- *I will eliminate criticism, blame and ridicule in all interactions with others.*

And just when you thought he was done, Stan let me in on his magic secret sauce. As a leader, he eats a lot of pickles. I know, if it were that easy, I'm sure many leaders would have been eating these long ago. In reality, the pickles Stan has been eating as a connected leader form his own way of defining how he has become and been a connected leader and then gone beyond the connected leader attributes framework.

"Pickles" is the mnemonic device Stan uses to employ his own connected leader model every day. It is as follows:

- *Passion for my work, my team, and my field*
- *Integrity in all that I do*
- *Communication—open, timely, thorough, effective, and well-crafted*
- *Knowledge of my field, my areas of responsibility, and my extended network*
- *Love of my work, my field, and my colleagues*

- *Empowerment—allow others to thrive, succeed, and advance*
- *Service—serve those who work for me, my colleagues, my company, my field, and my extended network*

Stan's fabulous leadership style is a perfect conclusion to the connected leader component of Flat Army. It is also a nice segue to the next section, dealing specifically with collaboration—something Stan does for a living.

CHAPTER SEVEN

THE PARTICIPATIVE LEADER FRAMEWORK

THE UNTUTORED EYE

Stan Brakhage was a filmmaker like no other. Of the 370-odd films he made (in 8 mm or 16 mm formats) in a career that spanned more than five decades, most were silent and ranged in length from nine seconds to four hours. Brakhage was a believer in the act of seeing. His films were not the norm in terms of having protagonists and antagonists. Nor did they consist of typical Hollywood-style treatments, story arcs and denouements. Some say his films are light-filled poetry, highly subjective and metaphorical reflections on vision that make you think beyond what the film is about, to take you to where you should be.

Think of Brakhage's work as visual stimuli. He wanted you to think, but what he really wanted was for you to see. He wanted you to see differently. He was a precursor to Apple's now-ubiquitous slogan "Think Different." Brakhage's art is as cerebral as it is groundbreaking. His goal was to liberate your eye and to blatantly suggest you have no limits. Think of it as unconventional illusion.

Brakhage didn't want the viewer to see his films within the conventional boundaries of perception. He saw the world as fluid, in four dimensions rather than two or three. He felt society had self-imposed limitations, and his films are not only anti-establishment; they are anti-habitual. They not only break the mold; they make you think. And they make you think deeply. The films question viewers' perceptions and challenge the status quo.

His definition of perception and concept can best be summarized by a piece he penned in 1963 for the journal *Film Culture*, entitled "Metaphors on Vision":

Imagine an eye unruled by man-made laws of perspective, an eye unprejudiced by compositional logic, an eye which does not respond to the name of everything but which must know each object encountered in life through an adventure of perception. How many colors are there in a field of grass to the crawling baby unaware of "Green"? How many rainbows can light create for the untutored eye? How aware of variations in heat waves can that eye be? Imagine a world alive with incomprehensible objects and shimmering with an endless variety of movement and innumerable gradations of color. Imagine a world before the "beginning was the word."

To see is to retain—to behold. Elimination of all fear is in sight—which must be aimed for. Once vision may have been given that which seems inherent in the infant's eye, an eye which reflects the loss of innocence more eloquently than any other human feature, an eye which soon learns to classify sights, an eye which mirrors the movement of the individual toward death by its increasing inability to see.

But one can never go back, not even in imagination. After the loss of innocence, only the ultimate of knowledge can balance the wobbling pivot. Yet I suggest that there is a pursuit of knowledge foreign to language and founded upon visual communication, demanding a development of the optical mind, and dependent upon perception in the original and deepest sense of the word.[1]

When I think of Brakhage, I immediately find my mind wandering toward today's state of leadership. The untutored eye, in Brakhage's opinion, is one that refrains from looking at the world as being static or fixed. In today's state of leadership, the participation among teams and employees doesn't parallel a Brakhage film; it screams of the formulaic way in which mainstream films have been and continue to be written and produced. Each of today's Hollywood films starts with an opening scene that introduces the main characters (protagonists and antagonists) along with the imminent crisis that needs to be solved or worked out. From there, the plot shifts to various hiccups and hurdles, only to close with the protagonists smiling in a wild embrace of success and the antagonists spiraling away in fits of rage. Cue the ending credits and an orchestra of violins. It's been that way for years and it rarely deviates.

What if we applied Brakhage's films and his thinking to the context of leadership and participation? The accepted, tolerated and habitual vision of leadership that emanates command-and-control behaviors and a general lack of inclusiveness is a modern-day crisis. If we were to use, however, Brakhage's analogy of the camera lens to explore participation as anti-establishment and thus anti–traditional leadership, would we be on the right track? What if we didn't have a history of organizational examples that perpetuate a command-and-control leadership style that denies participative behaviors? Perhaps we simply need leaders to *see* leadership in a new, innocent light.

I would prefer us to let go of the current practice of leadership criticism, which is to view leadership through the lens of poor execution and examples of such. Where has that got us? We have a proclivity to exacerbate current leadership messes by deepening our inability to actually see them differently. We are not viewing leadership as Brakhage did his films; we view leadership as it is currently and historically perceived. It's the same old plot.

Leadership is in need of a shift. In the Brakhage analogy, it is in need of a new camera lens. The singular nature of leadership perception, where we point fingers, hide in offices and generally bark orders as a measure of being a leader, is not only anachronistic, but also an affirmation of hierarchical anthropocentrism in our organizations.

I argue that leadership is for all to borrow from Brakhage; the act of participating can provide this new camera lens. For purposes of Flat Army, the Participative Leader Framework is the lens for our untutored leadership eye.

SAY IT FORWARD

You've no doubt come across the term "pay it forward." It is a phrase that dates back to a play by Menander, *Dyskolos,* circa 317 BCE, but its most famous adaptation—outside of the movie *Pay it Forward* in 2000—came when Benjamin Franklin described its intent in a letter sent to Benjamin Webb dated April 25, 1784:

I do not pretend to give such a Sum; I only lend it to you. When you meet with another honest Man in similar Distress, you must pay me by lending this Sum to him; enjoining him to discharge the Debt by a like operation, when he shall be able, and shall meet with another opportunity. I hope it may thus go thro' many hands, before it meets with a Knave that will stop its Progress. This is a trick of mine for doing a deal of good with a little money.[2]

We might think of the term "pay it forward" as referring to a way in which employees—regardless of rank—help others in the organization without prejudice. If, for example, we could employ this concept through all roles and job descriptions, employees might pay forward their knowledge, insight and ideas without concern for something in return. If, as *pay it forward* suggests, good deeds get repaid by having a subsequent good deed applied to someone else not within the original exchange, perhaps the corporate version of *pay it forward* is *say it forward*. And thus, perhaps *say it forward* is part of being a participative leader.

Some sociologists also liken the *pay it forward* concept to the term "generalized reciprocity."

Reciprocity, according to the Cambridge Dictionary Online, is defined as the "behavior in which two people or groups of people give each other help and advantages."[3] Generalized reciprocity, according to sociologist Nancy Bonvillain in *Cultural Anthropology*, is "the exchange of goods and services without keeping track of their exact value, but often with the expectation that their value will balance out over time."[4]

We might suggest, therefore, that *say it forward* at its core is the act of participating in the organization—the equivalent of organizational reciprocity—and thus everyone, regardless of role, should employ participative behaviors to achieve personal, team, unit and organizational goals through projects, actions and deliverables. If we believe that we might exchange knowledge, insight and ideas without keeping track of their value, I argue that with the *say it forward* and *organizational reciprocity* concepts we are now redefining the term "participation" through this new level of mutuality.

GUANXI

In 1975, Charles Lee started his career at AT&T as a marketing manager. His new executive marketing boss, Archie McGill, had been parachuted in from IBM, and McGill quickly realized that the company, despite being a monopoly at the time, was doing zero business outside of America. He subsequently asked Lee (a Chinese citizen living in America) to explore business opportunities and contacts in China. As Lee relates in his book *Cowboys and Dragons,* "That is how I found myself as an entry-level marketing manager reporting directly to the guy one level down from the head of the AT&T empire! It felt like shooting to the top of a tall skyscraper!"[5]

With orders in hand to drum up business opportunities and contacts in China, Lee quickly invoked a concept that is familiar, if not innate, to the Chinese: *guanxi.*

What is *guanxi* and what has it got to do with participation or Charles Lee?

Emanating from China but in use across many Asian cultures, when loosely translated *guanxi* means connections, networks and community relationships. It describes a very basic dynamic: your personal and professional circle of contacts is your center of influence, and, thus, the more you build your network, the more likely it is that you achieve results, answers or knowledge. It is the ultimate "It's not what you know, it's who you know" philosophy. I have often said when public speaking, "I store my knowledge in my network," and the concept of *guanxi* aligns nicely to this philosophy.

Guanxi also comes with a deep-rooted level of responsibility. *Guanxi,* therefore, can also be thought of as employing reciprocity, as per our prior definition. Each person in the community (be it internal or external) and each type of direct relationship (be it a family member, friend or colleague) that one considers to be in his or her network now becomes a partner in reciprocity. Those two people that are now connected have established a set of obligations and expectations between one another.

- Need some help with a business idea? Tap into the network.
- Worried you don't have enough information about a client opportunity? Tap into the network.
- Unclear what project management company to employ for a time-sensitive project? Tap into the network.
- Seeking advice on your next career move? Tap into the network.

The obligation and expectation in *guanxi* is that you too will be there in a moment of need, hence the alignment to reciprocity. *Guanxi* is not a one-sided relationship. It is a social circle on performance-enhancing drugs. In China, *guanxi* has always been and continues to be a form of participation. Through the act of reciprocity, and by working with one another, China itself is a giant, cohesive node of connections helping one another get business done. The size of your *guanxi* network and how well you employ the act of reciprocity can dictate your level of success in the country. Key behaviors outlined in Chapters 4, 5 and 6 include *trusting, involving* and *developing*. It's these and other attributes that should remind today's leaders in the Western world that *guanxi* is not only working, it's demonstrating business results.

In *Networking Guanxi* by Barry Wellman, Wenhong Chen and Dong Weizhen, the authors solidify my point that *guanxi* is a summative example of concepts we have discussed thus far. It is part reciprocity, part participation, part *say it forward* and part Brakhage's new camera lens. Wellman et al. suggest that *guanxi* relationships are:

- *composed of strong or weak ties; kin or friends; characterized by gender, lifestyle and age; symmetrically reciprocal; made up of local or dispersed relationships, between status equals or patron-clients*
- *broadly supportive ties providing a variety of assistance or specialized relationships in which different network members provide different types of assistance*

- *better understood as discrete two-person dyads or as relationships that can only be understood as contingent parts of multi-person networks and groups*
- *bound up in densely knit groups or spread out in more sparsely knit networks*[6]

Charles Lee, our newly minted marketing manager at AT&T, knew exactly what to do when his gregarious boss instructed him to find new business in China. There was a problem to solve and, by habit, Charles tapped into the network and participated. His steps were as follows:

1. Utilize *guanxi:* find someone within his networking circle who might initially help.
2. Lee contacted a Chinese scientist he knew working at Stony Brook University in the state of New York.
3. Professor Yang Zengning, in turn, invoked his own *guanxi* and through past ties, reached out to the business attaché at the Chinese Liaison Office in Washington.
4. From there, the business attaché arranged for meetings with the Chinese Ministry of Post and Telecommunications (MPT).

By tapping into the network, by a "say it forward" attitude, by demonstrating reciprocity and ultimately by participating in the relationships, Lee's business quandary was solved and high-level meetings occurred between AT&T and the MPT. From out of thin air, with no prior relationship between the two entities (and back in 1975, when relations between China and America weren't exactly as warm as they are today), *guanxi* bore business fruit.

Guanxi is a remarkable concept and has provided many successful examples of personal and professional success across Asia. There is no sense of confinement or control when *guanxi* is employed. It acts like a method of networking osmosis, spreading to fill the infinite volume of relationship-building possibilities. It is a supportive model that enacts reciprocity. It is a behavior as much as it is a process. It is bound by quid pro quo, akin to "I'll be there for you so long as you're there for me." The responsibility is mutual. The expectation is shared. The result is not as important as the act, for the culmination of all actions is the evidence of *guanxi* itself. Isolation is unacceptable. In other words, my network is my net worth, as long as I'm participative.

AUTOPOIESIS

Autopoiesis is an ancient Greek term that is derived from the words "auto" and "poiesis," which can be defined as "self" and "production." In the context of an organization, we can think of autopoiesis as a recursive interaction of processes and exchanges among employees. It's these interactions that cause employees to ultimately determine how to beat the competition as opposed to beating each other.

In a paper entitled "Autopoiesis and knowledge in the organization: conceptual foundation for authentic knowledge management," Professor Aquiles Limone of Pontificia Universidad Católica de Valparaíso in Chile suggests that autopoiesis in the organization is

a network of processes of production of labor, technologic and economic acts that, upon interacting among themselves, return to produce the processes produced through the generation by those processes of relations that specify the conditions and operation of the economic community, which is the domain where the acts are produced.[7]

It's a tongue-twister, but at its root Professor Limone is stating that an organization brings economic benefit to itself if it knows how to work with itself. The organization becomes a kind of self-maintaining or self-defining system that allows personnel, knowledge, information and data to flow uninterrupted among everyone. It creates consistency.

The community becomes the exchange system, but because it's such a collaborative force, it has the means to self-regulate, driving efficiencies and coherencies at all times. It's participative panacea with positive business outcome.

In 1999, J.F. Keane and colleagues studied the effects of autopoiesis at Disneyland in California. They came to summarize the Disneyland environment as *an autopoietic system [that] acquires the radical autonomy of a living organism when it has the following qualities: it has its own operating code; it defines its own boundaries; it reproduces its own elements in a closed circuit and it obeys its own law of motion.*[8]

Let's hypothesize and then imagine that the organization has the following characteristics:

- its own operating code; through the Participative Leader Framework (which will be introduced later in this chapter), it stands to reason it can improve the internal and external value chain success rate
- its own definition of boundary through the Connected Leader Attributes (CLAs), ensuring consistency of behavior (see Chapters 3 through 7)
- its own circuit, such as the Collaborative Leader Action Model (CLAM), which establishes a common language across the organization in which to communicate and get things done (see Chapter 8)
- the ability to reproduce its own elements by establishing the necessary communities, both internal and external, to mimic the conditions of *guanxi*
- the wherewithal to obey its own law of motion; the organization and its leaders have successfully crafted and deployed organizational disciplines that will ensure both current and future success

Could it be that by employing more participative behaviors, both individually as a leader and pervasively across all units, the organization might become an autopoietic entity?

KNOW WHO YOU KNOW: NEIGHBOR NETWORKS

If ever I was knocked off my feet by a book—and plenty have seriously jolted me—it was by *Neighbor Networks: Competitive Advantage Local and Personal* by Dr. Ronald S. Burt, professor of sociology and strategy at the University of Chicago Booth School of Business. I'll get to Professor Burt's book in a moment.

For a few years, however, I had been a devotee of Mark Granovetter's 1973 paper entitled "The Strength of Weak Ties." This research paper is one of the most influential in social science and has been cited more than 20,000 times. When it comes to social network analysis, this is considered the preeminent work. It is a key piece to Andrew McAfee's book *Enterprise 2.0*, a seminal work you might also know.

Key points that surface from Granovetter's paper include:

- The definition of a tie, which he calls "a combination of the amount of time, the emotional intensity, the intimacy (mutual confiding), and the reciprocal services which characterize the tie."
- Ties, specifically those that are weak, will act as a "bridge," spanning parts of a social network connecting disconnected social groups.
- "No strong tie is a bridge." For example, if an individual has a strong tie with another individual, anyone else will be tied to them and thus the ties will be redundant.
- In order for true dissemination or diffusion to occur across a network, the weak ties provide this service and therefore are those that prove the most valuable. [9]

Weak ties are much more likely to connect different groups and therefore can provide ways to link content and information from small groups with more macro discussions.

In plain English, Granovetter's research asserts that the organization is healthier if employees are connected—not necessarily directly to one another, but indirectly. It's not as important to focus on your strong- or direct-tie network as it is to ensure you're plugging into the second-, third-, and fourth-level indirect relationships. Having read the paper a few times, I really wanted to believe it. I really wanted weak ties to be part of the answer to organizational engagement.

But they're not.

It's always bothered me. As a corporate organizational anthropologist, at least one that is self-proclaimed, I've never been convinced of the "strength of weak ties" argument even though I've written in favor of it previously. Although on occasion an employee might profit or prosper from someone within the organization they don't know, in my experience it rarely happens. Tests I've performed at organizations I've worked for, including TELUS, suggest corporate altruism only goes so far. That's not to say people aren't willing to share or exchange information, but networking has more to do with direct access to knowledge, information and corporate intelligence than it does some whimsical or vicarious route. Although important, the health of an organization cannot rest solely on "weak ties."

Then along came Dr. Burt and Neighbor Networks.

I now believe Granovetter is outdated. He may have been right for the time in 1973, but 40 years later, his theory doesn't seem to hold true. This has considerable implications for leaders aspiring to lead better. His research also creates significant ramifications for leaders looking to coach their teams to ultimately become better members within their team and throughout the organization.

The bottom line that Burt presents is starkly sobering in a world of Facebook, Twitter and Google+. No matter the scenario, says Burt, it is a person's own direct network—his immediate set of contacts—that bring benefits to any given situation. It has nothing to do with what Burt calls "secondhand brokerage" contacts, those second-, third-, etc.-level connections into other people's networks that bring the benefits.[10] Neighbor Networks directly opposes Granovetter's research and after thinking it through and performing my own analysis, I believe it's absolutely correct.

Burt investigated myriad examples—a product launch network, supply chain managers, investment bankers, senior analysts and human resources—and in each case, he proved "secondhand brokerage" showed no relationship with an increase in social capital, information exchange, performance improvement or advancements of any kind. His research proved indirect contacts—or as Granovetter would call them, "weak ties"—have no bearing on the positive competence or performance delta of an employee. Rather, competitive advantage lies with the personal, local or direct network of the individual. It's about how participative a leader is in building her network.

Consider the following scenario. How many times, as a leader, have you tried to coax other employees (leaders or otherwise) to help you on an initiative that you knew was right for the organization? In a situation where you knew everyone, and they you, was it relatively easy? I state "relatively" because given the alternative—when you were in a situation where you didn't know other stakeholders—how much longer did it take? Did everyone take the initiative and outcome at its word (i.e., your word) or did you have to politic, coerce and schmooze first before you could gain liftoff? Did it ultimately take longer and did you suffer more stress, time lags or budget overruns? Be honest with yourself.

Let's look at things somewhat differently. Imagine for a minute that your organizational network for a particular project includes a colleague—call her Denise—and seven other team members. As luck has it, Denise is a direct-network ally to each of the seven team members, but only Denise knows the seven. The others don't know one another. What does Denise bring to the table? She is a direct connection to those seven individuals, and you are not. Denise is a direct-contact juggernaut. Burt would articulate that Denise was the networking ticket; leaders need to find team members much like Denise because she is the interlocutor, the one to create new direct connections among others. It is this ability to bolster your direct connections that makes life easier in an organization and get the work done, not the proliferation of "weak tie" relationships.

Burt's research has considerable implications for organization silos. If a leader, for example, simply stays put within her business unit (or worse, her team) and doesn't branch out, communicate or participate with others, it has a negative effect on her team, her career, overall engagement and possibly the goals of her team. Alternatively, a leader who does connect with other leaders, pushing for more direct contacts and relationships (as opposed to second- or third-hand ones), not only synthesizes ways in which to prosper with other new connections, but she also gains exposure to new ways of doing things as well as contacts for future initiatives.

If you're thinking about career development, how is this not a good idea? If you're bringing a new employee into your team, how too is this not a fantastic idea? I'm reminded of the arrival of a new employee at SAP one year. He was hungry to learn and eager to perform. Not surprisingly, one of his first questions to me during the first couple of days was, "Dan, can you provide me a list of key people I need to meet with so I can build my own relationships?"

If we decouple the question, we can see the following assumptions and implications:

- An enthusiastic new employee assumes the leader has already built up a direct network for him to plug into.
- As a new employee, he is someone who knows the value in building direct network contacts to get things done.
- Dan, as the leader, better already have established a direct network to pass on, otherwise his credibility with the new employee will be tarnished.

As a leader, it is incumbent upon you to develop as many direct network contacts as possible. It is not only about access to information, it is clearly about access to direct network contacts who in turn have access to information. Burt's findings state well-connected people through weak ties do not necessarily have the same benefit when compared to direct relationships or contacts. That is, weak ties are possibly irrelevant when you need to get things done in your organization. What is critical, however, is the direct network contacts that both the leader possesses (and continues to build) as well as the team that she is leading. She must coach, nurture and implore her team to increase access to a direct network as well. Not simply within the organization, but outside it as well. She must instill a credo of being participative.

I started my career as a high school teacher and for two years I worked with a witty Italian. His most enduring quotation to me was, "God makes them, and they find each other." In the context of this book, it's the antithesis of leadership. You must seek out the network if you want to become a true Flat Army ambassador. The Participative Leader Framework fails if you don't.

✻ ✻ ✻

PUTTING IT ALL TOGETHER

Earlier in this chapter we explore concepts that may seem disparate, but hopefully you've now caught on and are connecting the dots I'm proposing. I apologize for taking this long, but I feel it important to dig deep before bringing the actual framework to the surface.

The new organizational camera lens—referring to the Brakhage analogy used at the opening of this chapter—is in fact the Participative Leader Framework. It comprises concepts that include Neighbor Networks, autopoiesis, *guanxi* and the notion of *say it forward*.

But we shouldn't use this camera lens reference any longer. As we define, to be an organization that is participative is to allow and encourage employees to contribute and consume knowledge, insight or ideas with any direct relationship via professional or personal networks. What does that look like?

THE PARTICIPATIVE LEADER FRAMEWORK

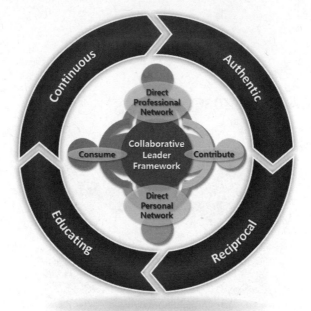

The Participative Leader Framework is a model for leaders to use as they contemplate the actions necessary to become more inclusive and to become more direct-network driven. The PLF acts as a handy guide for leaders, who should use it both as a personal framework for themselves and as a way in which to encourage their team to become more participative in relationships, content, knowledge and information. It contains four key behaviors, two actions and two target audiences.

The four behaviors to deploy make up the acronym CARE. A leader must demonstrate these holistic behaviors with his team and the organization; he must be

- continuous;
- authentic;
- reciprocal; and
- educating.

These participative behaviors help leaders exhibit the concepts we outline above, particularly *guanxi* and *say it forward*.

The two actions a leader should employ to become more participative include *consuming* and *contributing*. It's no use doing only one—they form the yin-yang relationship of the Participative Leader Framework. These also loosely align with the concept of autopoeisis.

Finally, the two audiences to target include your direct professional and personal networks. Efforts to spend time tapping into second-, third- and fourth-level contacts are unadvised. Rather, to be truly participative, a penchant for improving and working with direct connections is the most productive path forward. This links to Burt's theory of Neighbor Networks.

Continuous

Being *participative* is not something that should happen once, or even occasionally. It must be continuous; it must occur with relative frequency such that knowledge, information and ideas continue to be given and gained, networks steadily increase in size, our personal engagement stays on an upward trajectory, and lastly our performance ability prospers. On the flipside, if participation is too intermittent, the framework doesn't have a chance to be successful. When we're sleeping, we're still breathing. It's the same concept.

How? Your action cadence as a leader will speak volumes to those you lead. Determine the correct level of frequency that you will employ with your team on all matters. How regular are one-on-one meetings? What is your cycle-time to respond to emails, blog posts, etc.? Do you recognize achievement as well as mistakes? How often will you coach? Is it open to everyone or to a select few? Do you connect with a few on your team or are you consistent (and continuous) with everyone? Think of being continuous as defining your level of leadership cadence. Participation is about being consistent. You cannot go on holiday from being a participative leader.

Authentic

Without authenticity, you're a fake. If you're a fake, you are a participation hypocrite. The PLF requires users to be genuine, real and honest. What you write, how you communicate, who you attribute, and why you're participating are all questions one must ask to, in fact, be authentic. Be true to yourself, your abilities, your knowledge and your network, and engage as someone who is unpretentious and indisputably sincere.

How? Nobody likes a fake. Be real in your communication with the team. Show pictures from your vacations. Tell people you're having a bad day when you're having a bad day. Superhero syndrome is no badge of honor; the more you relate to your people, the more they like you for being an actual person. Eddie Vedder, lead singer of the group Pearl Jam, wrote the lyric "I shit and I stink, I'm real, join the club."[11] It's a tad crude, but it exemplifies my point.

Reciprocal

Participation is not about one-sided opinion. It is being receptive to and reciprocal with ideas, knowledge, input and thoughts. It is having the willingness to listen, the aptitude to synthesize and the capability to reflect before opining. It is binding. As much as participation is about giving, it is about taking—but not unless you are naturally receptive to diverging sentiments. To be participative is to be reciprocal; otherwise, it is a one-sided conversation, however you look at it.

How? Answer that email. Respond to that voicemail. Don't hide behind an executive assistant; get out of your office and dialogue with your people. Your team needs the guidance, wisdom and insight you've been hired for. Demonstrate it by giving back in a timely manner. Ask for feedback. Ask for opinions. Ask your team to contribute as well. If you are the only one talking or coming up with ideas, that's not reciprocity either. There are further mechanisms and tips on how to share and demonstrate reciprocity in Chapters 9 and 10.

Educating

Each of us has strengths, and it is foolish to believe we can be all things to all bodies. To be truly participative, however, we must demonstrate with conviction that we can, in fact, improve ourselves by believing we can enrich a body of knowledge, a network, our level of engagement and, ultimately, our performance. This happens through the behavior of educating. If you have personal belief in yourself that you can inspire, elevate, improve or enhance any given organizational scenario, then you are educating those around you.

How? Commit to teaching. Host a webcast series, or organize some lunch-and-learns, or dedicate time to facilitating a leadership forum. Open your team to the opportunity of having think-tank education sessions with one another. Coach someone on your team and encourage others to do the same. Be a mentor. Start a book club or, at a minimum, highlight books, articles or blog posts that help others with their learning. Be committed to the learning process itself and take an interest in the career development of people on your team.

Direct Professional and Personal Networks

According to a joint MIT and IBM research study in 2009, each person you have a direct relationship with in your email address book at work is associated with $948 dollars in annual revenue.[12] As per the work of Burt and Neighbor Networks, it is incumbent upon leaders to carry out two actions:

- commit time to building your own direct professional network at work; and
- encourage and help your team to do the same. By assembling a cadre of direct contacts at your place of work, you are making your work life inherently easier in the process. Don't ever stop, either. The more people you can call upon at work to help you, the better off you will be trying to actually employ the Participative Leader Framework.

As a leader you must at least encourage, if not coach, and help your people do the same. The more direct professional network connections your team has, the more connected everyone is going to be. And when that occurs, it makes the Participative Leader Framework that much easier to employ. How do you think I was able to land a writing contract with a bona fide publisher like Wiley? That's right, through my direct professional network.

You and your team should apply the same modus operandi to your external or direct personal-network connections. A workplace does not become successful based solely on the myopic view of internal-only direct connections. There is so much to be gained and learned when direct contacts are made outside the sphere of the workplace.

How? Get networking. Ask to be introduced to people—internally or externally—by those you already know. Commit to meeting two new people both internally and externally every month—for a total of at least 48 per year. Start using something as simple as LinkedIn to host your contacts. It's a fantastic resource that helps you keep your contacts organized. Mine the address book at work. Comb through the hierarchy and review job titles. Ask to be included in all newsletters that come from your corporate communications teams and research the stories, the names, the teams. Harvest those names and reach out. Get on Twitter, LinkedIn and Google + to find those in your profession as well as those outside of your profession. Nancy MacKay saw a need and formed MacKay CEO Forums, a group dedicated to the sharing of ideas, information and knowledge strictly among CEOs. It's a perfect example of executing the direct personal network component of the Participative Leader Framework. Networking is like flossing; it has to be done, otherwise decay is certain to occur.

Contribute and Consume

The final component to the Participative Leader Framework is how we ingest and convey knowledge, information and ideas. True organizational engagement can occur only when we consume and when we contribute back to the network of direct and indirect networks. I liken this concept to a term Stephen Downes of the National Research Council of Canada coined: "Connective Intelligence."[13] Quid pro quo.

As Robert Cialdini writes in his book *Influence: The Psychology of Persuasion:* "To engage in this sort of arrangement with another is not to be exploited . . . but to participate fairly in the 'honored network of obligation' that has served us so well from the dawn of humanity."[14]

Regardless of which network—professional or personal—and dependent on the situation, it is imperative that one follow the CARE principle and contribute back one's knowledge to the network if one truly wants to achieve Flat Army status. The level of depth and breadth will obviously depend on the scenario, but it's not participative if you're not contributing your knowledge, your opinion, your insights or your ideas to the two direct networks.

You also have a responsibility to consume the knowledge and ideas of others in your direct network, thus assisting you to become more engaged, increasing your connections and ultimately your performance. Think of it this way: if leaders are only contributing and not consuming, how does that demonstrate the CARE principle? Consuming the ideas, concepts and thoughts of those in your direct network permits you the opportunity to increase your own knowledge base first and foremost. We can't really participate (or contribute) unless we are equally consuming.

How? More to come in Chapters 9 and 10, but the use of collaboration-based technologies such as wikis, blogs, micro-blogging, leader-generated videos, discussion forums, instant messaging and, yes, even email, are critical. You must be present with your team and your organization. Your contributions must come in the form of these new technologies. Similarly, you should find ways in which to contribute through the previously mentioned element of the CARE principle *educating*. You have knowledge and it's your duty to contribute that knowledge back through whatever means are possible. To consume, you must be conscious of the content that comes directly or indirectly into your workflow. If a team member needs your feedback, read the report or slideshow they've sent you; don't pretend you did, because you'll get caught. If there are conversations going on in the organization (virtually or physically), insert yourself into the process to listen, to consume and to understand what is going on. Make the time—it's important.

PARTICIPATIVE LEADER FRAMEWORK IN ACTION

A study published in *Journal of Medical Marketing* in 2009 entitled "Collaboration in research protocol design: A case study exploring knowledge creation for the pharmaceutical industry and prescribing physicians" suggests that the pharmaceutical industry needs to be more participative with physicians in order to bring innovative products to market. Their findings "support the importance of knowledge creation between physicians and pharmaceutical companies."[15] The research demonstrates elements of the Participative Leader Framework in action. Pharmaceutical industry representatives, for example, need to create better direct professional links and connections with physicians. To be successful, they have to do a better job of consuming the knowledge, data and information from physicians as much as they have to contribute back to the physicians' own knowledge banks. With a professional distance between the physicians and the pharmaceutical industry already in existence, leaders from Big Pharma had to employ the CARE principle in order to ensure the physicians were onside with the project. This is progress in my opinion.

In Oakland, California, the Participative Leader Framework was demonstrated at an elementary school called Fred T. Korematsu Discovery Academy. More than half the second grade students at the school in 2009 were close to illiterate. Math skills were no better and it was generally the same story across other grades. In an interview with *Converge Magazine* in 2012, principal Charles Wilson said, "There was a lack of focused teaching."[16] What Wilson brought in was a more inclusive approach to the workplace. He had teachers working with one another more directly, building educational practices and techniques together, reading professional books as a group, among other participative workplace techniques. They were employing the CARE behaviors while contributing to and consuming each other's development. Rebecca Akin, a teacher at the school, stated, "There was resistance, as there usually is when people have to work together." In the end, literacy scores were up across the board. Nineteen percent of second-grade students at the school are now at advanced reading levels and 49 percent are at the basic level—a marked improvement from 26 percent the year prior. Akin went on to say, "I think the collaborative nature of our work and the leadership really accounts for a lot." If an elementary school can utilize a concept like the Participative Leader Framework to improve results, can't we all?

At TELUS, leaders continually remind team members to build their networks, both in the company and outside of it. It is a firm believer in the "direct professional and personal network" adage, so much so that there are clubs and groups across TELUS that support the company, its employees and its clients even though the objectives of the club or group may not directly link to the day-to-day functional roles of its members.

Introduced in 2006, Connections is a national initiative supporting the professional development of women at TELUS. The group has ten different chapters across Canada and more than 3,000 members. The intention is simply to connect with each other, employ the behaviors of CARE, consume and contribute knowledge, information and ideas, as well as be a place to build additional direct professional and personal contacts.

Another example at TELUS is Spectrum. Launched in 2009, Spectrum is TELUS's lesbian, gay, bisexual, transgender and queer (LGBTQ) group. The group meets on-site or off-site, during business hours and outside of them, not only to share, learn and plan for volunteer events but also to support efforts to reach LGBTQ customers and assist with LGBTQ community investment initiatives. It's another example of the Participative Leader Framework in action as all members and supporting leaders must employ the underlying concept in order for it to be successful.

✳   ✳   ✳

Inspiration doesn't happen in isolation. The same can be said of participation.

The Participative Leader Framework is both a mindset and an activity for leaders. Inclusivity might be thought of as an altruistic, proactive as well as reactive information-and-knowledge-exchange loop. It doesn't happen, however, unless the Participative Leader Framework is put into motion by the leader.

Lynn Wu of MIT and several of her colleagues presented a paper in 2009 at the Winter Information Systems Conference in Salt Lake City, Utah, entitled "Value of Social Network: A Large-Scale Analysis on Network Structure Impact to Financial Revenue of Information Technology Consultants." In it, the authors state the following:

We find that both network diversity and betweenness are strongly correlated with performance. This demonstrates the importance of distinguishing one's social network not only by its network topologies but also the content of the network such as the cumulative human capital inside the network and the strength of ties connecting to this type of capital.[17]

That is, assemble those direct network connections and treat them well—via the Participative Leader Framework—and you just might improve your own performance and that of your team. Truly demonstrate the CARE principle—be *continuous, authentic, reciprocal* and *educating*—in an effort to get both you and your team participating regardless of the situation.

CHAPTER EIGHT

THE COLLABORATIVE LEADER ACTION MODEL

Whosoever desires constant success must change his conduct with the times.
—Niccolo Machiavelli[1]

In a stirring blog post, Dr. Stephen Rhinesmith—author of several books including *Head, Heart, and Guts: How the World's Best Companies Develop Complete Leaders*—brings to the surface an argument concerning the paradox of corporate profits and the leadership required to ensure its continuance.

Rhinesmith states the following:

While philosophically many would agree to the expansion of corporate responsibility from maximizing shareholder value to creating shared value for society, the current forces in place allow little deviation from a corporation's original responsibility to maximize shareholder value. The vast majority of these forces are not Wall Street greed (although this is obviously a factor), but the fact that our global economic system has built a dependency of investors, including pensioners around the world, on a consistent return on investment from the corporate sector. As a result, the pressure from the investment community to keep corporations focused on maximization is relentless.[2]

He believes, as do I, that a new definition of leadership is the answer. Rhinesmith goes on to indicate the only way to solve our paradox is through "leadership that is committed to managing the paradoxes of profit and purpose and short-term vs. long-term needs." But what is committed leadership? In part, it is what we've already uncovered to this point in the book. There are fifteen leadership behaviors under the aegis of *becoming, being* and *beyond* that must be part of a leader's DNA. A leader—and his or her team—must also become more participative, through the Participative Leader Framework.

But to continue the pursuit of Flat Army, to ensure corporate revenues and profits continue amid a need for enhanced employee engagement practices—our paradox—we must now discuss the act of collaborating. It's my ongoing belief that by collaborating more effectively, organizations become both healthier and more productive. And it's this third act to the Flat Army play—collaboration—where we might provide a solution to the paradox Rhinesmith alludes to.

Let's first explore the history of collaboration. As many words do, the word collaborate originates from Latin— in this case, from *collaborare*, which means "to work with." The prefix *col* means "with" and, of course, *labore* is familiar to us as "to work" or, in today's lexicon, "to labor." Thus, to collaborate is to work with.

Unfortunately, the word collaborate, in terms of its modern-day definition, took a turn for the worse circa World War II. The negative connotation took shape during the occupation of Europe in 1939 when factions of Europeans began "working with" the Third Reich in very traitorous ways. Civilians might have collaborated on an individual basis with German soldiers by offering community details, doing laundry for German soldiers or being part of locally based militias. Perhaps the most famous organized example of what I call "misfortunate collaboration" occurred in July of 1940 when the Vichy regime was established by Marshal Pétain as a result of establishing collaboration practices with Nazi forces.

Pétain made the decision to collaborate with the occupying forces of Germany so that France might remain undivided. At the time, I suppose it might have been his only move. How did the Vichy Regime carry out its act of collaboration with the Germans? Pétain and his Vichy authorities aided in the rounding up of Jews and others, handing them over to the Reich. This indeed can be defined as collaboration—the French were "working with" the Germans to achieve a goal—but this act of misfortunate collaboration resulted in a negative connotation of the word. And rightly so. Thankfully, we're well aware of what happened in 1944 with the Allied invasion coupled with the efforts of exiled French General Charles de Gaulle, who just might have begun a more positive interpretation of the term collaboration.

If, as is suggested in Chapter 2, most of our current leadership behaviors are based on past practices of hierarchy, controlling, commanding, hoarding and territorialism, we should define collaboration so that it has plausible use for anyone in the organization and for years to come. We need to take back the word "collaboration." For the purposes of achieving a Flat Army, collaborating in the organization is defined as follows:

> **Collaborating:** The unfettered allowance and encouragement of employees to both contribute and consume knowledge, insight or ideas with any direct relationship via professional or personal networks to achieve an outcome.

Let's think back to Chapter 7 and the example of marketing manager Charles Lee of AT&T. Indeed, collaboration is the twin sister to participation, albeit fraternal, not identical. Can we compare our definition of collaboration against Lee, and determine if he was not only demonstrating the Participative Leader Framework, but also collaborating?

- Was Lee provided unfettered allowance and encouragement? Yes.
- Was he able to contribute and consume knowledge, insight and ideas? Yes.
- Did he tap into his relationships among internal or external communities? Yes.
- Did Lee achieve an outcome? Absolutely.

Collaboration itself is not the point; the outcome through collaborating is what we're trying to achieve.

HETERARCHY IS NOT ANARCHY

In Chapter 7 we introduce the Participative Leader Framework (PLF), the essential life cycle that ensures leaders, workers and members of all walks of the organization have a model with which to participate more effectively. To further improve our levels of engagement (as we discuss in Chapter I), leading to an increase in productivity and then profitability, and to recalibrate our organizations away from silos, hoarding and blind hierarchy (as per our examples in Chapter 2), we need to talk about leadership in the context of *daily* leadership.

Talking about leadership by the minute, hour or day is not as simple as merely introducing social media tools into the organization and assuming everyone is going to become instantly more collaborative. Don't be naive. There are questionable social media technology companies purporting to aid your organization's culture and productivity simply by having your organization launch their platform or apps. Do not listen to them. Your goal is to redefine the behaviors of leadership as per the Connected Leader Attributes in Chapters 4 through 6 and to ensure all employees see themselves as part of a cohesive and inclusive team. Hence the introduction of the Collaborative Leader Action Model.

In 2011, McKinsey Global Institute issued a paper entitled, *Big data: The next frontier for innovation, competition, and productivity.* Among other points of reference, the authors find there could be somewhere between a $900-billion to $1.3-trillion value spike to the economy by virtue of employees working more communicatively and collaboratively through the use of social media.[3] This purported value comes almost solely by virtue of increased productivity. If there is going to be that big a positive hit on the economy by collaborating better through social technologies, imagine if we simply focused on the behavior of collaboration first? I don't doubt the researchers at McKinsey, but it seems to suggest technology is the savior, whereas I posit it's the behavior that must be enhanced before any value will be realized. And if it is, dare I say quadrillions of dollars of economic value will be realized?

It's time, therefore, to introduce you to the CLAM. The Collaborative Leader Action Model is an action process for leaders and employees alike to become more collaborative in their projects, actions and decisions. It is nonhierarchical and can act as an interaction manifesto between members of all walks of the organization and applies to any type of opportunity. It can help bring this economic value McKinsey purports to actual fruition.

- Has someone tasked you with a project to complete in three months? Invoke the CLAM.
- Are you considering a way to save money inside your business unit? Invoke the CLAM.
- Do you think a reorganization of several units might cut down red tape? Invoke the CLAM.
- Want to know if there are operational efficiencies that can be driven out of your team? Invoke the CLAM.
- Not sure what your objectives should be for the next fiscal year? Invoke the CLAM.

The CLAM is a daily leadership habit as much as it is a collaborative process to be initiated when starting something new. It's an interaction process for everyone in the organization and it moves both the organization and leaders away from ingrained hierarchy to a combination of heterarchy and situational hierarchy. How cool is that?

"Heterarchy" as a word isn't well understood. It's not about making the organization and its employees responsible for the same tasks. Nor is it about giving everyone a consensual vote on every single action or decision. It is about understanding an employee's or leader's inherent responsibility for contributing to the success of the mission, of the task, or of the goal. Heterarchy permits relationships to form between employees and leaders without a focus on positional boundaries. The benefit to a concept like heterarchy is that leaders and employees alike can allow relationships to build, and connections to become stronger as a result of value and outcomes, not because of position, power or rank. Heterarchy permits an open culture to grow in the organization and it does so when models like the Connected Leader Attributes and the Participative Leader Framework are utilized in parallel.

The CLAM might be construed as a way in which to drive daily heterarchy in your organization and within your own personal leadership style. But it's a way in which to get things done, too.

Situational hierarchy, however, should not be confused for outright hierarchy. Situational hierarchy is important for decisions and actions in an organization that quite simply can't involve the masses or a team in general. If your executive board and senior leadership team are contemplating a merger or an acquisition, it's unlikely the CLAM is going to be employed across the organization. If you have to approve an expense report or vacation schedule in your managerial tasks, it's overkill to use something like the CLAM, so situational hierarchy comes into play. But let us not mistake situational hierarchy for heterarchy. By the end of this chapter, we'll learn how to utilize the CLAM as often as we can within our teams. The CLAM enables opinion and outcome through the process of inclusion.

HAT TIP TO WIREARCHY

We mustn't press ahead any further with the CLAM without paying deep respect and acknowledgment to Jon Husband, founder of the term "wirearchy." Quite frankly, Jon was ahead of his time. Through a storied career working in the U.S., Canada and the U.K. in the banking industry and in firms such as Hay Group and then as an independent and appropriately self-titled techno-anthropologist and organizational-change consultant, Jon connected the dots between collaborative culture, organizational engagement and positive business results far earlier than the present-day musings from yours truly. There are only a few in his class.

In 1999, after working as an independent for five years, Jon formulated his organizational-behavior futuristic thoughts into the concept known as "wirearchy," defined as follows: "A dynamic two-way flow of power and authority based on knowledge, trust, credibility and a focus on results enabled by interconnected people and technology."[4]

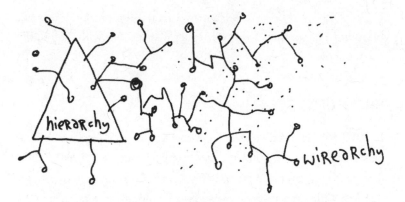

I've been lucky enough to spend some time with Jon over the years. He doesn't believe hierarchy should go away; rather, wirearchy—as an organizing mechanism for the people of the organization to regulate the flow of work— complements hierarchy. Wirearchy is an overarching behavior much like what we've been discussing throughout *Flat Army*. An organization that permits information, data and knowledge to freely flow throughout the organization can become an engaged organization. Wirearchy is not a nebulous or nefarious term. Its hypothesis suggests works gets done better—and perhaps faster—through altruistic behavior, and that behavior is built on the reciprocal and credible flow of knowledge and trust.

In a 2007 interview with *CIO Magazine*, Jon was asked about wirearchy and the changing nature of organizational structure. Here is his response:

Increasingly, employees seek meaning and/or satisfaction in their work and want to be able to connect their values and aspirations to what they do. Customers want authentic and honest responses to their needs and the purchases they make with their money. Both sets of voices will be heard. People connect, talk and link. They talk and link about what they buy and about their work . . . why, what for, how they think it should be, how things could be better. These are all democratizing forces, key elements of engagement organizational leaders can use as levers to enhancing and sustaining performance in service to vision and mission.[5]

Hat tip—or HT to those in the Twitter world—to Jon Husband, the founder of wirearchy. (He once even gave me a shirt with the graphic you see above.)

SHELL OF THE CLAM

In 2010, IBM released a research report entitled "Working Beyond Borders: Insights from the Global Chief Human Resource Officer Study."[6] The findings germinated from surveys and discussions with over seven hundred CHROs across the globe. Two key points were raised that fit nicely into the theme of Flat Army. CHROs believe there is:

- a shortage of creative leaders; and
- ineffective collaboration and knowledge sharing among leaders.

Not surprisingly, fewer than 33 percent of CHROs who participated in the research felt their companies were adept at leadership development itself. Furthermore, 78 percent of those same executives didn't think their organizations were effective at collaboration.

Today, many organizations have leadership-development training programs for their employees. But do those same organizations follow a leadership-action model that encourages everyone in the organization to connect and contribute? Is the leadership-action model a part of those same training programs? Do those leadership-development programs include a new attitude, a new DNA, a new bedrock that starts first with the notion that everyone at the company is in fact a leader? Can they even pronounce "wirearchy"?

Implementing Flat Army and the CLAM starts with the principal tenet that we need to open our doors, tear down the cubicles, and invite the entire organization to the table before making decisions or inventing the next new shiny object. Do you remember the Connected Leader Chasm from Chapter 3? It's the harmonious leader zone all leaders should be trying to attain. The CLAM helps achieve this.

The Collaborative Leader Action Model is a process that brings heterarchy to the surface within situational hierarchy. It provides those CHROs mentioned above with a simple leadership and collaboration behavioral model that drives cooperation, knowledge sharing, creativity and development—the very same traits the CHROs believe are currently in dire straits within their organizations.

Imagine for a moment you're in a rather large organization with several business units spread across multiple geographies. One leader in a product marketing unit instructs his team to design a go-to-market strategy for a product line that spins a new message the organization has never seen before. Meanwhile, in the corporate marketing team, they are busy like beavers, building out a new campaign that stretches current messaging but builds off of a previously agreed-upon theme. In a third part of the organization, another team—product management—is just about finished a new line of products, with the leader taking the proactive measure with her team of establishing the name of the product. She has also crafted the message, key themes and tagline. She sticks firm with her belief this is key to product success. Her team rocks, or at least that's what she thinks.

What's really going on?

- Team #1 comprises a dictatorial leader who has instructed his team to do his will, and his team must listen (or else).
- Team #2 has a team that is following previously established practice, but isn't involving anyone else despite good intentions.
- Team #3 is eager and innovative but sees no need to include others across the company in the naming or messaging process.

This scenario, or a reasonable facsimile, happens all the time in organizations. Time, budget and people pressures push leaders to dictate, to take the easy way out, or to proclaim their ideas or innovations are the best way: No one else can be as clever as me. There's no need to change. There's no need to involve anyone, is there?

But what is the end result?

- Team #1 is scared to death to confront the leader, thus members acquiesce and do as they're told.
- Team #2 is following standard practice, but who says this is the best way to proceed?

- Team #3 contains employees who may be collaborating among their own team members, but are blind to ideas or opinions elsewhere.

Collaboration isn't easy; in fact, it's quite difficult. Through this chapter, please root yourself in the know-how that collaboration—as good as it is—always takes longer, but in the end, your leadership style, growth, team unity and organizational prosperity are better off.

The cyclical stages of the Collaborative Leader Action Model are as follows:

- connect (with others)
- consider (all options)
- communicate (the decision and action plan)
- create (the result)
- confirm (the result met the target)
- congratulate (through feedback and recognition)

The CLAM

CONNECT (WITH OTHERS)

You've got an idea. A project has been initiated. A process must be redefined. There's a problem in customer service. What's going on in procurement—a new approval system needs to be introduced. These and countless other opportunities for action or decisions surface on a daily basis in organizations.

The default mode for many of us is to solve the problem or complete the task as quickly as possible. Our thought process goes something like this: "Speed is good. I need to look great in front of my peers. Somebody is there to replace me. My boss wants this done yesterday."

Who would disagree that organizations are plagued by "fire, aim, ready" syndrome, which is, of course, the exact opposite of "ready, aim, fire."

But that's the epitome of how leaders are getting it wrong from the beginning. Leaders jump to solving and acting on a problem, task or opportunity before stopping to think who they should connect with first. Therefore, the first stage of the CLAM is to connect with others before going down a path of regret. It's the way in which leaders can immediately break down hierarchies and nurture a collaborative culture across business units and teams. It's the initial step leaders should take to open up the realm of possibilities and to avoid duplication of effort.

How to *connect*

Key actions:

> STOP . . . don't start anything. First thing is to think about connecting with others who might be impacted. Who is it that may need to be involved or who could assist? Who needs to be part of the process or the decision? Are there individuals on your team, other teams, partners, customers or elsewhere? Invite them to the table so they can be a part of the next stage.

Result:

> You have passed the first stage of the CLAM. More importantly, you have demonstrated being a collaborative leader. By

reaching out, you are openly suggesting you don't have all the answers, and you require input before proceeding with decisions or actions. It's the first step and the most critical.

I've seen too many leaders over the years forget to connect with others first. It's such a simple action to take, hence the reason why it sits at the top of the CLAM. By default, it is the expected first action to take. One nutty example comes at the expense of the National Basketball Association. After the 2005–06 season, the commissioner of the league, David Stern, announced its teams would use a new basketball for the next season. The new ball—a microfiber ball—was to replace the leather basketball. You might guess the problem I'm about to let loose, right? You got it. The league didn't bother to meet with the players and discuss the transition, resulting in a huge outburst from fans echoing player complaints about the new ball. Players claimed it became difficult to handle and was the cause of an increase in turnovers. For some there was a decline in shooting percentages. By January 2007, the leather balls were back in play and the microfiber ones sent to the bin. Imagine if the commissioner had connected with players beforehand, inviting them into the entire CLAM process?

CONSIDER (ALL OPTIONS)

The word conversation is fascinating. Its earliest use in the 1300s meant to deal with or live among others. The word conversation derives from the Latin *conversari* ("to move about or to keep company with"), which itself came from *convertere*, which means "to turn about."

These days, if we converse or have a conversation with someone it means something totally different. A conversation is an exchange of thoughts, words and information between one or more parties. Some refer to it as a dialogue, a conversation's stepsister. We purport to have open, transparent and honest dialogue in the workplace, yet many employees believe conversations are closed, off limits or, in fact, dishonest. Some are never a part of them, ever.

Perhaps we need to rethink the history of the word "conversation" and use it in a slightly different way, particularly in the Collaborative Leader Action Model. Perhaps conversations need to be thought of first as the way in which we *consider* options through dialogue before moving forward. A conversation, therefore, is not simply an exchange of words—it is a behavioral attitude that defines our ability to consider what we should do before we actually do it. To consider is to discuss options that are fruitful, positive and purposeful. It is professional debate and discourse that leads to a decision. To converse is to consider options before deciding what should actually be accomplished. This is the second stage of the CLAM.

How to *consider*

Key actions:

> With the right players now involved (however large or small) this is the proverbial whiteboard, brainstorm and ideation phase. Consider your options. Contemplate the pros and cons of doing something, or not doing something. Are other groups working on similar projects? Engagement, productivity and financial options should be weighed. You are hypothesizing not only options but what may come as a result of completing the initiative. With other smart people around you, encourage them to bring their considerations to the surface; it's your responsibility as a leader.

Result:

> You and the connected team members have brought up a series of options. By already connecting with them, those that have been included feel good about being part of the up-front planning and discussion, which will improve levels of engagement. You also have options of better quality than if devised solely by yourself. Simultaneously, you've considered a variety of options that can help spur other projects or initiatives unrelated to the task at hand. The connected team members feel positive and optimistic, the options are plentiful, and you're ready for the next CLAM stage.

Cam Crosbie is the CIO of Equitable Life Insurance Company of Canada, represented by more than 10,000 independent producers across Canada and Bermuda, who in turn are supported by more than 500 staff at their head office in Waterloo, Ontario. When Cam is considering options before moving forward he tries not to shy away from asking lots of questions including, as he says, "even the so-called 'dumb ones.'"[7] As a CIO, Cam believes it's important to reach out to others and inquire before pushing ahead. Cam said to me, "I hope that in some small way if people see the CIO unashamedly asking the simple questions, it clears the way for clearer and more meaningful discussion." That's a CIO who gets the stage of *considering*.

To consider is to stretch one's thinking to the thinking of many. Greek philosopher Aristotle was quoted as saying, "Two good men are better than one."[8] It's not only about the number two and it's not solely about men—rather obviously—but you hopefully get the point.

COMMUNICATE (THE DECISION AND ACTION PLAN)

According to Google Ngram—a viewer that displays a graph showing how one or more phrases have occurred in a corpus of books over time—the term "communicate" hit a high-water mark around the year 1830. It's at this point in time when authors were using the term the most (see the graphic below). Both it and the term "communicating" tailed off to a low point in 1940. Since then, it has been on the increase, but we're beginning to see it decreasing again as of 2002. I personally find it troubling and hope Flat Army helps to stem the tide. I'd like to see the terms "communicate" and "communicating" rise not only on Google Ngram; I'd like them to become ubiquitous among Flat Army leaders.

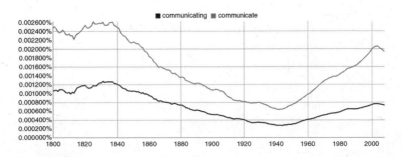

To communicate in the CLAM is to a) decide what action is to be taken followed closely by b) that decision and accompanying information or action plan getting into the hands of any relevant stakeholder. Once you've connected with the right people and considered the options, it's time to make a decision and to communicate it. Too often a decision is made and communicated without taking into account the stages of *connect* and *consider.*

In terms of the decision itself, there are myriad ways in which it can be handled, but which is chosen depends on the scenario or opportunity. There are times when situational hierarchy must be invoked—where the ultimate leader makes the decision and owns it outright—and there are times when consensus might be applied to a relevant group. Let us not confuse the *communicate* stage with fairness, though. The Flat Army concept is not about mutual decision making throughout an organization; rather, it is about becoming more engaged, productive, connected and collaborative so that employees feel part of the equation and not simply numbers in a database. Employees are not the ultimate decision makers but they need to be part of the process.

Once the decision has been made, it's time for part two of this stage, which is to inform others of the direction. Warren Bennis and Burt Nanus in *Leaders: Strategies for Taking Charge* insist when leaders communicate through meaning, they are in fact creating a "commonwealth of learning."

They write: "What we see and experience in today's organizational landscape are cumbersome bureaucracies that more often than not betray the mismanagement of meaning."[9]

By inviting representatives into the process (*connecting*) and through the analysis of options (*considering*) we've broken down the bureaucracy while simultaneously providing meaning. It's not coming after the fact, but rather coming during the process itself, at least for those involved. Sure, not everyone is going to be a part of the *connect* and *consider* stages, so once the decision has been made, it's even more important to communicate the decision and the action plan to others to continue this level of meaning that Bennis and Nanus suggest. It's a critical step in the CLAM.

They further assert: "Communication creates meaning for people. Or should. It's the only way any group, small or large, can become aligned behind the overarching goals of an organization. Getting the message across unequivocally at every level is an absolute key."[10]

How to *communicate*

Key actions:

Part A

Once the *connect* and *consider* stages are complete, make certain the decision-making criteria have been established. The *communicate* stage includes decision making, and it needs to be clearly stated who owns or is accountable for the decision that must be made coming out of the previous two stages. You must decide on the deciders. Is it a project that requires a vote or is it through consensus? Is it up to the leader to listen to those that have been invited to share their ideas and thoughts to ultimately rule on the way forward. Depending on the situation, a number of ways to determine the decision can be applied; the simple point here is to identify it up front. Once that's cleared up, decide!

Part B

It's now time to get the decision, the message and the action plan out to those that need it. Yes, it implies you create the action plan—with targets—at this stage as well. Targets need to be specific as well; quantifiable and focused, not metrics that wallpaper every single aspect of the endeavor. To communicate includes anyone involved in the *connect* and *consider* phases as well as pertinent stakeholders who were not a part of the exercise. Is it a large enough project to warrant a wiki or community site? Get building it. Should a conference call, web meeting or town hall be conducted? Start booking it. Will an email suffice? Begin writing it. Whoever needs to know, needs to know as soon as possible. Hoarding the decision and the details does no good whatsoever. As George Bernard Shaw once said, "The single biggest problem with communication is the illusion that it has taken place."[11]

Result:

You have a game plan and (ideally) anyone that should know is in the know. You've now spent considerable time inviting people into a stage full of consideration; and coming out of it are your actions and quantifiable targets. You now have stakeholders who you have proactively reached out to communicating the decision and plan. There will be no misunderstandings, and their absence will help fuel your credibility and alignment. The bonus part is if you inadvertently missed a stakeholder's meeting but communicated the decision and action plan before beginning the next stage, you have a bit of latitude to remedy the error.

To communicate is to be like Gene Kranz of NASA. He was both inclusive and direct. He was honest and open. If you've really been paying attention you will notice *communicating* is one of the Connected Leader Attributes at the *becoming* stage. No, I'm not repeating myself; it's that important for it to be both a behavior and an action in the Flat Army model.

CREATE (THE RESULT)

Larry Bossidy and Ram Charan, in their 2002 book *Execution: The Discipline of Getting Things Done*, articulate a set of three disciplines that ensure leaders get things done. We can compare the CLAM stage of *create* to their term of "execution." The ideas they posit are the following:

- Execution is a discipline.
- Execution is the major job of a business leader.
- Execution must be a core element of a business culture.[12]

To create, ergo, is to get things done. It's to *create the result*. It's to execute. This is the stage in which previous elements of buy-in, ideation, decision making, action planning and communication throughout allow the leader and the members of the team to begin accomplishing their intended goal. It's when the rubber hits the road. We'd need an entire book to delve into the mechanics of actually creating the result, and unfortunately we won't be able to provide it here. But, as Bossidy and Charan opine, "[It's] a systematic process of rigorously discussing hows and whats, questioning, tenaciously following through, and ensuring accountability."[13]

Truth be told, my hero is Terry Fox, a Canadian legend. His is a story of *creating the result* that cannot be matched. In 1977, Terry contracted cancer in his right leg. It was amputated, but this courageous and tenacious basketball player didn't let that stop him. In 1980, he set out to raise $24 million for cancer research—$1 for every Canadian citizen—by running across Canada under the banner of the Marathon of Hope. That's right—Terry intended to run a marathon a day in hopes he could attain his goal. His quest commenced in the spring of 1980 in St. John's, Newfoundland, which would take him across Canada where he would dip his leg in the Pacific Ocean in Victoria, British Columbia, at some point in the fall of 1980.

Cancer is inhumane; it came back to stop Terry in his tracks in Thunder Bay, Ontario, after 143 days and 5,373 kilometres of running. Do the math—it's just shy of a marathon a day for 143 days on one human leg and one prosthetic leg. I was 9 years old. Stunned, shocked and disappointed was how I was feeling back then. Nine months later, Terry succumbed to cancer and my nation and I mourned uncontrollably for the loss. Unjust doesn't begin to describe the irony. Some thirty years later, Terry's goal of $24 million has easily been reached with the annual Terry Fox Run—the world's largest one-day fundraising event for cancer research—bringing in well over $500 million to date.

During the Marathon of Hope itself, Terry was joined by his brother Darrell and good friend Doug Alward. It was here where Terry demonstrated the act of creating the result. Terry's pugnacious drive and hardened vision would not allow failure to be an option. He was resilient and always on top of Doug and Darrell to achieve the daily goal in hopes of reaching the overall objective. He was relentless. He was focused. He pushed his team when necessary. Terry was accountable to the team, himself and the mission. His stamina—physically and mentally—was unassailable. Were it not for the unkind fortune of a disease that didn't seem to quit, Terry would have accomplished his feat with dignity, engagement and a results-positive outcome. He inspired a generation (and now a second generation) to be bold, driven and at all times to *create the result*. I know he has done that for me and lately with our children. Can Terry be your inspiration to *create the result* too?

How to *create*

Key actions:

> Immerse yourself in the process of execution. Don't micromanage, but as per the Connected Leader Attribute of *delivering* utilize specific, measurable, attainable, realistic and time-sensitive actions (SMART) to cross the finish line. Are roles and responsibilities accurately depicted for the entire team? They had better be if you want to complete the stage successfully. An arc of accountability is also a must. Take responsibility, but engender an attitude of culpability—your team is looking up to you. Address issues as soon as possible, but remain flexible throughout the stage. Hiccups occur. Deal with them as necessary but motivate the team to stay on track as per the SMART action plan you've already devised. Most importantly, be there for the team. Chip in and lead by example.

Result:

> Yes, the outcome will be achieved at the completion of this stage. More importantly perhaps are the learning, the camaraderie, the engagement opportunities and the chance to achieve greatness. In creating the result, the result is being able to create. In a hierarchically driven command-and-control structure, executing a goal feels taxing, if not mind numbing. Too many leaders continue to bark orders expecting

the result to come to fruition with force, ego and fear. The result we should expect when utilizing the CLAM is a truly engaged and inspired team of people who will continue to create well into the future. It is these people who will stick up for the team and your wishes the next time it's needed.

According to The Conference Board's "CEO Challenges" report in 2010, 42 percent of CEOs believe "excellence in execution" remains a risk and is the greatest challenge among any other factor in the organization.[14] The CLAM helps you to rise above this rhetoric and stay focused to *create the result.* Don't let the hurdles, obstacles or naysayers get to you. Be like Terry Fox and execute with the team until the actions and goals are accomplished.

CONFIRM (THE RESULT MET THE TARGET)

Noted American science fiction writer Robert Anson Heinlein—often referred to as "the Dean of Science"—once said, "If it can't be expressed in figures, it is not science; it is opinion."[15]

There is truth to that statement, particularly in an organization focused on improving revenues, profits, customer satisfaction, employee engagement, etc. What's the point in the Collaborative Leader Action Model if you sail through the first four stages (connect, consider, communicate and create) only to send the result into the black hole of the unknown? Shouldn't the qualified be quantifiable? To confirm is to ensure the result meets the target whether by date, by level of quality, by budget amount, or by other measures. If you recall, the targets for the objective or project were set in the *communicate* stage during decision-making action. To confirm that you're hitting the mark, that the result has been achieved, seems like a sensible thing to do, doesn't it? I believe it is.

To avoid the *confirm* stage is to make a seriously misguided judgment of the Flat Army structure. Remember, to be an effective connected,

participative and collaborative leader, you must employ engagement
practices with precise execution actions. To simply think an objective
has met the mark is insufficient. To categorically qualify and quantify
that the result is commensurate with defined targets is to act like a true
Flat Army leader. Many leaders already do this very well. The point is
to ensure it is being done—or to continue doing it—otherwise, the collaborative practices and behaviors enacted up to this point are for naught.
Your team and cross-functional stakeholders utilized throughout this
stage will likely mock your leadership ability if you allow the creation
of the result to stand on its own without proper confirmation that the
actual intended targets and goals have been achieved. That cannot be
a good thing.

How to *confirm*

Key actions:

> Gather the team and various stakeholders to formally debrief
> once the project has concluded. Perform a clinical audit on
> two key areas:
> - the first four stages of CLAM
> - whether the various end goal targets were achieved as
>   set out in the *communicate* stage
>
> These two actions allow the team to offer opinions and positive
> or constructive pieces of feedback that can help you adapt
> mechanisms for the next time. It also allows the team to see
> how well the project has hit or is hitting the stated targets.
> This presupposes you have the wherewithal to have com-
> pleted this action prior to the debrief, so by implication, you
> as the leader have already accomplished this action. Nicely
> done. This can also become a learning experience for you
> and the team so treat it—like everything you do as a Flat
> Army leader—as a learning opportunity.

Result:

> The intention is not to deliver a Balanced Scorecard result. That
> is overkill. Don't do it. Blame Kaplan and Norton—the

architects of the Balanced Scorecard—on that one. The resulting effect of confirming is the recognition that what you—as a team—have accomplished is actually meeting the mark. It's important that the goal is achieved, and it's important for you as a leader to both confirm from the team that the first four Cs were effective. Also the team gains perspective about whether what they did and how they performed to help achieve the result was effective or not.

CONGRATULATE (THROUGH FEEDBACK AND RECOGNITION)

According to a Maritz study conducted in 2010, 80 percent of employees feel recognition strengthens their relationship with a company.[16] To complement the point, a 2006 study by Gallup finds that with an average increase of 10 percent in recognition practices, organizations witness a 6.5 percent higher level of productivity in addition to 2 percent higher level of customer engagement. In the case of Fortune 500 companies, each percentage point equates to hundreds of millions of dollars.[17]

To *congratulate* through feedback and recognition is the final stage to the CLAM, but it should be viewed with utmost importance. You've done everything right thus far through the CLAM. People feel engaged, they feel part of the solution and they've helped to develop something that they've not only bought into, they've knocked it out of the park with your omnipresent Connected Leader Attributes and Participative Leader Framework emanating at every turn. But you're not done. Just because the action might be complete doesn't mean there isn't another chance for learning or for engagement opportunities.

The CEO of TELUS, Darren Entwistle, speaks often about congratulations and thus recognition as an engagement opportunity. In fact, TELUS team members who receive timely recognition (within one week) have an 84 percent engagement score, whereas team members who believe they have not been recognized have an engagement score of 47 percent. Darren once said at an internal leadership forum,

Strong and innovative leadership means fostering a culture of appreciation and recognizing the behavior rather than just the outcome. It is important to recognize the how and emphasize it above the what. It is the how that you wish to see consistently repeated because this is the key ingredient to future successes.[18]

Whenever possible, Darren will also talk about a concept he calls "the tuition value of mistakes." He believes leaders and team members should recognize mistakes not as a witch hunt, but as a way in which to learn from. Those mistakes can then be shared and others will have the opportunity to learn as well. As we unravel the act of *congratulate* in the CLAM, don't think of it as merely a slap on the back or a high five. Certainly it's an opportunity to positively recognize and congratulate a job well done, but it's equally important to call attention to what went well and what didn't go so well in terms of the behavior. It's not enough to merely congratulate employees on the outcome.

How to *congratulate*

Key actions:

Before you throw a party or send out notes of commendation or issue thank-you cards or mail gifts as an expression of gratitude for a successfully completed action, take the time to sit down with those involved and congratulate the behavior. That congratulation can be positive and it can also be constructive, but the important thing to remember is to include the behavior with the outcome. Of course you'll want to congratulate the outcome—this is important—but if you only recognize the outcome, you're missing the chance to better the person. That's where the real transference of learning and the potential infusion of engagement lie.

Result:

Employees are begging for feedback and to be recognized. Failing this step in the CLAM might be disastrous both in terms of engagement as well as future successes. By congratulating, you have gone the extra mile and provided the example of being a truly collaborative leader. Your team will love that you recognized the outcome, but the members will absolutely be a better person for doing the same with their actual performance. This is a good thing for many cycles and projects to come.

To *congratulate* is to recognize the behavior and provide feedback on the process as much as it is the outcome. If you can perform this, you will have mastered and perfected the Collaborative Leader Action Model.

WHEN TO CLAM AND WHEN NOT TO CLAM

Simple tasks and actions do not need collaboration. If we collaborated on everything in the organization, two things would happen:

* murder
* anarchy

Employees would end up killing each other if forced to collaborate on every single action. This is not wise. HR and the legal department would be tied up in lawsuits for years. If we forced everyone in the organization to collaborate on everything, nothing would actually get done and there would be corporate anarchy. Nobody wants this, unless of course you are lead singer of the Sex Pistols or have organized an Occupy movement in recent months. So what to do?

Lynda Gratton of the London School of Business insists collaboration is unnecessary for every action or opportunity. She further asserts collaboration really is best applied when dealing with complex tasks.[19] I tend to believe the act of collaborating—and thus demonstrating the Collaborative Leader Action Model—occurs best in situations where the scope is medium or high. The following graphic depicts when you should apply the CLAM for given situations.

CLAM Usage Tree

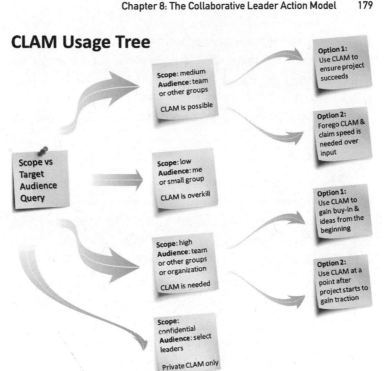

It really comes down to a question of scope and target audience when deciding whether the CLAM is suitable or not.

If the situation calls for a very low level of scope or the affected audience is simply yourself or a small group that may not have any care in the world for the action you're working on or the initiative you're about to kick off, the CLAM is definitively too onerous. It's overkill. It will conceivably hurt more than it will help, should you invoke the CLAM in such a situation. For example, if you're about to update an intranet page with fresh content that aligns to your portfolio, you don't need the CLAM. Thinking about improving the catalogue of offerings that partners are able to see because your organization's internal listing was updated? Don't apply the CLAM. This is simply being smart and proactive. Thinking about adding an invaluable service to a pre-existing external partner cloud-based application? Why not? Go for it. The

CLAM calls for judgment and particularly when the scope is limited and it doesn't detrimentally affect large numbers of people negatively (affecting them in a positive way is good news) my opinion is to act without the CLAM.

Of course the whole purpose of this chapter is to define and enact the CLAM; thus, there are several important scenarios in which you will want to apply it.

When the scope is medium in nature and there is the potential the idea or concept might affect other teams or groups—and their opinions might matter to enhance the end result—the CLAM may be a good idea. I state "may" because, again, it's a judgment call of yours to make as a collaborative leader using Flat Army. At this juncture you should be applying the Connected Leader Attributes along with the Participative Leader Framework, so that you've got a great vibe with your team and the organization. You should be able to tell the difference between an action or project that is low or medium in scope and whether or not you need to connect and consider with other employees in the organization before communicating or creating. If you don't need anyone and you're not going to ruffle feathers or the project will be fine without their input, your project speed will definitely go up. No one ever said that Flat Army or the Collaborative Leader Action Model was easier or quicker than our current command-and-control practices. Just ensure you develop your own scope-analysis method to help you decipher whether the project or action is low, medium or high in scope. It will aid your decision-making ability as when to use the CLAM or not.

But there is a scenario in which I personally believe the CLAM should be enacted in most, if not all, instances. In those scenarios where the impact is large—the scope is high—and the affected membership spans large parts of the organization, if not the whole organization, the CLAM should be instituted. Are you contemplating the purchase of a new technology that touches all employees across the organization? It's my counsel that you enact the CLAM from the very first meeting the idea is hatched. Have you got an inkling that the organization actually better define a risk-mitigation process for emergencies? It's best to invoke the

CLAM from the beginning and involve others as soon as you can. What if you're the CIO and thinking about switching laptop vendors for your employees? Should you make the call yourself or would it be wise to enact the CLAM? You see where I'm going with this: when the scope is high and it affects swaths of people, the CLAM can be initiated in two ways, from the onset of the idea or shortly after the project kicks off. Either way, I suggest the CLAM be put in motion well in advance of anything rolling out to anyone. Again, it may take longer, but it helps immensely in terms of execution and engaged collaboration.

The last possibility for the CLAM is what I call "private CLAM." Not everything in an organization can be open and democratic. Let's be realistic—that's a Grade 2 class, not an organization. So, somewhat unfortunately, the CLAM can't be applied to every action, project or opportunity in the organization. Nor should it. But a version of the CLAM—the private CLAM—can be applied when a leader requires confidentiality. If the subject matter needs to remain private—and there are many examples where this crops up in an organization, such as in mergers and acquisitions, payroll decisions, building closures, etc.—a leader would be wise to enact a private or closed version of the CLAM to appropriately steer through the process.

The CLAM, as a collaborative model of action, can be utilized in any situation whether open or private. A leader who may have to go through a difficult decision or process can utilize the CLAM as a way in which to better execute, but to do so within a safe zone. It can also potentially provide better options than simply remaining in a closed-door office deciding things in isolation. As a leader, when confidentiality is required, it doesn't mean you can't ask other leaders—with their hushed mouths assured—to participate in the CLAM process. I see this as a healthy component to an organization's culture when leaders can come back to its people and demonstrate that the CLAM was applied in a certain private or confidential situation. Imagine the employees' reaction when they knew it was being employed even in situations requiring that level of trust? To me, it's a sign of an organization's very mature culture.

DEGREES OF FLAWLESS EXECUTION AND COLLABORATIVE ENGAGEMENT

In life, there are good clams and bad clams. In Flat Army, there really is only a best-practice CLAM.

Once you've sorted out when to apply the CLAM, it's actually useful to contemplate how ineffective the model is if components are missing or out of place. The following diagram helps to illustrate my point.

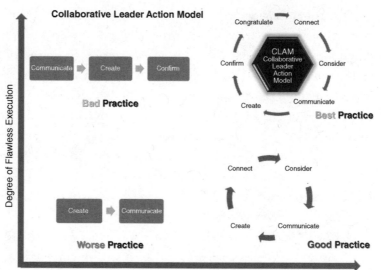

Worst Practice

A leader who *creates* first and *communicates* second not only has a lack of emotional intelligence but is representative of a truly command-and-control operating model. This type of leader has no business in our Flat Army. It's a horrible practice made worse by zero engaged collaboration. Your boss decides to enact a new edict stipulating everyone must start work at 7:30 a.m. instead of the normal start time of 8:00 a.m. It's then communicated by an email memo. How do you feel? A counterpart of yours in the same finance team you are a part of has just rewritten a process that negatively affects not only your own portfolio but that of your own team. He tells you it's been decided; it's in motion, and approved. You've been blindsided with no chance of recourse. How do you feel? This conduct still goes on in organizations—baffling as it seems.

In terms of execution, if the new edict or the imposed process were to have involved others, would things have been easier if others were at the table first? Would the path to execution have been easier, smoother or quicker if the instigator thought about connecting and considering first? Will there be buy-in to the new start time from employees? Will the new process be adopted quickly by others in the finance team? The absolute worst practice of a leader is to simply create, and then communicate the outcome, in situations where the combination of engaged collaboration and a more flawless level of execution could alter the outcome more positively. It's asinine. It's culturally abysmal. It's the exacerbation of hierarchy and management idiocy. Please don't do it in situations where the CLAM should clearly be invoked.

Bad Practice

A step up from the worst practice occurs when a leader sends out a somewhat proactive communication notice stipulating a project is going to commence, an action is starting or a decision has been made. Subsequent to the *communication,* action starts and people start creating results. Once it wraps up various stakeholders review the result and confirm how it went.

Why is it a bad practice? It's bad if other people should have been involved from the beginning. If the project is low or medium in scope and does not require the input of others, clearly this is not a bad practice. But if the initiative affects many and could use the input and advice of others before commencing, then this does become a bad practice. Proactive communication has gone out prior to the *create*-stage kickoff, which is good news. But the leader decided something in isolation and informed people of it before the *connecting* or *considering* stages could be applied. If others should have been involved, this is going to end up rather messy with hurt feelings, bruised egos and a lower level of engaged collaboration. Sure, the project may be executing close to flawlessly, but it may come back to haunt the leader in a future situation when assistance is required. It's not the best way in which to build a network, either.

Good Practice

If you're unable to use the Collaborative Leader Action Model at its full potential, the next best thing—a good practice—is to connect, consider, communicate and create. You have fully engaged collaboration by asking people to be part of the early stages. You suffer somewhat because you're omitting the final crucial stages of *confirm* and *congratulate.* This may detrimentally affect your level of execution due to the fact you are forgetting to circle back on the project to determine what went right, what went wrong and where the holes to fix lie. You have performed the first four stages marvelously, however, the fifth stage—*confirm*—ensures the project or action is in fact successful. Failing to confirm is akin to playing a baseball game without keeping score. Somebody needs to win.

By foregoing the *congratulate* stage you are also creating some risk in terms of future opportunities. It's your network that you rely on to execute on future projects and initiatives. If a leader misses the opportunity to congratulate members of the team for a job well done, or as mentioned earlier, providing constructive feedback and coaching, that leader might not ever have their buy-in again. To congratulate is to coach, provide feedback and say thanks. Other projects and actions will come over time; what you do with your people in terms of recognition—to congratulate—will play a large role in determining if they're going to assist you in the future or not. Be cognizant of the point: to congratulate is a best practice of the CLAM, not a good practice.

Best Practice

Of course, the best practice is the full implementation of the CLAM when applicable. I say "when applicable" because as much as I'd like to see CLAM in action all the time, it's simply not realistic. Please ensure you refer to the CLAM usage tree for more details.

Red Hat—a software company that provides open-source software products to enterprises—is one of those organizations that recognize the components of the CLAM as a part of its company-wide DNA.

It believes that collaboration manifests through an open culture, a place where employees, communities, partners, customers, and any other stakeholder, for that matter, feel free and comfortable to share ideas, best practices and thoughts. It wants its people and its stakeholders to value the process of working through ideas and problem solving by breaking the mold of top-down idea pushing and planning. Danielle Tomlinson, a senior director at the company, told me about something called "memo list"—a simple email alias discussion system—that any employee can post questions, thoughts, ideas and articles to and where reactions to and interactions with these posts are welcomed and encouraged. Through this act of the CLAM, there have been employees connecting and considering opportunities such as open-source industry ideas as well as feedback on holiday-shutdown policies. By instituting the behavior of openness and going through stages much like the Collaborative Leader Action Model, the company recognizes that the forum and the process itself elicits a healthy exchange of ideas, information and opinions at a global, cross-functional and cross-departmental level that leads to decisions and action. That is collaboration, and that is the CLAM in action.

✳ ✳ ✳

I absolutely love the story about TD Bank and its implementation of a social software platform for the organization. It is the CLAM in action. The bank's vice president of social media and digital communication, Wendy Arnott, knew back in 2007 that social media was becoming hot and thus the bank had better do something about it for its employees. Instead of choosing a social software platform herself, she devised a committee of many stakeholders from all walks of the business to help sort out what they needed and how it could roll out.

In an interview with *CIO Magazine*, Wendy said, "If it had just been the business going off and trying to do this on their own, we wouldn't have had a good solution. It's a partnership."[20] The bank now has more than 65,000 employees using the system, and over 4,000 communities, blogs and wikis are in action. Imagine if Wendy wasn't first connecting, considering and communicating before TD actually created the solution? Would there have been the same buy-in? I highly doubt it.

CHAPTER NINE

LEARNING AT THE SPEED OF NEED

Knowledge is of two kinds. We know a subject ourselves, or we know where we can find information on it.

—Samuel Johnson[1]

I thought about ending the chapter right here. Johnson makes so much sense it's ludicrous to think I can outdo him. But after intense discussions with my publishers, their advice was to delve somewhat deeper into the topic if I was ever going to write another book.

Reread that opening quotation again. When you stop and think about it, isn't he right? Samuel Johnson, the famous poet, essayist and speaker is credited as having said this on April 18, 1775, while visiting his colleague Richard Owen Cambridge's library. Johnson was intent on perusing the contents of the library shelves at his friend's new home and after Cambridge asked Johnson why his interest level was so high, he uttered this famous passage. Some 235-odd years later it still rings true. Where we find information, knowledge and help still comes via the library; although in 2013—according to our Flat Army thesis—the library is a metaphor for access via people and the Internet.

How prophetic, in spite of Nicholas Carr's objections through his book *The Shallows: What the Internet is Doing to our Brains*, in which he attacks the usefulness of easy and quick access to information and knowledge.[2] Although I learned a lot from reading his book, I'm not of the same mindset as Carr. In this age of the connected leader and in the context of our Flat Army thesis, we either have competence in a subject matter—with varying degrees of depth—or via our Burt-inspired neighbor networks and social collaboration tools we know how to find it. We learn at the speed of need. Johnson is right. Carr is, well, a tad cataclysmic in his thinking about the web, people and quicker access to information. Kudos to British Columbia's Ministry of Education, which recognized this exact paradox and now aims to undo decades of "sage on the stage" teaching and of rote memorization expectations of its students. In a report entitled *Update on B.C.'s Curriculum Transformation* it states:

[The curriculum] tends to focus on teaching children factual content rather than concepts and processes—emphasizing what they learn over how they learn, which is exactly the opposite of what modern education should strive to do. In today's technology-enabled world, students have virtually instant access to a limitless amount of information. The greater value of education for every student is not in learning the information but in learning the skills they need to successfully find, consume, think about and apply it in their lives.[3]

The arc of this chapter is to define a new kind of learning—Pervasive Learning—and how it should be deployed and employed in a Flat Army organization. More importantly, it articulates the modes a leader should be utilizing to enhance the behaviors of connecting, participating and collaborating through Pervasive Learning itself. Unfortunately, too many leaders have a premeditated view of learning; they still believe it occurs solely in a classroom from some resident expert. They unconsciously link classroom training to rigid forms of leadership. Why is that?

It's my belief we are conditioned as children—through the hierarchy of a centuries-old schooling system—to believe the oldest person in the room (the teacher) is the smartest. That works only for so long. We are further conditioned to believe that when we're extremely smart we'll be recognized by the highest authority—the school principal—through commendations and "bravos" on our report cards. Conversely, when things go awry, the teacher (or perhaps the manager in a corporate comparison)—and/or the principal (the vice president or CEO in a corporate comparison) may sternly call us out for unruliness, poor grades, or anything in between. Do you remember the absolute fear of being called into the principal's office? Particularly so if you hadn't a clue as to why you were being summoned to the office via the PA system, an office administrator or a student runner. Now *that* was stressful—and it was not unlike an archaic, antiquated and classically hierarchical annual performance review is in today's organization.

We are conditioned at a very young age, through the kindergarten-to-higher-education continuum, to believe that it is our individual accomplishments that allow us the chance to achieve great things in life. But success in today's world is not merely about academic prowess or individual accomplishments alone. Success is not about power, greed and stockpiling knowledge in a vault. Success can't be found by proficiently ruling in a silo. Nor is success found through a hierarchical, command-and-control philosophy.

If we're trained as children and teenagers to believe that it is the school system of master and apprentice that breeds success, is there any hope for a more collaborative work experience after high school or higher education? Is there any hope for a more creative, innovative and open-thinking organization? As Ralph Waldo Emerson once said, "You send your child to the schoolmaster, but 'tis the schoolboys who educate him."[4]

I hate the word "training." Each and every time I type those eight letters I cringe, because they hark back to seemingly endless drills during my soccer (football) training sessions as a youth. Those boring repetitive tasks that are meant to enhance or augment a skill. Google returns more than two *billion* hits on the term training. Two billion. I wish it weren't so. Training as we know it and live it, is to invoke the brilliance of Carol Dweck: it's a fixed mindset, not a growth mindset.[5]

To further assist leaders and organizations in the creation of Flat Army, I propose a concept called "Pervasive Learning":

Pervasive Learning: The switch from a "training is an event" fixed mindset to "learning is a collaborative, continuous, connected and community-based" growth mindset.

I liken it to moving from "sage on the stage" to "guides and strides from all sides." Think of it as my friend Dennis Callahan does through this simple yet powerful graphic he devised:

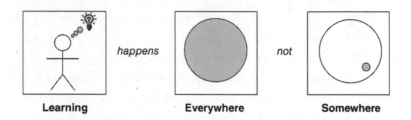

That's right—learning happens everywhere. It's like it functions through osmosis; it floats around and fills whatever volume it needs to. It should be encouraged. John Seely Brown, in his book *The Social Life of Information*, writes, "People learn in response to need. When people cannot see the need for what's being taught, they ignore it, reject it, or fail to assimilate it in any meaningful way."[6]

Put another way, "I learn at the speed of need." Everywhere. Anywhere. I learn through you, with you and around you.

DOES ORGANIZATIONAL LEARNING MATTER?

Santiago Budría, from the Universidade da Madeira, and Pablo Swedberg, from St. Louis University, published research in 2010 under the title "The Shadow Value of Employer-Provided Training." By using the European Community Household Panel data set (ECHP)—a survey of households and individuals containing labor-market characteristics—the researchers took into account 17,632 observations of organizational learning in various forms. They set out to prove whether organizational learning actually mattered; was there any benefit to it. Their results didn't surprise me. Four key points surfaced from their work:

- Taking part in organizational learning opportunities can be equivalent to a 17.7 percent increase in earnings.

- Short-learning opportunities are particularly relevant for job satisfaction.
- Formal learning courses attended on a part-time basis are roughly as rewarding as those attended full-time.
- Organizational learning is particularly rewarding among dissatisfied workers and when targeted to this audience has a large effect on the average job satisfaction level in the organization.[7]

Cagri Bulut and Osman Culha would agree with Budria and Swedberg's findings. In a research paper also published in 2010 entitled "The Effects of Organizational Training on Organizational Commitment," they set out to determine if organizational learning was in fact beneficial to the organization itself. Based on research on four- and five-star hotels in Izmir—the largest city on the Aegean in Turkey—they make four key observations:

- The willingness of employees to participate in organizational learning has a positive effect on organizational commitment.
- Employees tend to work harder, attach themselves to their organizations and display organizational citizenship when there is access to learning and they feel their organizations have been willing to invest in them.
- Employees who expect benefits from their participation in organizational learning activities are more committed to their organizations.
- Employees feel more attached to the organization when they receive support for organizational learning from their direct managers.[8]

In both cases mentioned above, we might argue that yes, organizational learning does in fact matter. Does it matter anywhere else?

At TELUS a similar positive pattern emerged. Employee engagement sat at 53 percent in mid-2008, but by the end of 2012 it had jumped to 80 percent. Interestingly, a similar spike in both the career development and learning sub-drivers tied to employee engagement occurred over this four-year period, reaching approximately the same levels. As TELUS added more organizational learning opportunities to the mix, the level of engagement rose. This may not be causal but there are indirect implications. Over this time period, formal learning opportunities rose by 85 percent, informal learning opportunities rose by 200 percent and social learning interactions went from zero to over 800,000 unique interactions.

To be sure, TELUS continued with in-depth formal courses, but the addition of shorter bursts of learning and short social user–generated nuggets helped to drive up—in Budría and Swedberg's language—job satisfaction. When organizational learning is shifted in its definition and deployment—and it is positioned in any form imaginable—it becomes a critical piece to the company's sustainable competitive advantage. Organizational learning is an investment in a company's people. By continuously improving on the modes, methods and opportunities involved in organizational learning, an improvement in both financial performance and employee engagement (and productivity) is realized. This is the case at TELUS. Voluntary attrition is down, financial metrics are up and a deep sense of organizational commitment is in motion. The story at TELUS confirms what the researchers from above posit.

70–20–10 OR 3–33?

Karen Kocher is one cool corporate leader. As the chief learning officer of CIGNA—a global healthcare-management company with $20 billion in revenue and over 30,000 employees globally—her job is to ensure CIGNA employees are smart, capable in their roles, and adapting to the challenges that surface—however and whenever. Karen believes flexibility in learning and a sharing mentality is key. In fact, her email signature says it all: "Let's GO SOCIAL . . . collaborate, grow and learn from each other!"

What's so cool about Karen and her organization? CIGNA believes learning and collaboration practices have a unique impact on overall employee engagement. Remember our Flat Army thesis from Chapter 1? "The working assumption by the majority of the population," Kocher said to me, "is that performance will likely be enhanced when working and learning with and through others."[9] Karen doesn't believe everyone has to collaborate or employ shared learning all the time, but she does believe "active listening, positive collaboration and continuous learning will improve employee engagement." CIGNA believes learning comes from myriad sources including instant messaging, blog posts and tweets, as well as multi-day online employee jams and face-to-face events. There is no one way or right way at CIGNA to learn.

Karen said to me that

achieving superior business performance on a consistent basis requires that the organization not only be a learning organization, but that the learning is actively applied to generate improved performance. If employees are not engaged, it is not only less likely that they'll learn but it is much less likely they'll apply the learnings and perform.

Karen as the chief learning officer, and CIGNA as an organization, have no time for a classroom-only learning strategy; it's important but not the sole way in which learning, engagement and performance is going to manifest. CIGNA has a learning culture that empowers and aligns to a model we might call the *3–33*.

Pervasive Learning (3–33)

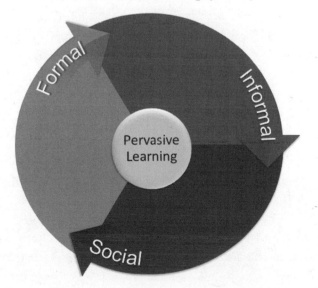

The Pervasive Learning model I'm proposing is another key component to the Flat Army model. It suggests that learning—and by extension, leadership—happens in three equally divided ways:

- 33 percent formal learning and leadership
- 33 percent informal learning and leadership
- 33 percent social learning and leadership

Pronounced "three thirty three," this model aims to highlight my personal belief surrounding the validity of the "70–20–10" model put forward by Robert Eichinger and Michael Lombardo from the Center for Creative Leadership in the 1980s.

The 70–20–10 model is broken down as follows:

- 70 percent learning from on-the-job experiences
- 20 percent learning from others
- 10 percent learning from formal courses[10]

To get to the 70–20–10 model, Eichinger and Lombardo interviewed senior executives and asked them to reflect back on their careers and denote where they believed meaningful learning, development or competence improvement came from, in the context of leadership. This could have been for themselves or their teams or their organizations. In essence, the research focuses on how these executives actually managed or led. Somehow, along the way, the learning profession has taken over the model to depict how workplace learning should occur. This is puzzling to me. D. Scott DeRue and Christopher G. Myers echo my puzzlement as they write, "There is actually no empirical evidence supporting this assumption [that learning maps to the 70–20–10 rule] yet scholars and practitioners frequently quote it as if it is fact."[11]

The executives being interviewed by Eichinger and Lombardo were reflecting on their leadership styles and how they learned to be leaders. To me, basing today's learning model on research that focuses solely on executives' learned leadership styles is incomplete. First off, the research was conducted in the 1980s, when the Internet was something chiefly people in the military knew about and it certainly wasn't deployed in organizations where the studies were conducted. Secondly, the 1980s seems to carry with them the weight of command-and-control leadership practices. Let's forget the Cold War rhetoric for a moment and think back to the era of Ronald Reagan, Margaret Thatcher, Lee Iacocca, Jack Welch and Roger Smith. Not exactly a collaborative-leadership decade in my books. Organizations are therefore basing a learning model on executives from the 1980s. It's time to evolve.

TELUS investigated this exact concept through the implementation of an updated performance model that linked learning and leadership. Over the course of two years the company asked its team members, across the organization on a quarterly basis, if they were learning in formal, informal or social ways. On the whole, 80 percent said they were learning through formal modalities, 82 percent, through informal means, and 55 percent, using social methods. By reviewing the amount of time spent learning, however, TELUS found each of the modalities equated to roughly 33 percent of time. That is, if a team member confirmed that she spent 120 hours learning per year, 33 percent was through formal means, 33 percent, through informal means and 33 percent, through social means. That's forty hours each in this example.

When asked if their leadership performance increased as a result of each mode individually, TELUS team members stated the following:

- As a result of formal learning, 82 percent saw a leadership performance increase.
- As a result of informal learning, 84 percent saw a leadership performance increase.
- As a result of social learning, 56 percent saw a leadership performance increase.

When averaged together, the return on performance increased in 2010 from 62 percent to 74 percent in 2012. But when leaders were specifically asked how they spent their time learning, not surprisingly, the breakdown of formal, informal and social was roughly divided equally. Which is to say, TELUS team members believe their performance varies between formal, informal and social modalities (as does their learning participation rate) but the way they spend their time learning and leading is roughly the same. It's a 3–33 model.

So what are these formal, informal and social modalities you ask? Glad you did.

FORMAL LEARNING

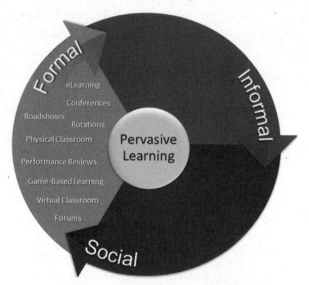

Pervasive Learning: Formal

I'd like to be crystal clear here—formal learning is not going away and it shouldn't. It is an essential component to the Pervasive Learning model. According to research put together by Global Silicon Valley (GSV) Advisors, there is currently a significant amount of investment happening with formal learning and according to their crystal ball it's only going to continue to grow.[12]

Sector	Market Size (2012)	Market Size (2015)	2012–17 Growth (CAGR)	Market Size (2017)
Global Education Expenditure	$4,450.9B	$5,508.7B	7%	$6,372.5B
K–12	$2,227.0B	$2,625.6B	6%	$2,930.3B
Postsecondary	$1,495.2B	$1,883.5B	8%	$2,196.9B
For-Profit Postsecondary	$96.1B	$146.1B	15%	$193.2B
Corporate & Gov't Learning	$356.6B	$449.3B	8%	$524.0B
eLearning	$90.9B	$166.5B	23%	$255.5B
Gaming	$2.0B	$4.4B	30%	$7.4B
For-Profit	$590.9B	$952.2B	17%	$1,311.0B

Formal learning is an integral part to the Pervasive Learning model. We can define it as follows:

> **Formal Learning:** A self-contained learning opportunity, occasionally scheduled, typically but not always tracked, providing a comprehensive and at times logical or sequential approach to a topic.

It's where we find everyone's favorite whipping boy: classroom instructor–led learning. Perhaps it's not everyone's; rather, it's mine. As I mention earlier, formal learning—and in particular classroom instructor–led learning—should always have a place in the Pervasive Learning model. It should not be positioned, however, as the sole way in which we learn. It also needs to become less of an event and more of an experience. It needs to be guided, not commanded. It is no different than hierarchical leadership or controlling leadership styles if used in a "sage on the stage" manner continuously. Flat Army leaders should use classroom learning as a way to discover, not to dictate. Employ it for deep discussions and analysis, not "my way or the highway" preaching.

Deloitte is a great example of how important face-to-face classroom learning can be if done in an experiential way. As opposed to developing a completely virtual learning model, Deloitte created Deloitte University— a thirty-five-classroom interactive learning center in 712,000 square feet replete with an amphitheater, ballroom, workout room and 800 hotel residences—where learning can be delivered to its almost 200,000 employees when necessary. The concept is marketed as follows:

At Deloitte University, face-to-face instruction by outstanding professionals is enhanced, but not replaced, by technology. Each of our 35 classrooms at DU are outfitted with the latest leading-edge technology, including wi-fi and video conferencing.[13]

Not everything in terms of their learning strategy is delivered at their Texas-based Deloitte University, as there are many informal and social learning examples and opportunities that are also made available. But the organization certainly believes that its $300-million investment pushes the needle forward on formal learning in a very significant and deliberate way.

If classroom learning is the whipping boy, eLearning is the ugly stepsister at the ball. You know she's there but you try dearly to avoid making eye contact. I believe eLearning is an important piece to the mix, but not if it's crap. What to do? Try the following:

- Make it relevant and context specific.
- Don't make it a page-turning exercise.
- Keep it to thirty minutes or less in duration (ten to fifteen minutes is ideal).
- Employ interactive elements that engage the learner.
- Don't convert classroom learning to eLearning (it's futile).

Why is game-based learning found in the formal-learning section? To be honest, I am not a fan of the terms "gamification" or "gaming" in the enterprise. The term freaks too many people out. You may understand it, but when you're trying to convince others about it, an uphill battle awaits. That is why I often pitch it as "interactive learning"—the next layer of eLearning. I've kept it in this section as "game-based learning" so you know what I'm referring to. The bottom line is that you should employ it in your organization. It's a fantastic culture builder and it really can assist the development of deep competences if formally developed correctly.

The virtual classroom—whether in the form of virtual-world technologies like AvayaLive Engage or web conferencing like Cisco's WebEx—is an excellent way to deliver on the interactive experience of formal learning. Through the use of avatars, polling, quizzes, and video sharing, among other engaging methods, the virtual classroom might be more useful in your situation than the physical classroom.

Ensuring you allow your employees to attend relevant conferences is also key. So long as you have instituted a way for your employees to share their learning with the team. Similarly, running internal roadshows or face-to-face forums helps develop bonds within the Flat Army structure. At TELUS, for example, the organization hosts senior-, director- and manager-leadership forums throughout the year in one- or two-day events. These are interactive, engaging and thought-provoking leadership development sessions often taught by TELUS leaders. In fact, CEO Darren Entwistle teaches four times per year—not for an hour or two each time, but for the entire day.

Permitting your team members to take part in formal rotations on different teams or business units is also beneficial to the 3–33 model and to the development of employees. Imagine allowing a team member to spend two or three months learning about another part of the business. What could she learn that would motivate her to do things more productively when she returns? What type of new direct contacts would she have made as a result of the rotation? How could those contacts help her in her current role? Think back to Burt's Neighbor Networks theory. It can have an amazing impact yet it's rarely found in organization's formal learning plans.

Formal learning provides depth as much as it can provide breadth. As a leader, I implore you not to focus on classroom instructor–led learning as the only way in which people learn. This is your largest hurdle to overcome. That stated, each of the modalities inside the formal learning triad must become a part of your Pervasive Learning strategy. To exclude is to prevent a rich learning opportunity within your team or actions.

INFORMAL LEARNING

Pervasive Learning: Informal

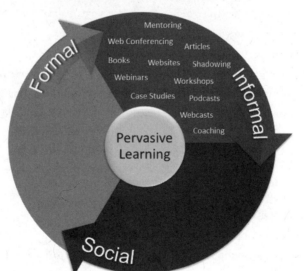

Anatole France is alleged to have said, "Nine-tenths of education is encouragement." This is a perfect way to begin the exploration of informal learning within the Pervasive Learning model. With such a fervent quest by many to predict that formal classrooms will become extinct and that learning will exist solely in a digital format, we forget learning often occurs via the vehicle known as motivation. Or, as France insists, by encouragement. Informal learning is the key link between formal and social learning. It is often overlooked yet it is one of the more critical pieces to the Flat Army model.

Take for instance one of the informal learning modalities—mentoring. Chief Learning Officer of SuccessFactors Karie Willyerd co-authored the book *The 2020 Workplace: How Innovative Companies Attract, Develop, and Keep Tomorrow's Employees Today* with Jeanne Meister, in which the authors state that Millennials actually prefer to learn through mentoring than any other formal, informal or social learning type.[14] So much for the digital-native assertion that people in this age bracket prefer to do everything online. In fact, Willyerd believes mentoring is quickly becoming an extremely important element in the workplace given this cohort is about to make up 50 percent of the actual workforce. Mentoring, like the other informal learning opportunities, are non-formal ways—devoid of any web-based interaction—to motivate, encourage, assist and educate and assist an individual, team or organization. What it lacks in depth it makes up for in personal interaction. What it lacks in formality it makes up for in creativity. Regarding mentoring specifically, we might define it as an informal relationship between two people—not in a manager-team member lineage—where the mentor helps the mentee through various issues, change situations or objectives. It really is an informal encouragement opportunity for both parties to learn.

For purposes of our Pervasive Learning model we define informal learning as follows:

> **Informal Learning:** An opportunity without conventionalism that provides guidance, inspiration, expertise or acumen typically in a non-formal environment.

Coaching is also a key action within the informal learning triad. Recall in Chapter 6 that we included the act of coaching to the Connected Leader Attributes. We stated that coaching is an ongoing informal conversation with the employee that focuses on providing the following:

- counsel on current objectives and actions to categorically improve the result
- feedback concerning their progress or improvements on Flat Army habits
- advice on personal and career advancement or opportunities

It is different than mentoring. Coaching is an attribute that functions between you and a member or members of your direct team. Mentoring, on the other hand, is your opportunity to provide motivated counsel and advice to others in the organization not situated within your span of leadership. Both are important.

Other modalities such as webcasts, webinars and podcasts provide you the opportunity to record your thoughts on any subject matter, making it available to your team or a larger audience such as the organization itself. These need not be two-hour sessions (nor should they be) rather short pieces of content that can be easily shared. Perhaps it's an update regarding your quarterly financials, or your thoughts on a recent acquisition, or you've got a leadership habit you'd like people to understand. Whatever the content area, it's an opportunity for you to motivate through interesting, if not short, nuggets of content.

Have you read an interesting or thought-provoking article or book lately that could be shared with the team? Why not? Have you been to a website that might help your team understand the nuances of your business? Ever thought about sharing it? Did you read a case study recently about one of your competitors that could help team members understand both your industry and the makeup of your competitor? Couldn't that be something you can motivate your team with? Each of these are examples of informal learning. You don't have to go to a classroom and there is no eLearning course to sign up for. It's a simple and hopefully enthusiastic action of yours to encourage the competence growth of your team and others. You've already read it or accessed the material. Is it really that hard to disseminate your findings to the rest of the team?

How often do you use web conferencing tools to conduct catch-up meetings or even one-on-one meetings with your team if you're dispersed or you're travelling? Do you lean on conference calls only, or, might you think about employing services like Cisco WebEx, Adobe Connect or Microsoft products such as Lync or Skype to conduct those opportunities. Webcams are your friend. Repeat . . . webcams are your friend. Yes, web conferencing is an informal learning opportunity too.

I love what Louis Franzese, vice president of Labor Relations and Human Resources practices at Hertz Corporation told Jathan Janove for a piece in the June 2012 issue of *HR Magazine.* When discussing the aspect of job shadowing, she says to her employees, "Wash cars. Spend time behind the counter. Get a real sense of what work life for employees truly is."[15] TELUS employs the same sentiment as outlined in Chapter 6 with its Closer to the Customer program. Spending time in other roles for a few hours once or twice a year keeps leaders and her team aligned with what's really going on in the organization. Why can't a university chancellor spend time with those in the internal information technology support team to see what it's like assisting thousands of students and faculty every day? Can't a vice president of marketing and his team shadow front-line retail agents in the stores where their marketing plans are alleged to actually sell more products? Shadowing is culture building and it's a critical element in the informal learning triad.

SOCIAL LEARNING

Pervasive Learning: Social

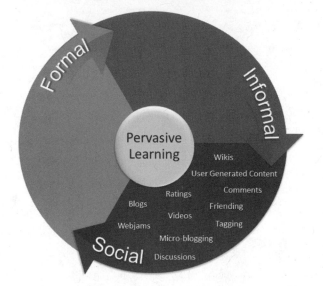

In 2005 there was no such thing as social learning. Well, that's not totally true. The education version of social learning is a recent phenomenon whereas the clinical-psychology version was first coined by Julian Rotter in 1954. We'll keep our thoughts here to the education version. It's a relatively recent term because most people believe it's tied to the influx of social media tools and technologies. I tend to agree. Community manager Aaron Silvers at Advanced Distributed Learning refers to social learning as

[t]he serendipitous learning that happens through social exchanges that results in a knowledge negotiation. Social learning works for people participating in social network-ing activities whether they exchange with each other for personal reasons or for larger collective purposes.[16]

For purposes of the Pervasive Learning model, we define social learning as follows:

> **Social Learning:** An exchange of ideas, knowledge or information via Internet-enabled services that provides initial or supplemental understanding through personal and professional networks.

Marcia Conner—former vice president and information futurist at PeopleSoft, worldwide manager at Microsoft, and fellow of the Batten Institute at the Darden School of Business—says, "social learning thrives in a culture of service and wonder. It is inspired by leaders, enabled by technology and ignited by opportunities that have only recently unfolded."[17] A perfect example to highlight social learning is the story of U.S. Army captains Nate Allen and Tony Burgess. Back in the late 1990s, these two friends were back from duty and began swapping stories about their time in combat. An idea surfaced that these stories ought to be shared. More importantly, they realized there were thousands more to be told by others. What they built was an online community of practice—a place to learn and share—for soldiers only. They called it "Company Command." The Company Command website contains the following description:

We are a grass-roots, voluntary forum that is by and for the profession with a specific, laser-beam focus on company-level command. By joining, you are gaining access to an amazing community of professionals who love Soldiers.[18]

With over 75,000 unique visitors per month and similar military forums that popped up as a result of the Company Command example, this just might be an example of a flat army demonstrating Flat Army.

Discussion forums like the one at Company Command are but one modality of social learning. As depicted by the graphic above, social learning comes in the form of wikis, blogs, micro-blogging, user-generated videos, commenting, rating, friending and so on. These collaboration technologies can be housed on the Internet—in the cloud—or they can be hosted inside your company's firewall. Specific detail on these technologies and their benefits are detailed in Chapter 10. What social learning can do, however, is act as the sweet jelly to your peanut butter sandwich (as first mentioned in Chapter 3). Imagine formal learning is the bread—an absolute necessity—and informal learning as the peanut butter. Informal learning sticks the formal learning together. It's the jelly—the sweetness—that makes the sandwich complete. That's why leaders should be both allowing and advocating social learning throughout their teams and organization.

When discussing the recent success of another type of social learning—MOOC (massive online open courses)—Stanford University President John Hennessy said,

We found that we were able to handle a lot of the Q&A through social networking. It's amazing that when you have 10,000 students in a class and a student puts up a question, the group quickly converges on the right answer: Several students put up an answer, other students come in and vote for what they think is the best answer, and there's a high probability that you'll converge to a pretty good answer in less than an hour. And if at the end of the two days there are three questions where the answers are not really clear, the instructor can come in and say, "This is the way you should think about this problem."[19]

This is the point at which the Pervasive Learning framework can meet the CLAs, PLF and CLAM in our organizations. Here we have 10,000 students participating in an online and interactive course. Through the behaviors and practices I outline in *Flat Army*, students are getting a business result achieved—in this case resolving questions about an assignment or theory—and it's being done in an expedited way. Social learning is assisting this to occur. There are videos, discussion forums, blogging and micro-blogging all in synchronous and asynchronous modes to achieve the result. That's where learning is truly becoming connected, collaborative and continuous. It truly is becoming pervasive. As Jane Hart of the Internet Time Alliances states, "true social learning is an integral part of working, not separate from it."[20] But, warnings must be heeded. As Mitch Resnick states in his seminal 2002 paper *Rethinking Learning in the Digital Age*, "while new digital technologies make a learning revolution possible, they certainly do not guarantee it."[21]

We must not solely base our Pervasive Learning strategy on social learning; it must become as a result of the 3–33 model—formal, informal and social.

✳ ✳ ✳

Pervasive Learning also leans heavily on Socratic learning, which itself is based on the idea that human beings have faculties that can be awakened through questioning, exploration, collaboration and self- or cross-examination.

It ties in so perfectly to the Flat Army thesis as well. Based on our learning requirements (individual, team, organizational, etc.), we must continuously connect the need that has to be filled to the learning modality, be it formal, informal or social. We have to question and explore which modality provides the appropriate amount of breadth and depth juxtaposed with the speed at which we need the information or new knowledge. How each can be utilized in parallel should always be at the forefront of a leader's learning strategy. Of course, the Pervasive Learning model is a natural extension to the frameworks I discuss earlier (CLA, PLF and CLAM) and thus there is clearly further alignment with collaborative technologies like wikis, blogs, micro-blogging and virtual worlds, among others.

Close your eyes and think of a capitalized letter T for a moment. If the top were considered breadth and the base depth, you'd have a relatively good depiction of how learning should be thought of in your organization as a leader. Breadth comes in the form of most social learning in addition to informal opportunities. The depth certainly comes from formal learning with spots of informal and social as well. Let's refer to it as the "Educational T."

The Educational T

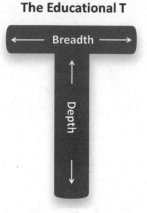

What would this look like if it occurred in an organization?

Matthew Wilder is an engineer at TELUS. He looks after myriad different technology innovations that affect TELUS customers and employees. One problem Matthew faced was something called "IPv6," the next iteration of Internet addresses. It turned out the world was running out of Internet addresses and it was Matthew's job not only to sort out what had to be done for the organization to overcome the issue, but he had to figure out how to educate various TELUS team members as well. Taking a look around at what was occurring at TELUS, Matthew decided to first build an open wiki that outlined what IPv6 was all about. From there, he created a discussion forum, a micro-blogging channel and a video channel, along with links to articles, books and webcasts. To complement the site, Matthew listed off a series of formal learning opportunities too. He certainly didn't offer a formal-only learning strategy to the organization. He had breadth and depth. He had formal, informal and social learning packaged altogether nicely. I had the chance to ask Matthew about his decision to go this route and he replied, "Dan, it just made sense. How else should we be learning and leading at TELUS these days?" If Matthew can be successful at generating understanding of something as complicated as IPv6 through both the Pervasive Learning model and the metaphor of the Educational T—much like Stanford University's Introduction to Artificial Intelligence MOOC—shouldn't we be able to employ this tactic for any type of learning requirement in an organization?

Pervasive Learning should not be treated as a commodity; rather, it should be treated as a way of being. Matthew didn't build a training course. You don't go *to* training, you learn wherever, whenever and however. Leaders should employ this model in an attempt to build engaging teams who also want to learn. Paying homage to John W. Gardner, author of the book *Self-Renewal: The Individual and the Innovative Society*, leaders need to become interested in Pervasive Learning, not interesting to others.[22] Remember this mantra: learn at the speed of need.

Pervasive Learning

CHAPTER TEN

TOOLS, RULES AND JEWELS OF BEING A FLAT ARMY LEADER

If you know me, or know anything about me, collaborative technology is arguably my favorite Flat Army ingredient. Although I care passionately and deeply about the material in this book, technology is both my hobby and my brain candy. In 1981, my dad came home one day with the TI-99/4A computer. Imagine the smile on my 10-year-old face upon realizing Gutenberg's invention could be more than a typewriter. Up until that point, I was hooked on the Atari 2600 gaming system—the first real interactive technology to enter our house back in 1979—as well as the IBM Selectric typewriter. When the TI-99/4A entered into the equation, I finally had the chance to go behind the coverings of the technology itself. Before, I was fixated on the Atari, particularly on how objects and characters could move on the screen from a twist of a joystick or paddle. Once that computer came into the house, I learned how to program my own games. I grew to understand the relationship between hardware and software. Additionally, I was fascinated by the connection of technology and human emotion. From the TI-99/4A and onward—including household computer upgrades to Commodore 64, IBM PC Convertible and Apple II—I've been hooked on technology as an enabler of the human experience. What an interesting upbringing indeed.

These days—and criticize me all you like—technology, both for work and play, has become a personal utility. I don't put it before physiological, safety or love requirements, but for me it's tied to esteem. Technology helps me connect, learn and lead, and therein it provides me with confidence. Without access to technology I don't feel as confident. Yes, I take breaks from it—I love cycling, for example, or mucking around on the beach with the children—but technology has become a way of being. It's not something I go do. I have an expectation that technology is mobile and at my command. I haven't had an office since 2002, so I'm certainly not the kind of leader that goes into a room, locks the door and pounds away on a keyboard in isolation. There is no way I would be the person I am today—rightly or wrongly—if it weren't for technology.

The 90,000 words that comprise this book were written using Evernote, a cloud-based application that I am able to access from any Internet-enabled device (and I used five different devices to write this book). How did I meet Marcia Conner, one of the most thoughtful and forward-thinking professionals out there? I wrote about Marcia in a blog post and she reached out to me. How do I set goals for the team I'm leading? I don't. We, as a team, utilize online discussion forums and other collaboration technologies to discuss, debate, debunk and decide what the goals should be for the subsequent year before we ever start them. How did I celebrate my father-in-law's sixtieth birthday that I wasn't able to attend in person? I put together a tribute video, posted it to YouTube and then Skyped into the party to see his reaction after he viewed it. How are my wife and I raising the 9-, 7- and 5-year-olds at home? By employing old-fashioned wooden blocks, art stations, toys, musical instruments, sports, dress-up clothes, plenty of field trips—and iPads. Each of our children has an iPad, connects through blogging on their own personal site (e.g., www.clairepontefract.com), and spread throughout the house are a Nintendo Wii, a Microsoft Kinect, three Apple TV consoles, three TVs, four terabytes of storage, Kobo online book accounts, digital cameras, laptops and a wireless printer.

At this point you may be thinking the author of this book is a tad eccentric. Although I do like to sing in the shower, I beg to differ. No Flat Army leader can truly be collaborative unless he or she awakes from the self-induced coma of technology ignorance and blindness. Technology plays a critical role in becoming a Flat Army leader. It can make sense of our world. Why wouldn't my wife and I blend physical-tactile learning (through toys, games, sports, art, music, etc.) with the latest technology opportunities to develop and raise our children? Do you really believe the amount of data and information or complexities in our world are actually going to ease up? Should we be preventing technology from invading our home or embracing it and teaching our children to do the same?

What about your work environment? Are you utilizing technology to assist your team's goals and actions? Has technology helped to enable your leadership habits or skills? It's my opinion that leaders must become adept to technology—particularly collaborative technologies—such that they treat it like a leadership utility. It should be as natural as turning on the light switch to see in a darkened room or turning a water faucet on to quench your thirst. It is an extension to our physiological needs.

By way of example, let me introduce you to Daniel Kligerman, a TELUS senior program manager based in Toronto. Daniel reached out directly to me and asked if I wouldn't mind chatting with his wife to discuss career change opportunities. My motto in life has always been a slice of "pay it forward" coupled with a dash of "quid pro quo" mashed with "the glass is half full" topped by "yes, I've got time." Sounds like the Participative Leader Framework from Chapter 7, doesn't it? So, after saying yes to the request, he had this to say a few days later:

In the past few weeks I've actually done a lot of reading of your previous [blog] posts. I have spent most of my career managing some of the technology (or leading the people managing the technology) behind enterprise collaboration, from LAN in the early days, to IP-Telephony and then Unified Communications. But until coming across your blog, and those of your peer group, I never really explored the world of how the enterprise was actually making use of that technology—to me, it was just a bunch of features we were providing. So it's been an eye-opening and fascinating experience, to say the least. Learning 2.0 in action, I suppose![1]

When at TELUS, I blog, micro-blog and submit all sorts of other content via videos, webinars, live chats and speaking engagements, but Daniel was viewing my external writing. It's the content found within www.danpontefract.com that helped him make a new connection and arrive at a new realization. What if I wasn't writing using collaborative technologies like an external blog? Would I have been able to help Daniel? What if I didn't believe—as a leader—in being open, transparent and a role model of Pervasive Learning? It's an example that demonstrates how through my own writing and thoughts, someone else is gaining, learning, and in turn, helping others to understand and utilize that knowledge and insight elsewhere.

More importantly, Daniel's observations underscore the overarching point of this chapter: Collaboration technologies are not about features, functions and cool enhancements. Collaboration technologies—at least in the Flat Army structure—are about enabling your collaborative, connected and participative leadership habits to become fully operational. Let's click on next to see how it's done.

CLICK NEXT FOR THE "CONS" OF COLLABORATION

For Flat Army leaders, utilizing collaboration technologies comes down to a Hobson's choice. Henry Ford—rather infamously—also utilized a Hobson's choice. When offering the Ford Model T for sale, he quipped, "Any customer can have a car painted any color that he wants so long as it is black."[2] Back in the late sixteenth and early seventeenth centuries, Thomas Hobson ran a business in Cambridge, England, renting out horses to locals—including Cambridge University students. He provided the animals to customers in an order that he chose. That is, he wouldn't allow a patron to select a horse. It was literally a "Hobson's choice" because, if the individual looking to rent a horse from Mr. Hobson didn't like the horse he was given, Hobson refused the rental and would forego the revenue. The customer had to take what was given or walk away empty handed. For Flat Army leaders, the same can be said of collaboration technologies. Your choice is to use them or not. If you choose the latter, good luck. You're choosing unwisely.

Collaboration technologies can be thought of as the means to bring applications of Flat Army to fruition. Earlier in this book we discuss the fifteen Connected Leadership Attributes, the Participative Leader Framework, the Collaborative Leader Action Model and the Pervasive Learning Model. Each of the aforementioned is an effort to illustrate the importance of adopting new leadership behaviors for yourself, your team and your organization. *Flat Army* could have been written about the ultimate importance of technology as the seminal focus. Obviously it's not. Those *other* books have it wrong. It is behavior first and technology second. We're here now, so let's dig into the correct Hobson's choice.

I'd like to introduce Collaboration Technologies in the *Flat Army* model around three key concepts:

- conversation
- context
- content

Each of the "con" components has five associated collaboration technologies found in each bracket. As of 2013, and in my opinion, these are the most influential collaboration technologies in each of the three categories. Of course, over time, these might change or there might be new ones, but, for now, we focus our efforts on a total of fifteen collaboration technologies and opportunities. Additionally, any of these can be applied to the social learning component of the Pervasive Learning model in Chapter 9 as well.

Collaboration Technologies

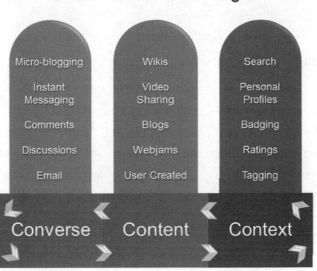

Micro-blogging

Instant Messaging

Comments

Discussions

Email

Wikis

Video Sharing

Blogs

Webjams

User Created

Search

Personal Profiles

Badging

Ratings

Tagging

Converse   **Content**   **Context**

CONVERSATION

A conversation involves participation through bi-directional dialogue using collaborative technologies. It is the antithesis of allodoxaphobia— a fear of opinions. Whether through synchronous or asynchronous means, when a leader converses, she is using Collaborative Technologies to dialogue, to opine, to confirm, to ideate, to share and to educate. To converse is to employ those Connected Leader Attributes we discussed earlier. Be trusting, communicating, clowning, coaching and engaging among other attributes as you converse with your team and others in the organization through collaborative technologies. The Participative Leader Framework I outline in Chapter 7 teaches us to use the CARE principle of participation (continuous, authentic, reciprocal and educating), but it also emphasizes the principles of consuming and contributing. When using collaborative technologies you are both consuming and contributing. In Chapter 8 we uncover the CLAM. Throughout the six stages, a leader should be having conversations via collaborative technologies as a way in which to connect, consider, communicate, create, confirm and congratulate. It helps to keep the conversation channels open and flowing through any project or action.

Micro-Blogging

What Is It?

Having first arrived on the scene in 2005, micro-blogging is the act of writing short quips, usually of 140 to 160 characters —such as updates, ideas, personal thoughts, links and even photos—through a form of collaborative technology that allows the entry to be viewed by anyone that uses the service. The posts can be written on a computer, laptop, tablet or mobile device. A common external example is Twitter. Internal organizational examples include products such as Yammer, Sharetronix, Socialcast and Presently.

How Do I?

Micro-blogging is a conversation mechanism. A leader uses it as a way to communicate and dialogue with the team about organizational issues, projects, goals and even non-work-related items like recipes or sporting events. It's a culture enabler. It's a form of conversing. "Micro-blogging isn't an elephant sitting in the room," Bert Sandie, senior director of technical excellence at Electronic Arts, said to me in an interview. "It's something that epitomizes tangible business value through the informal exchange of ideas and knowledge leading to improved results."[3]

Flat Army Benefits

Micro-blogging can truly humanize the pulse of the organization and a leader's team but it also can help drive benefits for the business. It's a running commentary of what might have previously been discussed at the water cooler, the lunch table, or in the classroom; only, now, the entire organization has access to the dialogue and can take advantage both by listening and by contributing back. It's a wonderful way for a leader to enact any of the Flat Army frameworks. It's economical from a time perspective, but it provides a real sense of genuineness that often gets lost in formal communication processes.

Instant Messaging

What Is It?

Instant messaging is a form of collaboration technology used when two or more people are conducting text-based communication (or video-based communication if a webcam is available) through the Internet or a network connection. Instant messaging can be found in many external products these days such as Google's Gmail, Facebook (through the chat functionality), Windows Live Messenger and Skype, to name just a few. Corporate or internal versions include the likes of Microsoft Lync (formerly Microsoft Office Communicator), Cisco Jabber and IBM Sametime.

How Do I?

Whether using consumer or enterprise instant messaging products, most come with a presence capability allowing you to indicate whether you're available, busy, out to lunch or in a position not to be disturbed. Use this feature whenever you can, particularly when you are on your laptop or computer. Your team needs to know if you are available to "chat," so don't hide from the presence function. Second, when your team or other organization employees contact you via instant messaging, respond to them. It's not email—the expectation is that you will answer the query immediately (hence the point about setting your presence status accordingly). Thirdly, why not randomly check in with others on your team via instant messaging? It's a great tool to create rapport and to support your team during spare moments and so on.

Flat Army Benefits

Instant messaging has the hidden benefit of the presence feature. This unheralded feature might actually outshine the advertised benefits of instant messaging itself. Use it continuously and you will note how engaged your team becomes regardless of whether they're in the same office building or in another city altogether. Instant messaging creates a bond between you and your team through the easy access to your brain and to the timeliness of your responses. It's not intended to be used for ninety-minute whiteboard or brainstorming sessions, but rather for quick messages to keep the ball rolling on projects, initiatives and actions. It's a perfect tool for the PLF, CLAM or parts of the Pervasive Learning model.

Comments

What Are They?

Over in the Content section you can read about collaborative technologies like blogs, video sharing and wikis. Most, if not all, tools come with a comment feature so that once a piece of content has been posted—like a new video—people have the ability to leave a comment. If you've ever visited an online travel site or an online newspaper, you have seen how comments are a way to engage the reader by offering an opportunity to provide his or her own personal commentary.

How Do I?

It's not overly complicated to leave a comment. You read a piece of content or view a video and write down your thoughts, feedback or advice in the appropriate box normally found underneath. There are two critical aspects to contemplate. First, do you make the time to view said content and provide a comment? You're busy and crises will never go away, so it may be a good idea to set aside time to peruse content and to leave comments as appropriate in your calendar—that is, if you don't get into a habit of viewing online content found within your organization when you have breaks or downtime. The second critical piece is tone. Don't use corporate jargon. Be real. Use humor and be humane. If you're going to leave a comment and it sounds like a glossy brochure from the marketing department, you will be ridiculed.

Flat Army Benefits

Comments prove you have read or viewed the content, but they also can be a wonderful way to provide additional insight. They provide a culture connection to the individual that posted the content in the first place. It's actually a wonderful example of the Participative Leader Framework. You are consuming content and you are contributing your own thoughts.

Discussions

What Are They?

Discussions (sometimes known as discussion forums or online discussions) are text-based, treelike conversations typically devoted to a single topic or subject using some form of browser-based technology. Within each topic a new discussion can be started, which is called a thread. Users may reply to the thread—where the discussion can take place—or a user may start another discussion altogether. Discussions are asynchronous; you can post or reply at any time, as there is no expectation you must respond with immediacy.

How Do I?

If you've mastered the act of commenting from above, you're able to participate in a discussion. As a leader, you can either start a discussion or you can participate in one. Think about initiating a discussion when you're in the *connect, consider* and *communicate* phases of the CLAM. Discussions are a great idea to conduct for project postmortems through the *confirm* phase as well. You can begin a discussion to gain feedback on an idea or to receive opinion on a recent organizational change. It's a magical tool to take advantage of as a Flat Army leader. But there are others on your team and in the organization who start discussions as well. As is the case with commenting, you need to find the time to participate in some of these discussions. And if you don't have anything constructive to add, don't bother writing anything.

Flat Army Benefits

In his book *Organizations Don't Tweet, People Do: A Manager's Guide to the Social Web*, author Euan Semple writes, "Social tools are personal. They rely on individuals like you and me finding our voice. Power is shifting from

institutions and corporations to networks and individuals."[4] Let the
Flat Army leader be a part of this democratization of hierarchy by participating in online discussions and breaking down the barrier between
manager and subordinate. In my opinion, those two words—"manager"
and "subordinate"—should be erased from the lexicon of the corporate
world. Participating in online discussions allows these benefits to manifest
in you as a Flat Army leader.

Email

What Is It?

No, this isn't a cruel joke. Even though email was invented before the
creation of the Internet as we know it today, it is in fact a collaboration
technology. Oxford Dictionaries defines email as "messages distributed
by electronic means from one computer user to one or more recipients
via a network."[5] The last portion of the definition explains what makes
it a collaborative technology. With the ability to converse one-to-one
or one-to-many, email can still be an effective way with which to enact
Flat Army behaviors.

How Do I?

I have to presume you've utilized email. According to an Ipsos poll
conducted in 2012, 85 percent of global respondents who are connected online report they use the Internet for sending and receiving
emails.[6] The question isn't one of how to use email; rather, it's of how
effective you are at using it as a Flat Army leader. First and foremost,
responsiveness is crucial. When your team member is waiting days
on end for an answer to a question she raises, you've lost your Flat
Army credibility. Conversely, when you use email as your only source
of collaboration, it is equally ineffective. Try to coach and encourage
your team to move "reply-all discussions" into discussion forums or
micro-blogging groups rather than clogging up email inboxes. If the
conversation is short-lived, then by all means encourage email, but
ensure you are part of the conversation as necessary rather than acting
as an ignorant bystander.

Flat Army Benefits

A leader can answer a team member's questions quickly, succinctly and with relative ease via email. These questions can also remain private, rather than finding a home in the public domain. In part, this is why email will never and should never die. If expectations are set up front that answers may be curt or even devoid of grammar, the more important aspect of gaining an answer quickly shows the benefit of email. Sending out short emails to team members in an informal way (e.g., "Hope you're having a good day" or "Enjoy your time off") suggests the leader is demonstrating some of the Connected Leader Attributes. This *is* collaboration and it is of great benefit when email is used wisely within the Flat Army construct.

CONTENT

Collaboration-technology content is made up of wikis, videos, blogs, webjams and other user-generated material. It's the creation of intellect, expertise and acumen—whether individually or collaboratively—that then gets shared throughout your organization. Have you ever visited CNN's iReport?[7] The site states that "iReport is an invitation for you to be a part of CNN's coverage of the stories you care about and an opportunity to be a part of a global community of men and women who are as passionate about the news as you are." We might loosely use this description pertaining to content in the organization. As a Flat Army leader, you—not just the C-Suite or corporate communications team—are responsible for the development of content. It is incumbent upon you—as per the Participative Leader Framework—to contribute content so others can gain and benefit. Be a CNN iReporter for your organization going forward.

Wikis

What Are They?

It's hard to believe wiki technology is well over a decade old now. We must pay homage to Ward Cunningham who invented the first wiki system (called WikiWikiWeb) in 1995, which was the first user-editable website—the simplest way to define a wiki. The most popular external example is likely Wikipedia, the online encyclopedia where global citizens work collaboratively to define the content through a wiki. According to Wikipedia's own Wikipedia entry, the site has over 365 million readers worldwide, more than 100,000 active contributors and over 23 million articles. There are organizational versions of wikis that can be bought such as Jive, Confluence and Socialtext and open-source technologies including MediaWiki, TWiki and Foswiki.

How Do I?

If you've ever used a document-editing tool like Microsoft Word or Microsoft PowerPoint, you more than likely have the skills to start, edit or populate a wiki. Wikis are WYSIWYG—an acronym for "What You See Is What You Get"—so you have little excuse from a skills perspective. Your major hurdle to overcome is determining when best to deploy a wiki according to the Flat Army leadership model. Rolling out a new initiative across your team or the organization? Why not establish an accompanying wiki? Trying to sort out all the acronyms in use across your business units? Why not set up an accompanying wiki? Wishing to extend your team's profile across the organization? You got it—a wiki can help that too.

Flat Army Benefits

Wikis are the antithesis of a locked-down non-editable intranet. They are open and available to anyone both to view and to edit. This is the essence of our engage-and-empower concept within Flat Army, so we might use the wiki as a metaphor, too. As a leader, you can engage with others across the organization using a wiki as much as you can empower your team to help co-edit and create any type of content all the while collaborating with one another. It can be used within the Pervasive Learning model with ease as much as being a part of the CLAM or the PLF.

Video Sharing

What Is It?

If you've ever stumbled upon a YouTube video, you are an experienced user of online video sharing. According to YouTube, every month there are over 800 million unique visits and over 4 billion hours of video watched. If you can believe it, seventy-two hours of video are uploaded every minute. It's evident, therefore, that, from an external or consumer perspective, videos are being developed, shared and watched by a large portion of people connected to the web. Inside the organization and closed to the rest of the world, video sharing can be a very powerful collaboration technology. Cisco's "Show and Share" technology, for example, allows an internal version of YouTube to come to life, whereas collaboration platforms like Jive, SharePoint and Connections have video capabilities built right into the suite.

How Do I?

Depending on the situation, the videos you create can range from short head-shot-only pieces to more elaborate amateur-edited video productions. Your tablet or laptop likely has a built-in webcam. To record a simple talking-head video, find the most appropriate software, click record, and then upload to the video-sharing service. If you have the time, creativity and skill, even more elaborate videos can be created using free programs like Microsoft Movie Maker or inexpensive solutions such as iMovie and Camtasia.

Flat Army Benefits

The earliest example of the phrase "a picture is worth a thousand words" is attributed to newspaper editor Arthur Brisbane when he delivered a talk to the Syracuse Advertising Men's Club in March 1911, where he said, "Use a picture. It's worth a thousand words."[8] We might extrapolate on the definition and suggest Flat Army leaders should say, "Use a video. It's worth ten thousand words." When a leader uses videos to share insights, skills, knowledge and experience, it's a wonderful testament to the power of the Flat Army model. When she uses video to *consider* options or *confirm* a solution (as per the CLAM), it does wonders. When a leader uses video to thank and recognize a team for a job well done, he is employing the *coaching, bettering* and *developing* Connected Leader Attributes as well as the *congratulate* stage of the CLAM. In any case, the use of video demonstrates you are *participative, connected* and *collaborative.*

Blogs

What Are They?

Blogs are the online equivalent of pontificating with others beside the water cooler. We often share thoughts over coffees, at dinners, and during elevator chats, hallway bumps and conferences about pretty much anything that transpires inside an organization. It could be a re-organization of business units, new technologies that are being launched to customers, changes to the travel policy or a recent acquisition. Why should those thoughts be shared solely with those within earshot only? Blogs allow your thoughts to be shared with everyone over an electronic and typically text-based and graphical format (and some are adventurous enough to video-blog).

How Do I?

If you've ever had an opinion, you can blog. If you've ever written a letter to Santa Claus or your mother, you can blog. If you've ever used a laptop to create a document, you can blog. The question a Flat Army leader must ask herself concerns when she should blog. A blog post—as it is typically called—can align with any of the aforementioned situations above and more. Perhaps you want to express your opinion about a recent project in the *confirm* phase of the CLAM. Why not write a blog post about your feelings and then ask others to comment on it? This action, in fact, is an excellent example of utilizing all aspects of the Collaboration Technology social flow (*converse—content—context*) because users can also rate your post for accuracy or quality. Perhaps you might want to blog about one of the Connected Leader Attributes every month? That's a good Flat Army idea. You might use the social aspect of Pervasive Learning and share your knowledge a few times a year via a blog post as well. In any case, it's as simple as collecting your thoughts, writing them down and potentially attaching a few photos or graphical representations of your thinking. It's that easy.

Flat Army Benefits

Based on a study of 2,396 employees over a fifteen-month period at a Fortune 1000 IT services and consulting firm, authors Anindya Ghose,

Yan Huang and Param Vir Singh find that "blogging has a significant long-term effect in that it is only in the long term that the benefits of blogging outweigh the costs."[9] Bottom line? Please don't think you can write one blog post and expect yourself to be a Flat Army leader. Like I've repeatedly stated, you must be *continuous, authentic, reciprocal* and *educating*. The benefits of blogging will come in the long term, but when they do, they will show you are open, transparent, connected and honest all of the time.

Webjams

What Are They?

The concept of a "jam" was first introduced in 2001 by IBM. Pioneering the use of the web to unite people and debate about particular topics or opportunities, IBM has hosted many internal company-wide jams—like their 2003 initiative called "Values Jam" to redefine their core company-wide values—as well as external ones involving people outside of IBM such as Innovation Jam and Habitat Jam. Through the use of collaboration technology that allows thoughts to be expressed in a thread format, complemented by ratings and polling, participants congregate online to solve whatever problem needs to be addressed.

How Do I?

Webjams don't require proprietary collaboration technology. The jams can occur in a discussion forum, blog, wiki or anything that permits conversations and other interactive and collaborative supporting mechanisms to happen. As a leader, if there is one happening in your organization, it would be prudent of you to participate. Again, it doesn't take much to review what's been said and to add your opinion. To initiate a webjam requires some planning in advance. Do you have an organizational issue you want addressed? IBM's 2003 example of the Values Jam is a good one. Instead of creating new corporate values in an ivory tower, the company decided to involve the entire organization in the creation of new values. It's the quintessential example of the application of a webjam. It blends technology with culture for the benefit of all.

Flat Army Benefits

Webjams involve connecting with the organization, participating, collaborating and learning while utilizing collaboration technologies to accomplish the goal. I'd argue this is a tremendous benefit for both leaders and the people working tirelessly across your organization. Using webjams can be a culture builder. They can cross boundaries and erase stovepipes. If you have an organizational issue that might need the involvement of all, a webjam is an easy way to gain credibility with your employees everywhere.

User-Generated Content

What Is It?

Have you ever created a document on your computer? What about a presentation with slides—have you ever designed one of those? Out of curiosity, have you ever developed a spreadsheet to help justify a business case or to create a fancy pie chart? I bet you have. This is user-generated content and it sits lonely—in isolation—begging to be freed from your computer and transplanted to the content megastore. One could argue blogs, wikis and videos should be similarly called "user-generated content" as might anything in our *converse, content* and *context* categories, but for Flat Army purposes, user-generated content pertains to the files you have sitting within your personal file system on your laptop. Anything that is non-confidential needs to be repatriated to the collaboration-technology mother ship.

How Do I?

Quite simply, Flat Army leaders need to devise a personal criteria assessment process that informally adjudicates whether user-generated content is confidential or not. From there, the next task is to save a copy of the file to the most appropriate place within your collaboration platform, presuming you have one to begin with. Microsoft SharePoint, for example, is a collaboration platform used by 78 percent of Fortune 500 companies in addition to commanding over 125 million seat licenses worldwide across all industries. With proper architecture and configuration, SharePoint is an opportunity for you to share out your files to your team and the organization, should it be deployed in your organization. Other platforms such as Jive, Confluence, Connections and Salesforce also allow content to be categorized and uploaded.

Flat Army Benefits

The Participative Leader Framework incorporates the adage "contribute and consume." By uploading your documents and files you are contributing. The benefit to this simple act is threefold. First, you are demonstrating reciprocity; no doubt your action will inspire others to do the same thus making it reciprocal. Second, who says what you have created is perfect? Perhaps others can take what you have and improve it for another project that pops up in the future. Third, don't we "learn at the speed of need"? How can anyone learn from your documents if they reside dormant on your laptop? Both your team and the organization can benefit from what you've already created by learning from your past efforts.

CONTEXT

Context is akin to an MRI—magnetic resonance imaging—in the Flat Army model. An MRI scan provides context for a diagnosis to the health professional in that it graphically displays the skeletal structures and organs of the body. Collaborative technologies enable a leader to mine ideas and creative strategies in their dealings with team members and the content itself. They extend the converse and content categories outlined above, such that a Flat Army leader might provide additional background as to her character, leadership abilities and interactions. To utilize collaborative technologies such as search, profiles, badging, ratings and tagging permits the leader to clarify his content and even his conversations. Context gives meaning; it shines a light on your leadership style and your leadership interactions.

Search

What Is It?

It's not what you think. When you read the heading above (search), I suspect your mind gravitated toward images of Google or Yahoo! and you thought that I was about to explain the virtues of saving your search results and sharing them with your team. Wrong. Search is what you have to do within your organization and outside of it to extend your network. Recall the Participative Leader Framework from Chapter 7; this is your chance to build your personal and professional contacts through the mechanism of search. Yes, it's a collaborative process as much as it's a technology.

How Do I?

Externally, you first must ensure you're a member of LinkedIn—the market leader in contact management. Once you're a member, begin searching for past and current colleagues. From there, be adventurous and join groups to see who you might befriend and become networked with. If you're not on Twitter, get an account now. Once you familiarize yourself with the environment, start searching the accounts of other people and who they follow. Research their profiles and previous tweets to see if they're posting garbage or if they remain focused on the passions you follow in the professional world. When you attend conferences, search the speakers and see if you can connect with them online. Inside your organization, the address book is your best friend. By searching each business unit and studying who reports to whom, you are setting yourself up for potential new direct ties in the future. Don't stop there, either. Search any of the other collaboration technologies that your organization may have to acclimate yourself to other leaders and team members across the organization. Search is important and the concept doesn't just refer to using a traditional search engine.

Flat Army Benefits

Search—at least in the manner I'm defining it—is of critical importance when building your various network circles. A strong network can provide context to an infinite number of work-related opportunities and actions. Recall our learning from Dr. Burt in Chapter 7; the Neighbor Network of direct relationships helps productivity, performance and to get the job done. If you search out additional contacts to increase your direct network size, you are bound to increase your Flat Army currency and both you and your team will ultimately benefit.

Personal Profiles

What Is It?

If you have a Facebook account—and at last count over one billion of us do—you now know what a personal profile looks like. You must consider LinkedIn to be a personal profile, too. Whatever the technology, be it internal or external, it's the place where you describe who you are as well as your skills, interests and past experience to others. It's your "about me" portfolio. I haven't possessed a business card since 2000. Although you may call me asinine, in this day and age, a personal profile that you create and make available online—be it internally or externally—is today's *nouveau* business card. It's who you are.

How Do I?

From an external perspective, as mentioned above, get yourself signed up for LinkedIn if you haven't done so already. Fill out every possible field there is, to let others know who you are, what you're about, and where you've worked. Similarly, if your organization has some form of personal profile available internally, please take the time to ensure you have filled out everything possible. Your name and mobile phone number is not enough, either. Put a photo up there of yourself. Describe your skills and the projects you're working on. It's a great time to invoke the *clowning* attribute from Chapter 5.

Flat Army Benefits

We've discussed often throughout *Flat Army* that you—as a leader— need to humanize yourself. If you truly believe that you can shift from command-and-control to engage-and-empower, by taking the simple step of populating your personal profile, you are in fact demonstrating that you're a real human being. As others through the organization—and your direct team of course—peruse the profile, they see how real of a person you are. It's a simple step but it's so often overlooked. It also enables reciprocity via the PLF. There is nothing worse than seeing team members with up-to-date profiles, and the leader's looking barren.

Badging

What Is It?

According to Mozilla's Open Badges project, a badge is defined as a "symbol or indicator of an accomplishment, skill, quality or interest."[10] If you were a member of the Girl Guides, Pathfinders or Boy Scouts as a wee tot, you're familiar with the concept of merit- or progress-based badges. Similarly, members of the military and police and fire services—from whatever country—are cognizant of badges and their importance in marking accomplishments, levels or assignments. With respect to collaboration technologies, badging takes on a similar definition; its intention is to provide context for those that come into contact with your online persona. Badges might denote education qualifications you have garnered, service anniversaries or even groups and clubs you belong to.

How Do I?

Badging as a collaboration technology is relatively new, so it's possible— or likely—your organization doesn't yet have it deployed. The first step is to visit the websites of Mozilla's Open Badges and Badgeville to fully understand the concept of badging itself for your organization.[11] Once the technology has been implemented, your next step is to ensure you— as a Flat Army leader—actually utilize the technology. There are often options for you to turn it off. Please don't do it. Depending on how the technology is configured you are able to highlight badges for the content you post (e.g., number of blog or micro-blog posts) or the skills you possess. Whatever the attributes they refer to, these badges expose your character and capabilities.

Flat Army Benefits

As the leader of a team, badging is another perfect example of providing additional context to your team and others in the organization. It's not an example of egocentrism; rather, it's further insight into you as a human—as a person. It's you being honest within the social flow of the organization. In their 2011 paper entitled "Badges in Social Media: A Social Psychological Perspective," presented at the 2011 ACM CHI Conference on Human Factors in Computing Systems, authors Judd Antin and Elizabeth F. Churchill of Yahoo! Research identify five key benefits to badging, which nicely summarizes how Flat Army leaders might think about using badging:

- *Goal Setting: Badges challenge users to meet the mark that is set for them.*
- *Instruction: Badges convey the notion that individual activities have value and create an awareness of a community of users.*
- *Reputation: By providing an encapsulated assessment of engagement, experience and expertise, badges can be an invaluable tool for determining the trustworthiness of other people or the reliability of content.*
- *Status / Affirmation: Badges mark significant milestones and provide evidence of past successes.*
- *Group Identification: Achieving badges can provide a sense of solidarity and increase positive group identification through the perception of similarity between an individual and the group.*[12]

Ratings

What Are They?

Most content delivered through collaboration technologies like wikis, blogs and videos provides opportunities for readers or viewers to rate the material. Some systems utilize a Likert scale such as a one-through-five rating with one denoting a not-so-good rating and five suggesting an excellent mark. Others might assign numerical points or a thumbs-up or thumbs-down mechanism. Amazon, for example, uses a five-star rating for the books it makes available to consumers. By contrast, YouTube uses a simple like-and-dislike function. These same opportunities can be realized in your organization's internal collaboration technologies.

How Do I?

Simply put, it's not difficult at all to rate content within your collaboration platform. So long as you are actually taking the time to review the content, you can place a rating at just about every opportunity. It's anonymous. There really isn't an excuse to absolve yourself from such an easy action of providing additional context for others in your organization.

Flat Army Benefits

Ratings provide a supplementary method for others to understand the validity of or approval given to content found within your organization. Rating is a simple act but it can further the experiences of others. Although anonymous, it's an expectation of Flat Army leaders.

Tagging

What Is It?

Much of the user-generated content that can be developed by employees and subsequently delivered via a collaboration technology system can be tagged. Tagging is the process of applying keyword attributes that identify what the content is associated with. For example, if I created a video detailing how to use Microsoft PowerPoint and uploaded it to an internal video-sharing service in my organization, I might use tags such as "Microsoft," "PowerPoint," "presentations," "graphics," "design" and "beginner" to appropriately label the content. In doing so, the tag makes it easier for others to find the content when they perform searches (i.e., for additional context) and it also provides additional information when looking at the description of the content in the first place. By clicking on a tag, a user can then discover other similar content.

How Do I?

You're a Flat Army leader, which signifies you're fully employing the Participative Leader Framework. That means you are contributing content in a continuous, authentic, reciprocal and educating way (CARE). In each case in which you contribute content back to the ecosystem, your duty is to tag it with the most appropriate labels. This content might include items like a blog post, a document or a video. Again, like rating or badging, tagging is a very simple step in the work flow and may add five additional seconds to the overall task. Just do it.

Flat Army Benefits

This is apt and perhaps redundant, but the benefit of tagging is context. If the content that you are uploading is simply that—content—it may not get the reach it deserves. Tagging the content allows others to potentially find it inadvertently. By tagging your content, you are helping others connect the dots between your content and that of others. You are demonstrating Connected Leader Attributes such as *developing, cooperating, communicating* and *bettering*. Tagging is a Flat Army staple.

COLLABORATION TECHNOLOGIES AND SALES 2.0

Some companies are beginning to see the link between collaboration technologies and culture in a business context. Jerry Nine is the chief operating officer at Skillsoft, a cloud-based company specializing in learning solutions such as eLearning courses, online books and videos. Skillsoft possesses over 5,000 global customers who form a part of the more than 13 million end users of its various products. Technology is important to Skillsoft as their workforce of over one thousand employees is dispersed across the globe. What's impressive about Jerry is that he believes that "an engaged workforce is always a higher-performing workforce." For him, engagement is important and it's enabled by collaborative technologies coupled with a culture of collaboration itself. Jerry filled me in on a new initiative rolling out across Skillsoft entitled "Sales 2.0." This blend of collaborative technologies and a culture of collaboration increase both engagement and performance at Skillsoft. Jerry said to me:

The Sales 2.0 initiative provides sales managers with the collaboration tools to support coaching across all Skillsoft sales and services employees. Through Sales 2.0, there are weekly performance goals and time allotted to coaching. Development plans as well as a mechanism for ongoing performance feedback is embedded into the system. It's an iterative process that becomes second nature on a continual basis, not something locked into an annual performance review. It also supports a healthy dialogue where no one should be surprised as ongoing candid feedback is paramount to the success of both the employee and the manager. Sales 2.0 truly is a way to marry technology with behavior.[13]

Wedded to the Sales 2.0 system are a number of additional tools and processes such as instant messaging, micro-blogging, texting, conference calls and their own product—InGenius—a social learning platform that allows employees to share knowledge and expertise among once another. Add it all up, and Jerry—the COO of the company—is demonstrating Flat Army in action at Skillsoft. The company doesn't roll out collaborative technologies for the fun of it; rather, it ties them into the culture of the company and the engagement of its people. Jerry believes in something he calls "participative management" where he is trying to ensure that he continuously supports and enables people throughout the organization to be successful. "It's built on delegation," Jerry said to me, "where I make it known that many people have more expertise than I have in their chosen area of focus and my role is to remove barriers and obstacles so they can reach their true potential. The use of technology is key." Spoken like a true Flat Army leader.

THE TECHNOLOGY STRIKES BACK

There is a potential dark side to collaboration technologies that all Flat Army leaders would be wise to understand, and they should also know how to take action when things go awry. Picture yourself on a conference call with eight people. You're in an office with a hands-free phone. The other seven colleagues on the phone are in similar situations. The meeting is sixty minutes and it's an operational review of each person's portfolio. There are five minutes allotted to each individual with roughly twenty minutes at the end earmarked for other business, questions and general roundtable discussion. You're slotted into the fourth spot on the agenda. As the conch is passed to you from updater number three, your briefing begins flawlessly. Well done. Just as you're halfway through, because you haven't shut down your email application, you notice a new email come into your account. Damn those notifications that pop up in the bottom right-hand corner over everything else on your laptop! Wait a minute; the email is from a colleague who is supposedly listening to your update. Did you want irony? The subject header reads, "Need Your Opinion." Sound familiar?

How about the "device prayer"? Imagine that, to your chagrin, in a face-to-face brainstorming session you've been ignored by your colleagues. Your passionate thoughts scribed on a whiteboard were not even misunderstood by those in the room—they weren't even ingested. When you began to add additional colors to your whiteboard SWOT analysis, those in attendance saw your back turn and it was at this precise moment that they grabbed their devices and begin answering emails, tweets, texts, etc. When you eventually spun around, unsuspecting, to your colleagues to ask for feedback on your masterpiece thus far, none of them actually broke eye contact with their devices. You stood there quietly for about two minutes, analyzing the situation until the tranquility was ended by the loud rattle of a dropped device from a rather clumsy colleague hitting the meeting room floor. Sound familiar?

Technology is a critical element to becoming a connected leader in our Flat Army model—however, not at the expense of people. Too often technology is consuming leaders but scenarios like the ones above are becoming the norm. Thought leader and former Microsoft vice president Linda Stone coined the term "continuous partial attention." By definition it is paying partial attention, continuously. Linda said to me, "In this state, we are constantly scanning and often attempting more than one activity that requires cognition. CPA is different from simply multi-tasking, and more similar to complex multi-tasking."[14]

When I asked her if it was affecting our organizations and the way in which we're operating, she said,

We apply continuous partial attention to many activities, throughout the day. For some activities, it might be a match. When we apply CPA to every activity, continuously, it's often a sign that we're in a state of chronic stress, and this can compromise our judgment and effectiveness.

She went on to describe the bane for many of us; meetings and technology:

It's time to be a little more intentional about meetings. New technologies, new rules. Just as a pilot uses a checklist to make sure everything is in shape before taking off in the plane, so it is for us, when we present or walk into meetings. First off, it's always a good practice to turn off notifications. Regardless of what you're doing, this interruption is like taking a gun to your attention, and really shocking your system. Consider how often that interruption really helps you and how often it's a disturbance.

Linda was adamant that both employees and leaders be intentional about their attention. "Some activities are best matched with simple multi-tasking," she said. "Some with continuous partial attention and some with full engagement or focus."

As a connected and collaborative leader you would be very wise to pay continuous *full* attention to the prospect of continuous *partial* attention having a detrimental effect on your team or organization. Don't let fancy technology become a dividing influence in your newly engaged corporate culture.

✳   ✳   ✳

I asked Tony Bingham, CEO of the American Society for Training & Development (ASTD), if he had come across any examples or stories where culture and technology seemed to blend nicely. He recalled a story about Booz Allen Hamilton, an American consulting firm with over 26,000 employees and $5.5 billion in revenues:

Walt McFarland, when at Booz Allen Hamilton, once told me that technology doesn't make a difference if the culture doesn't support collaboration. We had this discussion back when the idea of "social learning," some call it "collaborative learning," was really beginning to gain traction in the workplace learning profession. In an effort to better serve their clients, Booz Allen was using social technology tools to give their consultants the ability to reach across the organization and tap the knowledge of subject matter experts to solve complex problems. It's important to note that at Booz Allen collaboration is a corporate value. Working together is built into the company's DNA. In Walt's terms the technology, or tools, "actualize the culture."[15]

At the start of this chapter I mention Daniel Kligerman. Walt McFarland is of the same mindset as me and perhaps Daniel as well. Organizational culture and Flat Army leadership are complemented by collaboration technology, but you should recognize that technology is only an enabler. This is critical for you to understand before you set out to enact your Flat Army model.

On the other hand there is Sherry Turkle, the Abby Rockefeller Mauzé Professor of the Social Studies of Science and Technology in the Program in Science, Technology, and Society at MIT, who states in her book *Alone Together*,

Technology is seductive when what it offers meets our human vulnerabilities. And as it turns out, we are very vulnerable indeed. We are lonely but fearful of intimacy. Digital connections and the sociable robot may offer the illusion of companionship without the demands of friendship. Our networked life allows us to hide from each other, even as we are tethered to each other. We'd rather text than talk.[16]

Naturally, I disagree with Sherry. No employee I've come across is fearful of what I would refer to as "leadership intimacy." Employees want to feel part of the equation as well as being connected to their leader. This leadership intimacy is obviously of a platonic nature in the organization. It's supported by collaboration technologies.

To be sure, proper discipline and techniques must be taught and learned such that employees do not become addicted to such technologies nor, as mentioned previously, do they fall into the potentially negative vortex of continuous partial attention. But wasn't such cultural calamity predicted of the photocopier and fax machine when they arrived in the organization? Despite Turkle's central thesis, collaborative technologies are here to stay and they must become a key part of the Flat Army toolshed. It's not that employees would rather text than talk in the organization—they simply want to feel engaged with their leader as well as within their organization. Face-to-face contact and meetings are important, but so too is a leader who knows how to utilize collaboration technologies according to the Flat Army model. As I've reiterated throughout this book, it's incumbent upon you—the leader—to become collaborative, connected and participative through the various frameworks and behaviors we've discussed at length. But it's through the use of collaboration technologies where you can assist your efforts. These tools and technologies are not isolating, nor are they tethering us to noncommunication.

Collaboration technologies are as integral to Flat Army as they are to employee engagement and productivity. If you're not on board, please remember what Thomas Edison once said: "Many of life's failures are people who did not realize how close they were to success when they gave up."[17]

CHAPTER ELEVEN

FLAT ARMY IN ACTION

The greatness of the strategy is proven by the fact that in retrospect it seems obvious.
—Darren Entwistle

Over the course of my research and reading for this book, I've come across a number of interesting companies whose actions illustrate Flat Army ideas in action—or the reverse. You can be the judge as to whether each example features Flat Army in the field or an anachronistic hierarchy.

NHS

England's famous National Health Service (NHS) was featured prominently in the 2012 Summer Olympics opening ceremonies in London. The NHS was created by the National Health Service Act in 1946. As you might expect, it's the national health service for all of England. (Separate NHS operations are found in Scotland, Wales and Northern Ireland.) There were 1,210,784 people working at NHS as of May 2012, and roughly 47 percent are in support staff or infrastructure support roles.

A series of reports was released in 2011 and 2012 by the King's Fund Leadership Review that sought to determine the degree to which NHS managers and support staff were essential to the patient care cycle.

Were they as essential as doctors and nurses? What the reports found lays credible claim to the need for Flat Army at NHS. Four of the major points included:

- Leadership at the NHS needs to become shared and distributed.
- Leadership practice is currently overly reliant on heroic individuals, not on the effective use of teams and organizations.
- Leaders are operating in silos—not through others—to meet objectives.
- There is a need for leaders to motivate, engage team members, and operate across organizations and systems to successfully transform the NHS healthcare systems and operations.[1]

One of the reports encapsulates our Flat Army model in one succinct paragraph:

The dominant NHS approach is known as "pace-setter"—typified by laying down demanding targets, leading from the front, often being reluctant to delegate, and collaborating little—and is the consequence of the health service focusing on process targets, with recognition and reward dependent on meeting them. Truly high-performing leaders deploy a range of leadership approaches depending on the demands of each situation. There is growing evidence that the NHS needs to break with the command and control, target-driven approach.[2]

Kudos to the NHS for taking the steps to analyze its current leadership-operating model and for releasing the findings of the reports to the public. The reports are as indicting as they are hopeful. Prior to the reports surfacing, the Chartered Institute of Personnel and Development (CIPD) performed a three-year research study released in 2008 involving more than 6,000 NHS staff. One of the resulting outcomes was a model called "Engaging Leadership." The framework suggests that

[l]eadership is not about being an extraordinary person, but being open, accessible and transparent. It emphasises teamwork, collaboration and "connectedness," and removing

barriers to communication and original thinking. It reflects a desire to see the world through the eyes of others, to take on board their concerns and perspectives and to work with their ideas.[3]

Sounds like "Flat NHS" might happen one day if managers were to take the recommendations and fully implement them across its various healthcare platforms. I wonder what NHS would look like if the Flat Army pillars (CLA, CLAM, PLF, Pervasive Learning and Collaboration Technologies) were applied throughout the organization?

GOOD ROCKIN' TONITE

Why is it that leaders of any stripe are worried about the aging population, with respect to the accumulated knowledge and experience that is beginning to, as they say, walk out the door? A true collaborative culture in action—Flat Army in combat—is not one that needs to enact a plan to capture the knowledge of aging workers. If an organization needs to set up multiple task forces and initiatives to capture knowledge, that means that it hasn't built up a culture that inherently absorbs and transmits information from its troops, and therefore it's not incorporating Flat Army.

The Human Resources Professionals Association (HRPA) states that over 83 percent of larger companies (anywhere from 50 to 5,000 employees) acknowledge they are either "somewhat" or "poorly" prepared for the eventuality that baby boomers are leaving the workforce. Only 17 percent are in fact prepared for the rash of baby-boomer retirements.[4] Would you say that Flat Army concepts are deployed in those organizations that are marginally prepared? I didn't think so.

Consider the case of Terry David Mulligan. Over a forty-year period, the former music- and movie-industry schmoozing magnate held positions at MuchMusic (the equivalent of MTV in Canada) and CBC's *Good Rockin' Tonite* where he interviewed the likes of Jim Morrison, Cheech and Chong, Janis Joplin, Jimi Hendrix and members of The Beatles, not to mention actors and directors like Robin Williams, Jason Priestly and

Gus Van Sant. TDM—as he is affectionately known in music and movie circles—is a walking encyclopedia of entertainment knowledge. Shockingly, his employer at the time in 2007—CTVglobemedia Inc.—issued Terry a pink slip; his services were no longer needed at the organization. Remarking that he had just turned 65 years of age, the employer enforced mandatory retirement (with minimal severance) and TDM was let go after a remarkable—if not stunning—twenty-four-year career with CHUM, the group that had sold itself to CTVglobemedia Inc. To say this was a shock to TDM and employees at the organization was an understatement.

The key issue at hand is this: did CTVglobemedia or CHUM ensure that all of the knowledge that TDM possessed was captured or shared among his peers prior to his departure? I mean, aside from that which was contained in video and audio files. I bet many employees in that organization today would be soaking in a vast compendium of TDM knowledge had the culture been established to share and collaborate in the first place. But this is not a learning issue—it's a culture issue.

Second, if an employer is issuing a six-week termination notice because its employee was turning sixty-five years old, doesn't that make you think about the culture of the organization itself? Mulligan was right to feel incredulous about the experience, but the more powerful lesson learned here for aspiring Flat Army leaders in other organizations is not that culture eats strategy for breakfast, but rather that culture is the single biggest competitive advantage.

If the culture is—like it seemingly was at CTVglobemedia in 2007—one where decisions are being made in back rooms and employees are being treated like Terry David Mulligan, it raises the question of whether senior leaders had inculcated an organizational culture that was closed, commanding and conniving.

If the culture had been crafted from the beginning as a more collaborative and less hierarchical culture, Terry David Mulligan might have been in a place to share his off-the-record experiences more effortlessly than within a culture that potentially smacked of hierarchy and lethargy. Any culture that forces its people to retire probably isn't one that had an open and sharing type of culture in the first place. Maybe TDM would still be rocking.

Mercifully and thankfully, he moved on. In fact, he sued CTV-globemedia Inc. and won a settlement that allowed him to enter into a new phase in his life where he still thrives in the entertainment world. CTVglobemedia was eventually bought, and then split up, by Bell and the Thomson family.

It's my opinion that formal knowledge-transferring programs and forced retirement packages are antithetical to the culture we should be aspiring to build within Flat Army organizations from the onset. If a firm is spending time on formally capturing the so-called knowledge of baby boomers, then it hasn't done an effective enough job to establish an open culture. If it's forcing smart people out, in no way is it a Flat Army.

Don't be one of those leaders hellbent on transferring the knowledge of baby boomers to younger employees. Instead, think through how you can create a culture that ensures knowledge is being shared all the time, and that employees are really "learning at the speed of need" regardless of age. To do so is to manifest all that you have learned in this book. It is an example of bringing Flat Army into combat.

With respect to Terry David Mulligan, I wonder the degree to which current VJs, DJs and interviewers at the company's latest incarnation (Bell Media) might be better prepared to ask questions and mingle with entertainment stars of today if Terry had been working in a culture that encouraged knowledge sharing. Not many people had the chance to share drinks with Janis Joplin. Those types of stories and knowledge, at least in the entertainment world, should be easily shared so others can use them as insight or fodder for other situations. This example is analogous to situations in any industry or organization.

Knowledge sharing becomes a key component to the new company culture. It is Flat Army in action; silos are to be broken and organizational fiefdoms burned to the ground. This mitigates the need for so-called baby-boomer-knowledge-transfer programs. Imagine if CHUM had employed the Connected Leader Attributes throughout their organization.

What if staff knew how to utilize the Participative Leader Framework or the Collaborative Leader Action Model? What if Pervasive Learning and Collaborative Technologies were in operation throughout the company? What would have been the verdict? Would TDM have been retired? Would knowledge- and idea-sharing be prevalent throughout the company today? I suppose it could have been a case of "good rockin' tonight," but unfortunately it wasn't.

RESEARCH IN MOTIONLESS

Now we have another example, this one dealing with Research In Motion, more commonly known as RIM—the makers of the iconic BlackBerry smartphone. Pundits from San Francisco to Siberia to Sydney have written off this Canadian company since 2008. Many claim RIM is no longer relevant in a smartphone ecosystem dominated by Apple, Google, Samsung and Microsoft. According to Canaccord Genuity Estimates, RIM's global market share dropped from 19.7 percent in 2009 to 10.8 percent by the end of 2011. It further predicted a market share drop to 6.1 percent by the end of 2012 and 4.9 percent by the end of 2013.[5] Whether you're a shareholder, a customer, an executive or an employee, those numbers are difficult to digest. Gloomy is one word that comes to mind. What happened?

Kara Swisher is co–executive editor of the popular Silicon Valley–based media organization AllThingsD and has been outspoken about RIM on several occasions. In September of 2012, for example, while speaking at a Women in Film and Television event, she stated the following:

RIM is a perfect example of failing to respond to consumer changes. Lazaridis is a genius. But RIM missed so many consumer trends because they were protecting an old business. In the end, they broke their consumer relationship by not innovating.[6]

The "Lazaridis" she refers to is ex co-CEO Mike Lazaridis who, alongside fellow co-CEO Jim Balsillie, helped bring RIM to the forefront of innovation and success only to see it—and their roles as co-CEOs—vanish before their eyes. Through a twenty-year span, it could be argued both men helped launch the smartphone industry itself. Blindsided by the success of the Apple iPhone, however—which launched in 2007—it could be argued Lazaridis and Balsillie were the reason for both RIM's success and its recent collapse. They knew what worked up until the height of RIM's dominance, but rather than adjusting and having the foresight to alter course, they remained shackled to what worked in the past. By doing so, their stock price went from roughly $140 to $7 in a four-year period. Gulp.

Rather than being rigid and inflexible and incapable of change, what if the elements of Flat Army had been employed at the company? Would it have made a difference? There is reason to suggest RIM was a company of command-and-control habits. There is also reason to suggest Lazaridis and Balsillie didn't listen to or engage their employees. For this type of close-minded behavior the company is clearly paying a price. Could introducing the Flat Army model help turn it around?

By way of example, in the summer of 2011 an anonymous letter from a high-ranking RIM executive was sent to Jonathan S. Geller, founder of the popular mobile and telecommunications website BGR. Geller verified the source and proceeded to publish the letter on the site. The letter starts out as follows:

To the RIM Senior Management Team:
   I have lost confidence.
   While I hide it at work, my passion has been sapped. I know I am not alone—the sentiment is widespread and it includes people within your own teams.[7]

With confidence and passion lacking not only with this leader but alleged to be widespread, it really comes back to our thesis in Chapter 1—this employee has become disengaged, and if disengagement is afflicting others, there is no doubt the company could be in for future worrisome troubles.

The letter goes on to state that the following actions should take place:

Reach out to all employees asking them on how we can make RIM better. Encourage input from ground-level teams—without repercussions—to seek out honest feedback and really absorb it. We should also address issues surrounding making RIM an enjoyable workplace. Some of our offices feel like Soviet-era government workplaces.

Does this sound to you like the makings of a Flat Army organization, or a leadership team in a state of denial and disorder?

Marc Weber of the University of Waterloo—which coincidentally is in RIM's backyard—asserts that given the choice between following their own path and the pre-existing situation, people will naturally adapt to the situation rather than maintaining their own individual beliefs or natural behaviors. In other words, if the behaviors of an organization are, for example, like RIM—hierarchical, rigid, closed, non-collaborative and uncooperative—even if an individual employs the opposites of these traits at a personal level from their arrival at the company—the employee will, over time, act more like the organization (the situation) than how they might have behaved prior to joining the organization.

What was the *situation* at RIM? It was an organization where the leadership and leadership behaviors were clearly closed. There was no evidence of collaboration once the Apple iPhone arrived on the scene. Communication channels seemed to be nonexistent between staff and senior management. The situation was a giant example of groupthink. To many, RIM seemed to morph from an innovative and flexible organization to one that was rigid, blind and hierarchical. It has landed the organization in the deepest of all crises leading to the reduction of its workforce by over 5,000 employees and operating expenditure by over $1 billion in 2012 alone.

There are some interesting developments at RIM, though. Firstly, Lazaradis and Balsillie heeded the calls to resign and did so in early 2012. Thorsten Heins—RIM's COO at the time—took the reins and has been leading the charge to turn around the company and brighten its future outlook. In the summer of 2012, Heins wrote an editorial in *The Globe and Mail* where he states:

RIM has chosen to pursue a strategy that eschews the homogenized sameness of competing ecosystems. To help with that task, we have reshaped the executive team and recruited telecommunications industry veterans with proven track records of success.[8]

I found it compelling, if not confirming, that the leadership of the organization had to be both "reshaped" and "recruited." This says to me Heins is in the midst of reshaping and recruiting a culture that is potentially diametrically opposed to the *situation* that used to envelope the organization. It seems as though the *situation* is in need of a change. Perhaps Heins is in fact about to deploy Flat Army concepts such that RIM can pull off a similar turnaround like that of IBM, Apple or Ford—the stuff of corporate-change lore. With new devices launched in 2013, only time will tell.

THE SPIRIT OF HITACHI

In Chapter 4 I discuss the Hitachi Spirit: *Wa, Makoto* and *Kaitakusha-Seishin*. It's this spirit and a ubiquitous level of openness and trust that allows the company to be so successful. They already are a Flat Army organization.

Nick Howe, vice president of learning and collaboration at Hitachi Data Systems (HDS) is well aware of how important openness, trust and a sense of community is with respect to *Wa, Makoto* and *Kaitakusha-Seishin* at HDS. He said to me,

While people may be intrinsically or extrinsically motivated to perform, the ability to execute in a complex global organization for anything other than trivial tasks relies on networks of people working together—often despite rather than because of systems.[9]

On the topic of linking trust to engagement, Howe said, "It's built on trust of each other, and trust that the company will do the right thing—especially when times are tough or difficult decisions need to be made."

Nick's belief is that a common set of leadership behaviors that compare to the Connected Leader Attributes discussed in *Flat Army* are key to any sort of organizational success. And when things need to get done, it's the pioneering spirit of innovation, openness and trust that avoids duplication and accomplishes the goal.

From my discussions with Nick, it became evident culture had already become a competitive advantage at Hitachi. For example, after the organization deployed a certain collaborative technology platform that was viewed by many—including Nick and his team, after the fact—as too controlling and closed, it implemented Jive Social Business Software, a more open and collaboration-sharing platform in Nick's eyes. He said, "We built it on a governance model [in which] everything is open by default, and closed by exception—180 degrees from how Microsoft SharePoint was deployed." Imagine that. Having one collaboration platform and realizing it wasn't collaborative enough for your employees. That's Flat Army in combat.

Another example at HDS speaks to Nick's own uncannily Flat-Army-like leadership style. Within his existing team, Nick decided to create another one focusing specifically on collaboration and facilitation. He hired Jeff Maaks as the director of collaboration, and together they immediately enacted something Jeff calls the "Barn Raising." Nick explained it as follows:

Much like the Amish come together to build a physical structure, the Barn Raising approach, facilitated by my team, brings together individuals from different functions and geographies who have a common goal. This is not a "meeting" or a talking shop session. Over the course of two to five days, leveraging Jive and our culture of sharing, the individuals source or co-create content like best practices, reference guides, checklists, videos, and so on, populating Jive along the way. The content may be new, or may have been locked away. By the end of the Barn Raising exercise we have:

- *concrete deliverables accessible to the entire company that adds real business value;*
- *a tight community of committed individuals with a new global perspective; and*
- *a broader community who can benefit from those deliverables.*

Wow. I couldn't help myself, I had to ask Nick about his own personal leadership style. He broke it down into seven key components:

- *Informal: anyone can talk to anyone.*
- *Inclusive: seek input from and delegate to the entire organization, regardless of level.*
- *Authentic: walk the talk.*
- *Trusting: assume good intent; do not blame.*
- *Open: share as much as possible; err on [the side of] too much communication rather than too little.*
- *Responsive: "yes" is the default response.*
- *Supportive: take the blame for failure; ensure praise goes to those who deserve it.*

Let's recap. First, here we have an organization, HDS, that recognizes leadership is for all and which employs an eerily similar leadership construct to that of the Flat Army Connected Leader Attributes. Second, we have an enterprise-wide team under Nick's direction that is pushing culture-changing behaviors akin to the Participative Leader Framework and Collaborative Leader Action Model alongside Pervasive Learning (formal, informal and social) and Collaborative Technologies. To top it off, Nick's own personal style maps onto the entire suite of Flat Army ideas.

You now get a sense of why Nick is so happy in his role and engaged at Hitachi. You also can see how important concepts like we've discussed in this book can become normal business practice even for a large high-tech company. It really is a fine example of Flat Army in combat.

LESSONS FROM SCOTIABANK

Scotiabank is a company that fully understands why a common leadership framework and diverse and inclusive culture can benefit even those organizations that are already hugely successful. As Canada's most international bank, Scotiabank has more than 81,000 employees and serves some 19 million customers in more than fifty-five countries around the world. With assets in excess of $670 billion, Scotiabank is a highly successful organization and continues to grow both in Canada and internationally. Strong leadership has been an important part of that success.

With a firm view of the future, several years ago Scotiabank listed leadership as one of its five strategic business priorities. A bank-wide leadership development process ensures that employees with leadership potential are developed to their full potential through training, project opportunities, and responsibilities that expand their scope of competencies and experience. A Scotiabank Leadership Profile, available to all employees, clearly outlines the competencies, experiences and education that Scotiabank believes are essential to becoming a leader at the bank.

Recently, Scotiabank retooled its employee-competency model— shifting from twenty-two competencies to ten that are directly aligned with leadership competency—and introduced to the organization a unique leadership development approach known as iLead. Through the introduction of streamlined competencies and iLead, Scotiabank is saying to its employees, partners and customers that leadership is for all and that it is being facilitated through a coaching culture.

Shazia McCormick is director of global performance and learning at Scotiabank and in this role is responsible for the success of iLead. In a discussion I had with Shazia, she talked about the importance of building leadership competencies globally:

"We're unifying our leadership behaviour to one common approach globally. Furthermore, iLead is breaking down traditional barriers and silos between business lines. The feedback tells us we are on the right track. Employees are telling us "this is changing my career" and "I understand how much coaching can impact my team's results." For an organization with Scotiabank's size and geography, we're encouraged by the level of engagement and application we are already seeing from our employees.[10]

Not surprisingly, it was the bank's top leadership that indicated three years ago that a globally consistent approach to management and leadership development was in order. Previously, only vice presidents and above were consistently given leadership-development opportunities.

Now, through the introduction of bank-wide competencies aligned to leadership competencies, iLead, and a pervasive coaching culture, Scotiabank is building a "leadership at all levels" mentality while at the same time building their leadership pipeline and talent pool. This is a Flat Army habit and a lesson other organizations would be wise to emulate.

ZAPPOS

If you're unfamiliar with Zappos, it could well be the poster child for how an organization should be run and how its leaders should lead. It's the real deal when it comes to Flat Army in combat.

The spirited, if not culturally futuristic, CEO of Las Vegas–based Zappos is Tony Hsieh. Zappos itself is the self-proclaimed "best selection in online shopping" dot-com retailer. You name it, they sell it. Tony believes culture trumps everything, regardless of what you're selling or making. His mantra at Zappos has been to take care of the 3,000 employees who work there and let the results speak for themselves. He's a bit of a corporate renaissance man; a leader who fully understands the relationship of engagement and leadership to culture and business results. In my opinion, he has employed each of the five Flat Army segments.

Tony states the following:

What's the best way to build a brand for the long term?

In a word: culture.

At Zappos, our belief is that if you get the culture right, most of the other stuff—like great customer service, or building a great long-term brand, or passionate employees and customers—will happen naturally on its own.

We believe that your company's culture and your company's brand are really just two sides of the same coin. The brand may lag the culture at first, but eventually it will catch up. Your culture is your brand.[11]

In November of 2009, Amazon bought Zappos for $1.2 billion on the condition Tony remained CEO and that Zappos remained independent of Amazon so that it could keep its very unique and successful culture and it could continue driving business results. (Both were terms Tony put into the deal.) Asked at the time why the deal occurred, Tony stated, "It seemed clear that Amazon had come to appreciate our company culture as well as our strong sales."[12] In 2000, revenue at Zappos topped $1.6 million, but twelve years later it inched closer to $2 billion. Zappos has since leapt to #11 on *Fortune*'s "100 Best Companies to Work For" list.

The Zappos way, which seems quirky to some, is a testament to getting the job done with an employee-first attitude. It's an example of instilling the right leadership model where employees are able to breathe, feel a part of the company direction, and in return deliver fantastic customer experiences. This continuum is wrapped in a bow called "phenomenal financial results." It is an example of Flat Army in combat.

HCL TECHNOLOGIES

Zappos has a twin brother located halfway around the world. It truly is an uncanny resemblance.

Vineet Nayar is the CEO of HCL Technologies, an India-based global information technology services company. It provides IT-outsourcing services, business-process outsourcing services, and infrastructure services. There are more than 82,000 employees who help produce over $3 billion in annual revenues. HCLT, as it is known, is also the fourth-largest IT company in India. HCLT wasn't always this successful, though.

In fact, until Vineet came along, HCLT was an example of those organizations that symbolize the current status quo of cultural futility. Vineet wrote a book in 2010 entitled *Employees First, Customers Second: Turning Conventional Management Upside Down*. It documents the cultural and employee-first transformation at HCLT. Specifically, Vineet describes with resonating fervor what steps had to be taken to shift the culture and engagement of the company and how it got accomplished.

Vineet absolutely saw the relationship between employee engagement, culture, technology, learning and leadership and as a result, business results have dramatically improved at the organization. There are two examples that depict Vineet as a quintessential Flat Army leader.

When at an off-site meeting with many leaders across the company, Vineet floated the idea of opening up all financial data to one another in the company. He states:

At the time, our people had access to the financial information that pertained to their own projects, but they had no way of knowing how their business unit and the whole organization were doing. Nor could they compare the performance of their team to that of others in the company. What if we allowed everybody to see all the business units' and the company's financial data? Wouldn't that be an important step toward greater transparency? Wouldn't it help build a culture of trust—showing that we had nothing to hide and were willing to share both the good and the bad, just as one would in a strong family?[13]

Vineet worked with the information technology department and they went about opening up this important line of data access. It's truly demonstrating our becoming, being and beyond Connected Leader Attributes while blending portions of the Participative Leader Framework and the CLAM.

Another example demonstrated Vineet's passion for learning and collaborative technologies interspersed with his penchant for being a connected leader. He had always enjoyed meeting with employees in town halls and one-to-one meetings for feedback, but back in 2005, no less, he thought perhaps this could be complemented by a more efficient, open and web-based method. Vineet states:

While I was working with my social networking group, we came up with an idea we called U&I—an online forum where any employee could post any question, which I, along with my leadership team, would answer. The idea was to build an open site where everyone would be able to see the question, the questioner, and the answer. It was a simple idea that we hoped would foster a culture of open conversation, with fewer rumors and less misinformation, and that would thus create more trust.[14]

Needless to say, HCLT has been named "Best Employer in India" and one of the "Top 25 Best Employers in Asia" by Hewitt Associates.[15] As well, *Businessweek* listed HCLT as one of the five emerging companies in the world to watch.[16] Not bad for an example of Flat Army in combat.

FLAT ARMY AT TELUS

There are moments in your career when you bash your head against the wall thinking, "Why has it come to this?" Other times, you sit back in wonderment and regale to yourself the narrative of a recent win or a positive outcome. When you're firing on all cylinders, you feel as though nothing can go wrong. You are triumphant. Pack the car, kids, we're going to Disneyland. Such a scenario happened to me in the fall of 2012.

On this particular day, an interview with TELUS CEO Darren Entwistle had been published in *T+D Magazine.* Never one to mince words or hide behind a half-truth, Darren spoke candidly about the culture and leadership philosophy that had taken hold at TELUS prior to his arrival in 2000. Not only was he expansive about his beliefs regarding culture and leadership—which incidentally have a lot to do with being connected, participative, and collaborative and are interwoven with formal, informal and social learning means—he spoke passionately about collaborative technologies and social networking in general. One section resonated with me, particularly because of what happened later that day. With respect to social technologies and their relationship to the learning model at TELUS, Darren states:

Another important thing about social networking is that people learn from each other, peer-to-peer. Sometimes peer learning has even greater authenticity than more traditional teaching paradigms. It also creates greater cultural connectivity, and that is important within the matrix structure where you want people to feel they're all rowing the same boat. Social media is happily ignorant of the functional silos in the organization and also ignorant of geographic distance. Intellectual property, peer-to-peer learning, skills, experience, and creativity flow across the organization at speeds that ignore time and distance and organizational boundaries, and that's extremely cool.[17]

I had the fortune of sitting in on that interview in early July of 2012, and reading it for the first time on a bright and sunny morning in early September was, as Darren said, "extremely cool." But the story actually gets better.

Although I'm obviously biased, I think TELUS has done a remarkable job implementing collaborative technologies across the organization to connect its people, to reduce the cycle time of competence gain and information transfer. It's obviously a key piece to the overarching learning model as well. From wikis, to blogs, virtual worlds, gaming, badging, tagging, ranking, commenting, discussions, webjams, etc., the organization is never one to pass up anything that might help the team member experience. One of those tools, Buzz, is a popular micro-blogging platform. How popular, you ask? As of September 2012, more than 50 percent of the organization uses it regularly with some 2,000 unique posts and 5,000 discussion comments happening monthly. That's a lot of sharing.

On this particular day after reading Darren's interview, I went trolling through Buzz to see if I could learn anything, or if I could be of any assistance to fellow team members. If I'm going to write about Flat Army, I sure better be enacting it. Through my Buzz mining, I spotted a post from Lito, a member of the TELUS call center team based in the Philippines. The Buzz post read as follows:

Finally, I got the blog working.

That was it. Other than a link to his internal blog post he had written within the TELUS personal blogging platform, his Buzz post was short, crisp and to the point. Naturally, being ever the interlocutor, I clicked on the link and traveled off to his blog. It read, word for word, as follows:

Many of us have been part of many teams, and my thought of what a team is has changed ever since I joined this industry. All I thought qualified a team was a mere group with members and a leader. A group that can either influence you in a good or in a bad way.

I have been in this industry for roughly 5 years and still counting. I have been part of many other companies and already had several team members. The protocol was, they come and they go. But this one is different. They all stay. Yah, I'm telling you they all stay. My team and I have been together for more than a year now. Can you just imagine that, a year? You think I'm kidding, right?

We started May of last year. We were like a psychologist trying to read everyone's character and personality. Is she strict, did she / he like me? Is he / she fun? Well lots of questions right? That's what we always do before the getting to know each other stage right? Well anyway after all the long introductions and the smiles made for everyone, we were tied since then, and until now we are still together. Striving together for excellence and respect. A lot of struggles came and may come our way but we don't let any single negativeness ruin our bucket of positiveness.

We are brothers like sam and dean in the series supernatural and we are sisters like the movie the sisterhood of the travelling pants. We care for one another. We cheer for every success that anyone can get. And that defines the true meaning of a team.

And then it hit me like a brick to the head. I used Buzz (a micro-blogging platform) to connect to Lito's post (on a blogging platform) which helped me understand and learn about his feelings regarding his team. Lito, on the other hand, didn't have to share, didn't have to post to Buzz, but he did. I am better for it. I now know how he feels about his team, how cool it is to work with them, and it helped me understand just exactly who Lito is as a person. It made me want to learn more about this team. It made me want to learn more about Lito. It made me feel connected to Lito some ten thousand kilometers away. As Darren notes above, indeed, it does create a greater cultural connectivity. It was the Connected Leader Attributes in action between both Lito and I. It too demonstrated how the PLF and Collaboration Technologies can connect the dots between behavior, culture and output.

But it gets better.

After reading the post, I in turn decided to write about Lito. I whipped together a blog post and uploaded it to a blogging platform. From there, I went over to Buzz and sent a note out to the organization with an accompanying link to my post as follows:

A quick story about Lito #tlp #leadership #culture #teams

From there, a pile of team members across the globe commented on the story about Lito through the Buzz comments section. A few of those Buzz responses included the following:

@dan and @lito #culture #customersfirst #YOU Thanks for sharing this, Dan. It's great to read about Lito! I really enjoy meeting other TMs (team members) through Buzz. A recent "wow moment" I had: I called CS (Customer Service) a few weeks ago and had to give them my account info (my name, phone number, etc) and the agent says "are you Gina from the Customers First team? I just joined the Buzz group!" How amazing is that?! She's part of TELUS International team. . .and so far away, yet we connected without ever meeting. Very cool :)

Good vibe on your blog @lito—human leaders inspire others to become Human leaders too. That's contagious for sure . . . Keep at it!

@lito I sent you an invitation to join our "Customers First" group in Buzz. I hope you will join! Cheers :)

To recap, one short Buzz post and a couple of blog posts (Lito and me) turned into a swell of collaboration. It demonstrated pervasive learning, and it certainly displayed elements of the Flat Army Connected Leader Attributes, the PLF and the CLAM. This entire exchange occurred without anyone leaving their desks, wherever their desks might have been. To top it all off, Lito was invited to a group where he is now contributing and assisting the Customers First program at the company. Lito came back to Buzz later on and quipped:

thanks @dan, I never thought someone would take the time reading my blog. It was just one idle moment on the operation floor when I realized I should be writing something about my team, you know just something to do while waiting for the shift to end. Thanks for appreciating and for the good feedback.

How did this all happen? TELUS launched something it calls the TELUS Leadership Philosophy (TLP) in 2010 that defined and promoted a more collaborative, inclusive and engaging way of leading at the company. In fact, TELUS believes "leadership is for all." In parallel, the company deployed a litany of collaborative technologies alongside a formal, informal and social learning strategy. It's through this merge of culture, leadership, behavior, learning and technology that an example like the one described above can surface.

Darren also emphasized within the piece that culture is the single biggest contributor to the bottom line. He stated within the interview:

[my passion for culture] comes from a deep-rooted belief that when your peers and competitors are able to emulate your technology, you realize the one thing that is difficult to copy is your culture. That's something to invest in because you can build a sustainable competitive advantage through your culture that outlasts anything you do at the product or technology level.[18]

The day started with that interview and it ended with the real-time example of Lito, the call center agent from the Philippines. At least on this day, all of the cylinders were firing.

✳   ✳   ✳

Former VISA CEO Dee Hock introduced a concept known as the Chaordic Theory, which is a new organizational form he calls "simultaneously chaotic and orderly." Hock describes it as follows:

Chaordic is any self-organizing, adaptive, non-linear, complex system, whether physical, biological, or social, the behavior of which exhibits characteristics of both order and chaos or, loosely translated to business terminology, cooperation and competition.[19]

Flat Army is a quest to create the connected organizational culture through leadership traits that must become the de facto behavior of all employees regardless of rank, title or jurisdiction. It's a quest that simultaneously drives organizational clarity with precious innovation, participation and collaboration. Flat Army leaders who demonstrate reciprocity also must insist upon a consistent strategy. It is order among chaos, and chaos among order.

Our quest to paint a Flat-Army-organizational Picasso, in its simplest form, at the same time orderly and chaotic, refers to the point at which a leader thinks of the organization as a singular corporate organism. As an individual, she thinks not about herself; rather, she acts with the greater good of its people and the organization itself in mind. An organization, in totality, mixes with business units, teams and projects such that duplication is negated and a selfless amount of contribution is the norm to achieve shared goals. Ultimately, Flat Army is the point at which chaos meets order coupled with an infinite and unobstructed flow of corporate commonality. It is a professional panacea. It is organizational communitarianism, if you're a Goodwyn Barmby fan.

HDS, Zappos, TELUS, Scotiabank and HCLT are sublime examples of Flat Army in combat. Each organization instinctively knows that its success revolves around its people. Treating them unfairly or not utilizing them appropriately is antithetical to its own philosophy and approach. National Health Service is at least recognizing there is a better way. I personally will be watching that organization over the next few years to see if they can invoke Flat Army across all facets of its business. Although CHUM is no longer and CTVglobemedia was sold, the Terry David Mulligan situation provides an excellent example of what not to do to your organization's culture. Which leaves us with Research In Motion, a Canadian darling that may just face the same ominous fate as Nortel and Kodak did several years ago. I truly hope Thorsten Heins sorts it out. It would be a remarkable turnaround no different from Apple when Steve Jobs returned in 1997 or IBM from 1993 onwards with Lou Gerstner at the helm.

Albert Einstein once said, "A new type of thinking is essential if mankind is to survive and move toward higher levels."[20]

Flat Army is not an oxymoron; it is a way in which to solve organizational problems that are the residual effects of a troubled past.

CHAPTER TWELVE

THE CULTURE QUEST OF FLAT ARMY

What exactly is organizational culture? Why does it matter to our notion of Flat Army? Why should you care?

According to George Stonehouse and Jonathan Pemberton of the University of Northumbria at Newcastle, organizational culture "consists of the values, attitudes and beliefs that steer the actions and behaviour of the individuals making up the organisation."[1] Noted cultural dimensions researcher Geert Hofstede defines organizational culture as "the collective programming of the mind that distinguishes the members of one organisation from others."[2] Robert A. Cooke, CEO and director of Human Synergistics International and associate professor emeritus of management at the University of Illinois at Chicago, defines the culture of an organization as "the way employees behave at the workplace to ensure stable future and growth." He further subdivides organizational culture into constructive, passive-defensive and aggressive-defensive types.[3] And the "dean" of corporate culture—Ed Schein—defines corporate culture as follows:

A pattern of shared basic assumptions that the group learned as it solved its problems of external adaptation and internal integration, that has worked well enough to be considered valid and, therefore, to be taught to new members as the correct way you perceive, think, and feel in relation to those problems.[4]

Unfortunately, the definitions don't cut it for me. I don't like them; let's look at some others.

Colin Powell once said, "Great leaders are almost always great simplifiers, who can cut through argument, debate and doubt, to offer a solution everybody can understand."[5]

Be that as it may—and Powell is mostly right—perhaps we should turn next to Marcel Proust to help those of us implementing Flat Army with our definition of organizational culture. He said, "The time which we have at our disposal every day is elastic; the passions that we feel expand it, those that we inspire contract it; and habit fills up what remains."[6]

The many studies and hours of research with respect to their theories by those who provided the aforementioned definitions are important and credible. The reason those definitions don't work for me, however, is in the positioning of culture with respect to the people of the organization itself. We need a clearer and more relevant definition. To reach all leaders and managers inside an organization, to assist all employees regardless of rank, we require a simplified definition of organizational culture such that everyone may better comprehend what it is and know how to improve it. We need a definition of organizational culture that—as Powell suggests—offers a solution everybody can understand.

> For purposes of our Flat Army central thesis, organizational culture is defined by one criterion, and one only: an organization's culture is defined by the manner in which employees are treated by their direct leader.

Treat your people and your team members like tools, numbers or subordinates, and you can merrily look forward to an organizational culture replete with apathy, disengagement and insubordination. Do you recall the examples of rigidity from Chapter 2? What about the harmful and hurtful cases from Chapter 3? Treat your people through the mechanisms of our Flat Army philosophy discussed in Chapters 4 and 10, and you give birth to an employee population that is excited, engaged and wedded to the quest—whatever that may be.

Amy Edmondson seems to agree. In *Teaming: How Organizations Learn, Innovate and Compete in the Knowledge Economy,* Amy posits that leaders in the organization must create what she refers to as "psychological safety" for there to be a healthy and productive organizational culture.[7] Just who is responsible, though, for establishing the safety zone?

If we're referring to the vice president of finance, it is her team of directors that supports the mission. If it's the CEO, it's his direct group of executive vice presidents and perhaps other chiefs who sit at the executive table. If it's a team leader in a call center operation, it's those people that are handling customer inquiries on a minute-by-minute basis. Amy states that

[t]he most important influence on psychological safety is the nearest manager, supervisor, or boss. These authority figures, in subtle and not subtle ways, shape the tone of interactions in a team or group. Therefore, they also must be engaged as the primary drivers in establishing a more open work environment. They must take practical steps to make the workplace psychologically safe.[8]

Microsoft's chief people officer, Lisa Brummel, indicated to me that culture trumps everything. "It's one where individuals and teams understand that the sum is greater than the parts," she said, "where the collective can drive better idea and solution generation." When I asked Lisa about her personal leadership style and how it relates to culture, she replied:

I am a leader "among the people," whether it be my team or the employees themselves. I enjoy helping people reach their full potential through observation, guidance, and direction. I am not heavy-handed in my style but am direct in my feedback on both the positive and constructive sides of my interaction with my team.[9]

Lisa has been with Microsoft since 1989, working through various product-management roles, engineering teams and software groups up to her current post, which she accepted in 2005. She is a card-carrying member of Flat Army and instinctively knows—and demonstrates— that how you treat your people and the example you set enacting the components of Flat Army ensures your direct team and your organization want to be there; that they want to achieve any stated goal and that they feel psychologically safe in which to do so. Lisa is a shining example of Flat Army in action, and Microsoft is lucky to have her as its CPO.

What strikes me most from Lisa's words is the phrase "I am a leader 'among the people.'" It is you—the leader of people within your direct span of influence—who is responsible for an improved level of employee engagement and thus a healthy, prosperous and psychologically safe organizational culture. Yes, organizational culture is determined not only by the engagement of employees, its accountability devolves to you—the Flat Army leader. It is you—if you're a leader who possesses skip-level reports of whatever magnitude—who is also responsible for that same scenario within a wider span of leadership. For example, perhaps you have responsibility for the entire organization.

Employee engagement and business results are what we're measuring, but organizational culture—through Flat Army—is what we're building.

FLAT ARMY PHILOSOPHY

A Flat Army culture is one that simultaneously enhances organizational engagement while incorporating equal parts effective execution. It is one that calls upon its leaders to demonstrate reciprocity alongside the executive team who insists upon a clearly delineated strategy. Flat Army in its simplest form refers to the point at which all employees act as a unified corporate organism through the use of clear and succinct goals. Individuals don't think solely about themselves, but rather act with the greater good of the organization itself and its people in mind. Hitting business financial targets is important, but so too is an organizational culture that promotes the well-being of its people. When an organization is united such that duplication is negated and a selfless amount of collaboration is the norm, Flat Army is in motion. It is no longer a culture of "command and control," but rather one of "engage and empower" combined with effective execution. A Flat Army organization is at the point at which there is an unobstructed flow of corporate commonality.

It's no longer a professional paradox; it's a highly engaged workplace. It's when the employee suggestion box becomes the organization itself. It's when each of the five Flat Army frameworks is in full swing—by leaders and the organization in general—and operating seamlessly. It is Flat Army philosophy in action.

Flat Army Philosophy

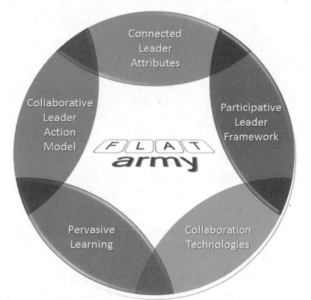

Over at the popular social networking company LinkedIn, vice president of human resources Steve Cadigan has his finger on the pulse and understands the need and execution of a Flat-Army-like philosophy. I mention LinkedIn in Chapter 10: It operates the world's largest professional network on the web with more than 175 million members in over 200 countries according to its own self-published statistics as of summer 2012. The company also employs over 2,800 people across the globe.

Does LinkedIn employ the Connected Leader Attributes? Steve thinks so. He said to me, "Core leadership values at LinkedIn are be[ing] open, honest and constructive."[10] Do leaders at LinkedIn employ the Participative Leader Framework, Collaborative Technologies and Pervasive Learning?

They absolutely do. In fact, Steve believes balance between technology, learning, collaboration and participation is important. He remarked,

We try hard to balance leveraging technology such as biweekly face-to-face company all-hands meetings where we cover key activities in the organization and field questions. We leverage video conference technologies and try to build a big community for a small event.

LinkedIn employees love it. The sharing and participation is infectious. Steve went on to say,

We make this all-hands meeting all the more meaningful by making it the most important delivery of business updates in the company. Everyone gathers around to listen and share the same experience and information all at the same time.

If that weren't enough, the all-hands meeting presents an opportunity to employ something similar to the Collaborative Leader Action Model:

We use that meeting to reinforce our culture of humor and transformation by sharing examples of what is special and great about our company. It's very positive reinforcement. We also discuss things we could have done better and are fairly open about it as we want to learn and improve.

It sounds eerily similar to the CLAM, where Steve and his team are connecting with the organization and considering options before they set out and create a result. It's also an opportunity to confirm with the team what has gone right and perhaps not so well, while using it as a platform to congratulate those deserved of a public commendation. Steve concluded by saying, "At LinkedIn, we have a company that is a constant stream of ideas, information, philanthropic offerings, product suggestions, [and] feedback on the food in the cafe and the flavor of coffee." LinkedIn is a fine example of employing Flat Army culture from the trenches. And Steve as a leader of his team is emblematic of what we're depicting with Flat Army.

Oh, and is LinkedIn simultaneously executing on and improving its business results as well? Judging from its results below, LinkedIn not only has a highly engaged, empowered and Flat-Army-like culture, but the company is also delivering on every possible business outcome as well. It will be interesting to watch LinkedIn grow over time—both culturally and financially.

Revenue

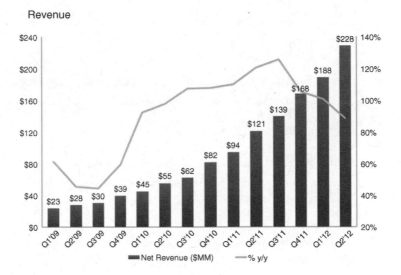

Adjusted EBITDA & Margin

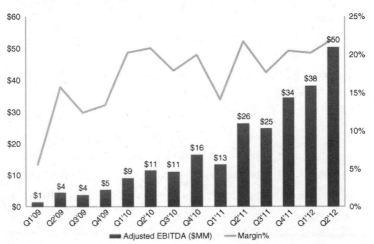

ROLLING OUT FLAT ARMY

This brings us now to the home stretch of this book.

Your Flat Army action plan can be bifurcated. Perhaps you're a leader who can directly influence others on a regular basis. Or perhaps you're a leader who can impact through indirect means. In the case of the former, practicing leadership is a relatively easy concept to understand if you have a team that you lead directly. Over at Microsoft, this would be Lisa's direct team of reports in the organizational chart. (By the way, if you're an individual contributor who aspires to lead a team, this applies to you as well.)

In the case of casting your leadership influence over a wider net, there are degrees of influence. In Lisa's case, she can impact the entire organization as its chief people officer. If you're a CEO, your span of control is also across the entire organization. If you're the vice president of a business unit, then of course your control spans those you affect in your business unit. If you're the manager of an engineering group, it spans whoever comprises the teams. Flat Army leaders who possess skip-level reports of any degree have significant influence over not only their direct reports but the direct reports of their direct reports and so on. Most importantly, any individual in an organization can have an impact on any facet of the organization, regardless of title or rank. That's the beauty of Flat Army. Therefore, Flat Army can be employed by you as an individual leader effecting change with those that you directly or indirectly work with anywhere in the organization. Review the following diagram, "Flat Army Influence," to see what I'm driving at.

Flat Army Influence

Direct Team
(I have direct reports)

Indirect Teams
*(I have direct reports +
I can indirectly affect
others in the
organization)*

The entire cadre of frameworks within Flat Army do not need to be rolled out organizationally at the same time. Similarly, if you're thinking about the direct team you are leading, addressing each of the five Flat Army frameworks simultaneously is sure to be ulcer inducing. In fact, it's my opinion that to become a full-fledged wearer of the Flat Army badge it takes roughly two to three years to be firing fully on all cylinders and using all five frameworks. The following paths for both your direct team—and, if applicable, the indirect teams you serve—are recommended for your implementation of Flat Army to be truly successful.

Impact: Direct Team

Flat Army Rollout (Direct Team)

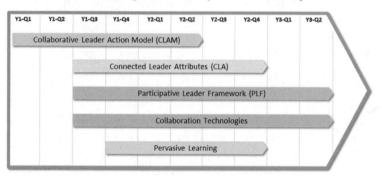

If you're thinking about your direct team, the first thing you may want to employ is the Collaborative Leader Action Model. It's an easy win, and it's an engagement- and culture-building step up front. If your personal leadership style has been relatively closed, where decisions are made and then edicts are issued down the chain, the CLAM is a fabulous way to immediately alter course. Your team will feel more included and engaged in the day-to-day processes of work than when they are simply told what to do. It's the first step to becoming a harmonious leader, as we discuss in Chapter 3. In retrospect, the CLAM may be a simpler way in which to operationalize the Vroom-Yetton-Jago Normative Decision Model. From autocratic to consultative to group-based decision-making modes, this model was devised to identify the various ways in which a leader and her team can get things done. It will take a while for you and your team to adapt to this new way of operating, collaborating and decision making. By giving yourself a six-month head start before you begin to implement the other four Flat Army frameworks, you will be well on your way to changing both your own personal leadership behaviour and the culture of the team. To connect and consider before creating is a potentially huge behavioral change; don't take it for granted and think the CLAM is an overnight fix.

Once you're relatively comfortable that you and the team are regularly employing *connect, consider, communicate, create, confirm* and *congratulate* as default day-to-day behaviors in projects, actions and decisions, you can begin thinking about the Connected Leadership Attributes, Participative Leader Framework and Collaboration Technologies.

The Connected Leader Attributes are exhaustive to say the least. I'm not expecting you to conquer all fifteen of them immediately, which is why you have roughly eighteen months in the timeline above to accomplish this step. You may already be pretty good at some of these behaviors. For the sake of your team's engagement and execution levels, you're going to review them all so you know which ones need attention now, later on in the cycle, or not at all. There are three ways for you to assess your own personal state of the Connected Leader Attributes. Each is offered as a way to help you determine which CLAs to pay attention to now—and later on in the "Flat Army launch" section.

Self-Assessment

Review each of the fifteen CLAs—particularly the "How to be" subsections in Chapters 4 through 6, and assess yourself. Give yourself a score of 1, 2 or 3, with 1 signifying a "poor or needs improvement" grade, 2 signifying an average score and 3 denoting an "excellent or high-performing" rating. For those who fall into category 1, you may want to take action and determine how you can improve the behaviors contained within the attribute definition. If the score is a 2, you may want to delay any performance development action until such time that you have enough time to fully address it. If you have some 3s in your self-assessment, congratulations. Keep it up.

Team Assessment

Have you ever completed a 360-degree assessment with your team? Perhaps you could devise one using the fifteen Connected Leader Attributes by taking the content from Chapters 4 through 6 as your baseline for questioning. Maybe you've never created a 360-degree assessment before. In that case, don't fret—there are countless companies that can assist. Simply type "online 360 tool" into a search engine and find one that can customize questions for you. Failing that, you can always utilize an online survey service like Murvey, SurveyMonkey or KwikSurveys to establish a team-based questionnaire on the CLAs. In both cases, you may want to utilize a Likert scale of 1 through 3 or 1 through 5 to benchmark you and the team. Either through the 360 or the survey, you should have a good idea of which CLAs to tackle first. I recommend working on your bottom five scores over the first nine months and the next five over the subsequent nine months. It's a good idea to assess again after a reasonable period of time to determine if you and the team are making progress.

Flat Army Assessment

What about your direct team? Although you are going to employ the CLAM with them—it's a team-based model after all—the Connected Leader Attributes may be something you utilize solely for yourself. I'm not suggesting the CLAs can't be applied to your team; it's simply a judgment call whether you use them for yourself or you want to have everyone on your team working on them and speaking the same leadership language. If you do choose to drive the adoption of the CLAs across your entire direct team, you may want to enlist the service of external (or internal) assistance. It's one thing to work on the CLAs based on your own assessment strategy, but if you have a team—large or small—you are adding complexity and time to your own plate. You don't want the process to feel as though you're pushing water uphill with a pitchfork.

The Participative Leader Framework is a change to your leadership behavioral model that is neither an easy fix nor ephemeral. The PLF is a long-term change to the way you network. It's also a big change to the way you might be consuming elements of, and contributing back to, the knowledge ecosystem. It's recommended you start employing this framework in concert with the rollout of Collaboration Technologies. You require several of these collaboration technologies to enhance the behaviors of contributing and consuming. They also come in handy when building your direct personal and professional networks.

Think about the intent of the PLF for a moment. How can you build up your direct network in the organization and outside of it, while contributing and consuming knowledge and intellect through the CARE principle: (continuous, authentic, reciprocal and educating)? It may take some time to alter your default leadership style, so the PLF is more like a marathon than a 100-meter sprint. You have to do some test runs at shorter distances before you can fully accomplish the 42.2 kilometers. This is the precise reason it spans a twenty-four-month period.

Remember what we stated about the impact—and influence—you have by building up your internal and external network? Further credibility comes from Ajay Mehra, Andrea Dixon, Daniel Brass and Bruce Robertson who illustrate in their paper "The Social Network Ties of Group Leaders: Implications for Group Performance and Leader Reputation" that a leader who is central to direct contacts and networked relations will increase both performance of the team and his or her own leadership reputation. They state:

Not only do [direct ties] appear to provide leaders access to resources that facilitate group performance, but [direct ties] also seem to help [leaders] secure favorable reputations for leadership in the eyes of their subordinates, peers, and supervisors.[11]

It takes time for you to fully adopt the CARE principle as it does for aspects like consume, contribute and the networking criteria of the PLF. Be patient; you will eventually be successful.

Collaboration Technologies in the Flat Army model—as we discuss in Chapter 10—primarily revolve around online tools and applications that help you to converse, to create content and to provide context. The first order of business is to take stock of the tools that are actually available inside your organization. In Chapter 10 we discuss fifteen different collaboration-technology opportunities. Your job is to decipher which of these is available to you, your team and your organization and which isn't. From there, make a judgment call. Can you be more collaborative, connected and participative with what's available today via your organization? If you can, that's fantastic. Begin a plan of action to incorporate whatever collaboration technologies you believe are critical to get you rocking in the Flat Army world. If there is a gap, sort out how you can make those technologies available to your team or organization.

Don't bite off more than you can chew; elongate the adoption and inclusion periods of collaboration technologies over the prescribed time period above. If your organization doesn't make these tools and applications available, it's your job to sort out how you might utilize cloud-based collaboration technologies to commence your plan. Remember how I wrote this book? That's right, I used Evernote. There is a business version of Evernote (www.evernote.com/business) with which you and your team could share documents, ideas and decisions. Another company called Jive has a cloud-based collaboration platform (www.jiveon.com) with which you can employ most of the *converse, content* and *context* technologies starting at $300/month. Atlassian is another collaboration platform company offering a product called Confluence (www.atlassian.com/software/confluence/overview/team-collaboration-software) for as low as $10 per month. You need to do your homework, but it might be a great idea to utilize the CLAM with your team to sort out what collaboration technologies to roll out and when. I'd call that "drinking your own Flat Army champagne," with your team playing the part of the ultimate arbiters.

Finally, once the first four frameworks are off and running, you can give consideration to the manner in which you and your team are learning. This is aided by introducing the Pervasive Learning model. From your own personal standpoint, ask yourself how you normally learn.

Are you waiting for that instructor-led classroom course to show up on a schedule, or have you bought into the Flat Army theory that learning is part formal, part informal and part social? If it's the former, you had better reread Chapter 9. If it's the latter, now is the opportunity for you to begin your own personal transformation. From there, you want to champion the changes needed within the team as well. Work with your team members—individually and as a collective—to determine what formal, informal and social learning methods will be utilized and by when. Again, your tactic depends on what is available within your organization, so devise a checklist to see what is available and what isn't. From there, decide which modalities make sense for you and the team and then develop an action plan to change the way all of you learn. That itself can be a Pervasive Learning experience.

You may be able to fully transform your leadership style in less than two to three years—to completely adapt the Flat Army model—and that's great. There is no prize for doing it quickly, though. If you cut corners or rush the process, you may find you're alienating the team and disappointing yourself. The five Flat Army frameworks are rather large. Don't fret. Relax and enjoy the process. You might want to consider yourself "at transformation" as per the words of my buddy Gord Downie.[12] And as Leo Tolstoy once said, "The two most powerful warriors are patience and time."[13]

Impact: Organization (indirect teams)

Flat Army Rollout (Organization)

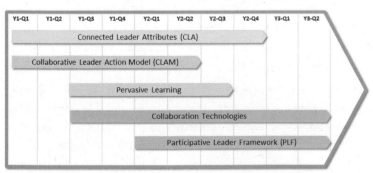

If you have responsibility for skip-level reports—a larger team that doesn't directly report into you but which you can highly influence—this section is for you. For purposes of simplicity, we'll focus our efforts on the organization in its entirety as opposed to a business unit. When you are contemplating the rollout of Flat Army organization-wide, it's the behavior of being a more collaborative and connected unit that should be the initial focus.

First and foremost, your organizational culture requires a common leadership lexicon. Whether it's the IT department, marketing, finance, human resources, product, engineering, or any go-to-market function such as sales, consulting or support, leaders and employees alike must be able to speak the same leadership language. This process comes in two parts, the first being the Connected Leader Attributes through the levels of *becoming, being* and *beyond* as depicted in Chapters 4, 5 and 6. Those fifteen attributes are the behavioral commonalities among all the members of your workforce. Your task is to embed these attributes into the workflow of leadership wherever you can. Make them a part of your hiring practices. For example, your recruitment team can use the CLAs to assess whether a candidate might be a good fit for your culture.

What about promotion or succession planning? Wouldn't you want to utilize the CLAs as the basis for giving more responsibility to an employee? How about performance development and its link to annual bonuses and additional remuneration? The CLAs together can act as an arbiter if the way in which your organization evaluates people on leadership through the performance development process actually utilizes those attributes. Devise levels of competence for each of the CLAs at four levels (individual contributor, manager, director and vice president) and publish them for all to see in the organization. Begin adjudicating leadership performance thereafter based on an individual's level. Build recognition practices around the CLAs. Develop formal, informal and social learning opportunities for each of the CLAs. Create even more pervasive learning opportunities that demonstrate the link between each of the CLAs. From an organization-wide perspective, the Connected Leader Attributes are its leadership DNA; be wise, expansive and methodical as you roll them out across your audiences. It takes roughly two years to properly align the entire organization to these attributes, so don't think you can make tremendous strides in only a few weeks.

The second way in which your organization can improve its leadership lingo such that everyone is in sync—improving engagement and culture in the process—is through the deployment of the Collaborative Leader Action Model. As depicted by the graphic above, the launch of the CLAM across your organization should occur in parallel with the CLAs. If the CLAs are the DNA of leadership for you and all of your employees, then the CLAM is the daily hygiene to ensure your organization is healthy and devoid of culture stove pipes. The CLAM becomes a daily leadership model for everyone to utilize across all divisions and geographies. You will require changes to your strategy-planning processes as well as your project-management methods. The CLAM should be embedded into each such that any strategy and project opportunities utilize the *connect, consider, communicate, create, confirm* and *congratulate* model. If it were the 1980s, you might call this action "Business Process Reengineering." Regardless, the CLAM becomes the important yin element to the yang of the CLAs, and your organization benefits greatly if you roll both out at the same time.

The CLAs and the CLAM can be followed six months later by two additional Flat Army frameworks across your organization—Pervasive Learning and Collaboration Technologies. Due to the Pervasive Learning model, consisting of formal, informal and social learning modalities, bridging the two frameworks—particularly because of the link between social and collaboration technologies—makes a lot of sense. Depending on your role in the organization, you want to involve current leadership within the departments of information technology, human resources and learning, to bring these two frameworks to fruition across all employees. Specific to Collaboration Technologies, and similar to the action needed for your direct team, it's wise to take stock of any existing technologies and then perform a delta gap analysis to sort out what needs to be implemented thereafter. Here's a tip—use the CLAM to involve your employee base by asking for suggestions and perhaps having them help make a decision on what collaboration technologies should be a part of your organization. Collaboration Technologies will always be changing. Don't think this action should ever stop, either; your organization will want to constantly be monitoring what other collaboration technologies might add benefit to your Flat Army implementation over time.

The Pervasive Learning model—although reliant on collaboration technologies—is really a behavioral shift in which everyone in the organization must understand and recognize that learning doesn't happen solely in a classroom. You require at least a year of change management action across all geographies to help employees synthesize the model and ultimately begin employing it for various programs and learning opportunities. The model can be applied to leadership, sales, business, professional development and any technology-based learning. You may want to, for example, reconstruct your employee-new-hire-orientation program if it's currently a 100-percent-classroom strategy. Based on the Pervasive Learning model, you could redevelop it such that it spans the first one hundred days of employment, encompassing some face-to-face sessions alongside mentors, discussion forums, virtual sessions, recommended articles and videos, among other Pervasive Learning options.

Once the CLAs, CLAM, Pervasive Learning and Collaboration Technology frameworks are in full swing—roughly a year into your organization's Flat Army evolution—it's time to launch the final piece, the Participative Leader Framework. At an organizational level, this can be treated as a leadership development opportunity for leaders across all units. It's an extension of the CLAs and the CLAM. not something diametrically opposed or different. Once employees are adapting to the attributes and behaviors of being more connected and collaborative, it's sensible to add the final behavioral component—participation. By focusing on the behaviors found within the CLA and the CLAM first, your employee population will have begun mastering the act of working more openly with people. From there, the next layer of evolution—through the PLF—reinforces what has already been learned and introduces the CARE principle alongside the acts of consuming, contributing, and building up personal and professional networks. It's a wonderful closing act to the Flat Army transformation in your organization.

Warren Bennis, in 1993, noted the following in his book *An Invented Life: Reflections on Leadership and Change*:

Given the nature and constancy of change and the transnational challenges facing American business leadership, the key to making the right choices will come from understanding and embodying the leadership qualities necessary to succeed in the volatile and mercurial global economy. To survive in the 21st century, we're going to need a new generation of leaders—leaders, not managers[14]

Through the rollout of Flat Army across your organization, perhaps we can make Bennis proud. After all, he did write those words in 1993; it's best we get a move on. I couldn't be more excited for such a shift to manifest in our organizations. In the end, it's up to you to make it happen.

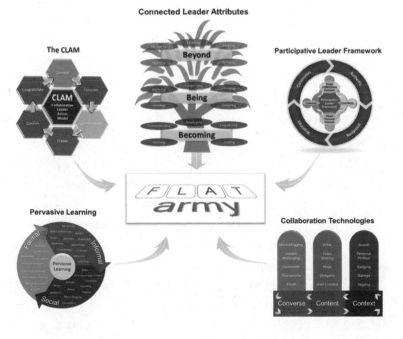

✲ ✲ ✲

I'm fascinated by various presidents of the United States of America. When you study their biographies and leadership practices, you can learn a lot. How was President Lyndon B. Johnson as a leader? On one hand, he was inspirational. He was unfortunately forced to pick up the presidential ticket after the assassination of John F. Kennedy and—among other actions in the mid-1960s—continue with Kennedy's vision of putting a man on the moon. On the other hand, he was a leader known for his command-and-control leadership style, often provoking rather than engaging. It is alleged that during a tour of the NASA Space Center, Johnson came upon a janitor at work in the building where the lunar module was being housed. When asked by the President what his role at NASA was, the janitor pointed at the lunar module and stated, "To help get that thing up to the moon."[15] That janitor was a great example embodying Flat Army; someone who was engaged, collaborative and productive regardless of rank.

In another presidential example, let's hearken back to May 1, 2011. It was a significant moment in the history of the United States of America, perhaps the world. President Barack Obama addressed the nation that night to announce the death of Osama bin Laden, the reputed mastermind behind various terrorist attacks including the infamous 9/11 tragedy. What caught my attention was one particular remark during the address: "Shortly after taking office, I directed Leon Panetta, the director of the CIA, to make the killing or capture of Osama bin Laden the top priority of our war against Al Qaeda."[16]

Do you recall who actually carried out the operation that day? It was the U.S. Navy SEALS from U.S. Special Operations Command. What this signifies, at least in my opinion, is that the CIA was working *with* the U.S. Navy SEALS as opposed to working in isolation. Collaboration, participation, connectedness and a different leadership mindset had a hold within the U.S. military in order to accomplish the goal the President set. With so much written—almost unilaterally critical—about the lack of cooperation, let alone collaboration between various U.S. agencies in the lead-up and lack of prevention to 9/11, it was encouraging to hear the President of the United States of America allude to the new normal—an anti-silo working model—within U.S. intelligence. This might well be an example of Flat Army in action and a lesson for us all. Old dogs *can* learn new tricks. The job was accomplished through a new and arguably more effective leadership playbook. Although they didn't use Flat Army specifically, the organizational culture had in fact changed. What a difference a decade can make.

And thus, if the U.S. military can undergo such a change, could it be that our organizations are in the midst of a real-world version of *The Divine Comedy*? Has our protagonist—Dante—finally passed through the hell of organizational hierarchy and rigidity only to find himself inching out of employee disengagement purgatory? Is the next step—through the implementation of Flat Army—to push into the heavens of connectedness, participation, collaboration and execution? Are we on the cusp of a more engaged and productive organization? Can the organization become a place that rids itself of "leaders without leadership" to instead embody a systemic Flat Army model that possesses "leadership through leaders"? Is organizational culture now in the hands of leaders who can lead using Flat Army techniques?

I don't know, but I hope this book can help in some form.

In the end, perhaps Flat Army can be guided by the Nisga'a.

The Nisga'a (pronounced nish-ga) are a small First Nations group of people based in the northwestern region of British Columbia, Canada, known as Nass River Valley.[18] They have thrived and lived in the region for over 10,000 years. Roughly 2,500 people currently live among four villages—Gingolx (Kincolith), Lakalzap (Greenville), Gitwinksihlkw (Canyon City) and Gitlakdamix (New Aiyansh)—with another 3,500 living in other parts of Canada and the world.

They believe in *"wo'osihl niga'a"*—which loosely translates to "one bowl that all will eat from." It's a metaphor, of course, but it ties nicely into our Flat Army thesis. The Nisga'a work together as a collaborative, participative and connected unit to achieve prosperity. Theirs is a story of human engagement. Their prosperity is life itself and the continuation of their culture, their history and their people. The vision of the Nisga'a people is *Sayt k'ilim genxhl luu-yoxgum ahl ts'im-sayt k'ilim goot*, otherwise known in English as "One Heart, One Path, One Nation." Through their vision, they believe the Nisga'a Nation is a place where

- language and culture is the foundation of their identity (known as "Ayuuk");
- learning is a way of life;
- they strive for sustainable prosperity and self-reliance;
- they inspire trust and understanding through effective communications; and
- their services evolve to meet the needs of the Nisga'a.

One Heart, One Path, One Nation—we'd all be wise to think of this in our definition of organizational culture and employee engagement, aided by the Nisga'a, as we strive for Flat Army in the place where we all work for a living.

Thanks for reading.

Tempus fugit.

Afterword: In Collaborative Conclusion

You made it.

With the right frameworks in place a leader needs to simultaneously execute and engage to be worthy of a Flat Army badge. But the key will always be whether you execute first in a fiefdom of individuality, or if you connect, collaborate, participate and share—while employing new leadership attributes—before anything else.

The main function of a leader, arguably, is to achieve a stated goal. That goal, however it is established, more often than not requires the assistance and input of team members (directly or indirectly) in order to be successful. This is the essence of Flat Army. Be inclusive rather than exclusive. Be a deliverer rather than a procrastinator.

That is, a leader must be able to execute while providing a nurturing, collaborative, supportive and open environment with all involved such that it's done on time, on budget, and to the stated level of quality. Maybe I'm a bit bullish, but this change is worth the effort. Change is in you.

These two disciplines often run into competition with one another due to rigidity, pressure or organizational cutbacks. Perhaps the leader is overly zealous on the execution plane and forgets to treat team members with dignity, with openness to ideas or feedback, with transparency, and with empathy and compassion. The Connected Leadership Attributes are the key behaviors to mitigate this scenario. The Participative

Leader Framework and the Collaborative Leader Action Model are two methods by which to operate as a Flat Army leader. On the other hand, perhaps the leader is too far removed from the execution plane itself, focusing not enough time on the actions, deliverables, processes and techniques that help the goal to actually be achieved. That's an out-of-touch leader.

We all know leaders who have been termed "too soft" as well. Equally so, there is a laundry bag full of leaders who have ruled through a culture of fear, focusing only on execution practices and not on their people.

So, what's a leader to do?

- Be transformational and transactional.
- Be collaborative and considerate.
- Be daring and decisive.
- Be inclusive and insistent.
- Be fun and formal.
- Be harmonious and humble.
- Be engaging and executing.
- Be Flat Army.

In collaborative conclusion, holistic leaders of today and tomorrow need to sort out how to both execute and engage with equal vigor. One can't spend their entire time in a command-and-control environment. It's about situational hierarchy interspersed with heterarchy. Conversely, one can't spend all of one's time simply being a kindhearted friend. Singing "Kumbaya" around a campfire all day is nonsensical. It is why this book is titled *Flat Army*. It is not an oxymoron.

In 1993, authors Bernard Bass and Bruce Avolio published the paper "Transformational Leadership and Organizational Culture." Focusing much on organizational culture, one paragraph in particular summarizes very well the quest of leadership today—let alone back in 1993:

In a highly innovative and satisfying organizational culture we are likely to see transformational leaders who build on assumptions such as: people are trustworthy and purposeful;

everyone has a unique contribution to make; and complex problems are handled at the lowest level possible. Leaders who build such cultures and articulate them to followers typically exhibit a sense of vision and purpose. They align others around the vision and empower others to take greater responsibility for achieving the vision. Such leaders facilitate and teach followers. They foster a culture of creative change and growth rather than one which maintains the status quo. They take personal responsibility for the development of their followers. Their followers operate under the assumption that all organizational members should be developed to their full potential.[1]

The intent of this book is to provide the tools, techniques, stories, anecdotes, analogies, metaphors and frameworks to bring Bass and Avolio's thoughts to fruition. It's to engage, empower and to execute.

What I would really like, however, is for Flat Army to become idiopathic. I want Flat Army to become a disease within the organization that has no known cause; it just happens. I don't want there to be a cure, either. Of course, for that to be true, leaders will employ the frameworks, thoughts and models suggested within this book, but between you and me, it should be with less fanfare and more by osmosis. It should be idiopathic.

I have stated repeatedly through *Flat Army* that leadership is for all, and that to become both a connected and collaborative leader, a camp mentality must not form. It is not us against them. It's not a game between those with direct reports and those without. Leadership is not found in an ivory tower; it permeates throughout, meandering like a river, reaching all banks of the organization. If you've missed that message, you may have wasted your money investing in this book. It too is not about a continuous group hug. Inclusivity is important and employee engagement is key, but getting things done is also critical. An equality between the two must form. This equality is the new organizational symbiosis.

Henry Mintzberg says in his book *Managing,*

effective managing can be seen as engaging and engaged, connecting and connected, supporting and supported. We need to rethink management and organization, as well as leadership and communityship, by realizing how simple, natural and healthy they all can be.[2]

When I had the opportunity to sit down with Henry and interview him for this book he left me with this: "No one wants to be led by someone that is not a manager and no one wants to be managed by someone that is not a leader."

I can't say it any better, although I still don't like the word "manager." Go McGill. I hope you've enjoyed the journey. I have.

Long live the Flat Army.

Ancora imparo

Endnotes

DEDICATION

1. Duncan Campbell Scott. "Enigma," in *The Green Cloister: Later Poems* (Toronto: McClelland and Stewart, 1935).

CHAPTER 1

1. Mike Johnson. *New Rules of Engagement: Life-Work Balance and Employee Commitment.* London: CIPD Publishing, 2004.
2. "State of the American Workplace: 2008–2010," *Gallup Consulting*, 2010, http://www.gallup.com/strategicconsulting/142724/State-American-Workplace-2008-2010.aspx
3. "State of the Global Workforce," *Gallup Consulting*, 2011, http://www.gallup.com/strategicconsulting/157196/state-global-workplace.aspx
4. "The State of Employee Engagement: 2008," *BlessingWhite*, 2008, http://www.blessingwhite.com/content/reports/2008EmployeeEngagementNAOverview.pdf
5. Jazmine Boatman et al., "Global Leadership Forecast 2011," *Development Dimensions International*, 2011, http://www.ddiworld.com/DDIWorld/media/trend-research/globalleadershipforecast2011_ukhighlights_tr_ddi.pdf
6. Ibid.
7. "Generation X: Overlooked and Hugely Important finds New Study from the Center for Work-Life Policy," *Center for Work-Life Policy*, 2011, https://www.worklifepolicy.org/documents/X%20Factor%20Press%20Release%20final.pdf

8. J.D. McAdams, "Generativity in Midlife," in *Handbook of Midlife Development,* M. E. Lachman, ed., Hoboken: John Wiley & Sons, 2001.

9. "Re-Engaging with Engagement," *The Economist,* 2010, http://viewswire .eiu.com/report_dl.asp?mode=fi&fi=987641483.PDF

10. J.S. Rain, I.M. Lane, and D.D. Steiner, "A Current Look at Job Satisfaction/ Life Satisfaction Relationship: Review and Future Considerations," *Human Relations* 44 (1991).

11. "'Paradoxical' decline? Another look at the relative reduction in female happiness," *Journal of Economic Psychology* 32, no. 5 (2011).

12. William H. Macey and Benjamin Schneider, "The Meaning of Employee Engagement," *Industrial and Organizational Psychology* 1, no. 1 (2008).

13. Thomas W. Malone. *The Future of Work: How the New Order of Business Will Shape Your Organization, Your Management Style, and Your Life.* Boston: Harvard Business School Press, 2004.

14. Sean Bakker, "A Study of Employee Engagement in the Canadian Work-place," *Psychometrics,* 2010, http://www.psychometrics.com/en-us/articles/ engagement-study.htm

15. Richard H. Axelrod, "All Aboard: Why Companies Still Don't Get Employee Engagement Right," *The Conference Board Review,* Fall 2010, http://www .axelrodgroup.com/articles/fa10AllAboard.pdf

16. Azka Ghafoor et al., "Transformational Leadership, Employee Engagement and Performance: Mediating Effect of Psychological Ownership." *African Journal of Business Management* 5, no. 17 (2011), http://www.academicjournals .org/AJBM/PDF/pdf2011/4Sept/Ghafoor%20et%20al.pdf

17. Laurie Bassi and Dan McMurrer "Does Engagement Really Drive Results?" *Talent Management Magazine,* March 2010, http://mcbassi.com/wp/resources/ pdfs/BassiMcMurrer-TalentManagement-Mar2010.pdf

18. Euan Semple, in discussion with the author in 2012.

19. T.A. Judge et al. "The Job Satisfaction–Job Performance Relationship: A Qualitative and Quantitative Review," *Psychological Bulletin* 127, no. 3 (2001).

20. Donna A. Dickson, "Fostering Employee Engagement: A Critical Compe-tency for Hospitality Industry Managers," *Rochester Institute of Technology,* 2008, https://ritdml.rit.edu/bitstream/handle/1850/7281/DDicksonConf Proc2008.pdf?sequence=6

21. "Gallup Study: Engaged Employees Inspire Company Innovation," *Gallup Business Journal,* October 12, 2006, http://businessjournal.gallup.com/ content/24880/gallup-study-engaged-employees-inspire-company.aspx

22. "Working Today: Understanding What Drives Employee Engage-ment," *Towers Perrin,* 2003, http://www.towersperrin.com/tp/ getwebcachedoc?webc=hrs/usa/2003/200309/talent_2003.pdf

23. 2012 Trends in Global Employee Engagement, *Aon Hewitt*, 2012, http://www.aon.com/human-capital-consulting/thought-leadership/leadership/2012_Trends_in_Global_Employee_Engagement.jsp

24. Mark Royal and Mel Stark, "Hitting the Ground Running: What the World's Most Admired Companies Do to (Re)Engage Their Employees," *Hay Group*, 2010, https://www.haygroup.com/downloads/ww/hay_group_fortune_2010_presentation.pdf

25. Mark Royal and Tom Agnew. *The Enemy of Engagement: Put an End to Workplace Frustration—and Get the Most from Your Employees.* New York: AMACOM, 2011.

26. "Driving Performance and Retention Through Employee Engagement," *Corporate Leadership Council*, 2004, http://www.mckpeople.com.au/SiteMedia/w3svc161/Uploads/Documents/760af459-93b3-43c7-b52a-2a74e984c1a0.pdf

27. L. Barber, S. Hayday, and S. Bevan, "From People to Profits: The HR Link in the Service-Profit Chain," *Report 355, Institute for Employment Studies*, 1999.

28. "The ISR Employee Engagement Report," *Towers Perrin-ISR*, 2006.

29. Sean Bakker, "A Study of Employee Engagement in the Canadian Workplace: Control, Opportunity & Leadership," *Psychometrics*, 2010, http://www.psychometrics.com/en-us/articles/engagement-study.htm

30. David MacLeod and Nita Clarke, "Engaging for Success: enhancing performance through employee engagement," 2009, http://www.bis.gov.uk/files/file52215.pdf

31. L. Worrall and C.L. Cooper, "The Quality of Working Life: Managers' Health, Motivation and Productivity," *Chartered Management Institute*, 2007, http://www.mbsportal.bl.uk/taster/subjareas/mgmt/cmi/qualitywl12.aspx

32. "Turbocharging Employee Engagement: The Power of Recognition from Managers," *Towers Watson*, 2009, http://www.towerswatson.com/research/629

33. "The Rage to Engage," *Time Magazine*, April 2008, http://www.time.com/time/magazine/article/0,9171,1731893,00.html#ixzz1vCI8e5Jz

34. Heather Mason Kiefer, "Federal Agency Explores Customer/Employee Link," *Gallup*, January 14, 2003, http://www.gallup.com/poll/7576/federal-agency-explores-customeremployee-link.aspx

35. "The State of Employee Engagement: North American Overview," *BlessingWhite*, 2008, http://www.blessingwhite.com/content/reports/2008EmployeeEngagementNAOverview.pdf

36. Greg Smith, "Why I Am Leaving Goldman Sachs," *The New York Times*, March 14, 2012, http://www.nytimes.com/2012/03/14/opinion/why-i-am-leaving-goldman-sachs.html?pagewanted=all&_r=0

37. Ibid.

38. "Talent and Organization," *Aon*, 2012, http://www.aon.com/canada/
products-services/human-capital-consulting/consulting/talent_
organization.jsp

39. Jim Harter, "Engaged Workers Report Twice as Much Job Creation," *Gallup Consulting*. August 9, 2011, http://www.gallup.com/poll/148883/
Engaged-Workers-Report-Twice-Job-Creation.aspx

40. Clay Shirky. *Cognitive Surplus*. New York: Penguin, 2010.

41. Thomas W. Malone, *The Future of Work*. Harvard Business School Press, 2004.

42. Gary Hamel and Bill Breen. *The Future of Management*. Boston: Harvard Business Press, 2007.

43. "Hewitt Survey Highlights: Cost Reduction and Engagement Survey," *Hewitt*, 2009.

44. Jonah Lehrer, "Steve Jobs: 'Technology Alone Is Not Enough,'" *The New Yorker*, October 7, 2011, http://www.newyorker.com/online/blogs/
newsdesk/2011/10/steve-jobs-pixar.html

45. Keith Davey. *The Rainmaker: A Passion for Politics*. Toronto: Stoddart, 1986.

46. Maurice Li, personal letter to the author in 2000.

47. Darren Entwistle, personal letter to the author in 2012.

48. Jim Kouzes and Barry Posner. *The Leadership Challenge*, 4th ed. San Francisco: Jossey-Bass, 2008.

CHAPTER 2

1. Stephen Denning. *The Leader's Guide to Radical Management: Reinventing the Workplace for the 21st Century*. San Francisco: Jossey-Bass, 2010.

2. Adam Smith. *An Inquiry into the Nature and Causes of the Wealth of Nations*. London: W. Strahan and T. Cadell, 1776.

3. Thomas W. Malone, "Decentralization Is the New Center of Command," *IESE-Insight* 4, no. 1 (2010).

4. Encyclopaedia Britannica, 11th ed., s.v. "the Roman army."

5. Thomas Hobbes. Leviathan—The Matter, Forme and Power of a Common Wealth Ecclesiasticall and Civil. New York: Simon and Schuster, 2008.

6. Henri Fayol. *Administration industrielle et générale; prévoyance, organisation, commandement, coordination, controle*. Paris: H. Dunod et E. Pinat, 1916.

7. Frederick Winslow Taylor. *The Principles of Scientific Management*. New York: Harper & Brothers, 1911.

8. Jeremy Rifkin and Ted Howard. *The Emerging Order: God in the Age of Scarcity*. New York: G.P. Putnam Sons, 1979.

9. Jill Lepore, "Not So Fast," *The New Yorker*, October 12, 2009, http://www.newyorker.com/arts/critics/atlarge/2009/10/12/091012crat_atlarge_lepore

10. Matthew Stewart, "The Management Myth," *The Atlantic*, 2006, http://www.theatlantic.com/magazine/print/2006/06/the-management-myth/4883/

11. Frederick Winslow Taylor. *Shop Management.* New York: Harper & Brothers, 1911.

12. Frederick Winslow Taylor, *The Principles of Scientific Management.* Harper, 1919.

13. Henri Fayol. *General and Industrial Management.* London: Pitman, 1949.

14. Charles Richard Williams, ed., *Diary and Letters of President Rutherford Birchard Hayes.* Columbus: The Ohio State Archaeological and Historical Society, 1922–26.

15. Henry Mintzberg. *The Structuring of Organisations: A Synthesis of the Research.* London: Prentice-Hall, 1979.

16. Milton Friedman, "The Social Responsibility of Business Is to Increase Its Profits," *The New York Times Magazine*, September 13, 1970.

17. Charles Handy. *Understanding Organizations.* New York: Penguin Books, 2007.

CHAPTER 3

1. Robert A. Guth and Shelly Banjo, "Gates, Buffett Goad Peers to Give Billions to Charity," *The Wall Street Journal*, June 17, 2010.

2. Chris Smith , "Open City," *New York Magazine*, September 26, 2010, http://nymag.com/news/features/establishments/68511/

3. Charlene Li. *Open Leadership: How Social Technology Can Transform the Way You Lead.* San Francisco: Jossey-Bass, 2010.

4. Luciano Pilotti, "Evolutionary and Adaptive Local Systems in North East Italy: Strategies of Localized Learning, Open Leadership and Cooperation. Towards Imperfect 'Communitarian Capitalism'," *Human Systems Management* 18, no. 2 (1999).

5. Ibid.

6. A.G. Lafley and Ram Charan. *The Game Changer: How Every Leader Can Drive Everyday Innovation.* London: Profile Books, 2008.

7. Ibid.

8. Larry Dignan, "HP's Ray Lane on why Leo Apotheker had to go," *CNET*, September 22, 2011, http://news.cnet.com/8301-1001_3-20110396-92/hps-ray-lane-on-why-leo-apotheker-had-to-go/

9. Ibid.

10. Thomas Carlyle. On Heroes, Hero-Worship and the Heroic in History. New York: Fredrick A. Stokes & Brother, 1888.

11. Adam Lashinsky, "Inside Apple," *Fortune*, May 23, 2011.

12. "Working Here," *Johnson & Johnson*, 2012, http://www.jnjcanada.com/working-here.aspx

13. "Legacy of Leadership," *Johnson & Johnson*, 2012, http://www.jnj.com/connect/caring/patient-stories/Legacy-of-Leadership

14. "World's Most Admired Companies: Johnson & Johnson," *CNN*, March 21, 2011, http://money.cnn.com/magazines/fortune/mostadmired/2011/snapshots/235.html

15. Charles Corace, "Engagement: Enrolling the Quiet Majority," *Organization Development Journal* 25, no. 2 (2007).

16. Trends in Global Employee Engagement, *Aon Hewitt*, 2011, http://www.aon.com/attachments/thought-leadership/Trends_Global_Employee_Engagement_Final.pdf and "Employee Engagement Report 2011," *BlessingWhite*, January 2011, http://www.blessingwhite.com/eee__report.asp

17. Charles Corace, "Engagement: Enrolling the Quiet Majority."

18. Cedric T. Coco, "From Employed to Engaged," *T+D Magazine*, November 2009.

19. Harold Jarche, "Work is learning and learning is the work," *Harold Jarche*, June 17, 2012, http://www.jarche.com/2012/06/work-is-learning-and-learning-is-the-work/

CHAPTER 4

1. Jack Zenger and Joseph Folkman, "How Bad Is a Bad Boss, Exactly?" *Harvard Business Review*, July 16, 2012, http://blogs.hbr.org/cs/2012/07/how_damaging_is_a_bad_boss_exa.html

2. Bill Sullivan, speech presented at CLO Symposium conference, October 13, 2011.

3. Simon Sinek. *Start with Why: How Great Leaders Inspire Everyone to Take Action.* New York: Portfolio, 2009.

4. JP Rangaswami, "The Role of Trust in Social Enterprise," *The Cloud Blog*, July 9, 2012, http://cloudblog.salesforce.com/2012/07/the-role-of-trust-in-the-social-enterprise.html

5. Stephen Covey. *The Speed of Trust: The One Thing That Changes Everything.* New York: Free Press, 2006.

6. "Trust Barometer 2011," *Edelman Editions*, January 25, 2011, http://edelmaneditions.com/2011/01/trust-barometer-2011/

7. Esther Kim, "Nonsocial Transient Behavior: Social Disengagement on the Greyhound Bus," *Symbolic Interaction* 35, no. 3 (2012), http://onlinelibrary .wiley.com/doi/10.1002/symb.21/abstract.

8. Ibid.

9. Daniel Goleman, "What Makes a Leader?" *Harvard Business Review,* January 2004.

10. Dev Patnaik. *Wired to Care: How Companies Prosper When They Create Widespread Empathy.* Upper Saddle River, NJ: FT Press, 2009.

11. William A. Gentry, Todd J. Weber and Golnaz Sadri, "Empathy in the Workplace," *Center for Creative Leadership,* 2007, http://www.ccl.org/ leadership/pdf/research/EmpathyInTheWorkplace.pdf

12. "15th Annual Global CEO Survey," *PricewaterhouseCoopers,* 2012, http:// www.pwc.com/gx/en/ceo-survey/key-findings/hr-talent-strategies.jhtml.

13. "Working beyond Borders: Insights from the Global Chief Human Resource Officer Study," *IBM,* September 2010, http://www-304.ibm .com/businesscenter/fileserve?contentid=221519

14. Robert D. Richardson Jr. and Barry Moser. *Emerson: The Mind on Fire.* Berkeley: University of California Press, 1995.

15. Marjolein Lips-Wiersma and Douglas Hall, "Organizational Career Development Is Not Dead: A Case Study on Managing the New Career During Organizational Change," *Journal of Organizational Behavior* 28 (2007).

16. Matt Lauer, "Apollo 13: The Real Story," *Dateline NBC,* April 13, 2010, http://www.msnbc.msn.com/id/36471007/ns/dateline_nbc-newsmakers/t/apollo-real-story/#.UM9x4GrHffE

17. Gene Kranz. *Failure Is Not an Option: Mission Control from Mercury to Apollo 13 and Beyond.* New York: Simon and Schuster, 2000.

18. Ibid.

19. "Hitachi Spirit," *Hitachi Data Systems,* 2012, http://www.hds.com/ corporate/careers/

CHAPTER 5

1. Nick Bloom et al., "Management Practice & Productivity: Why They Matter," http://www.stanford.edu/~nbloom/ManagementReport.pdf

2. Ibid.

3. Noel M. Tichy and Warren G. Bennis. *Judgment: How Winning Leaders Make Great Calls.* New York: Penguin, 2007.

4. "Gold Standards," The Ritz Carlton, 2012, http://corporate.ritzcarlton .com/en/About/GoldStandards.htm#steps

5. TELUS internal document.

6. Katharina Herrmann et al. "Return on Leadership: Competencies that Generate Growth," Egon Zehnder International and McKinsey & Company, 2011, - http://www.mckinsey.de/downloads/kompetenz/organization/Return%20on%20Leadership.pdf

7. Ibid.

8. Richard Branson. *Losing My Virginity: How I Survived, Had Fun, and Made a Fortune Doing Business My Way*. New York: Crown Publishing Group, 2007.

9. "History of IBM," *IBM*, 2012, http://www-03.ibm.com/ibm/history/history/history_intro.html

10. *U.S. Patent and Trademark Office*, http://patft.uspto.gov

11. Lynda Gratton. *Hot Spots: Why Some Teams, Workplaces, and Organizations Buzz with Energy and Others Don't*. San Francisco: Berrett-Koehler Publishers, 2007.

12. "American Time Use Survey Summary," U.S. Bureau of Labor Statistics, June 22, 2012, http://www.bls.gov/news.release/atus.nr0.htm

13. "Work-Life Balance," Organisation for Economic Co-operation and Development, 2012, http://www.oecdbetterlifeindex.org/topics/work-life-balance/

14. E. Wenger: *Communities of Practice: Learning, Meaning, and Identity*. New York: Cambridge University Press, 1998.

15. Cynthia H. Leslie-Bole. "Humor as a Communicative Strategy in an Organizational Culture" (master's thesis, University of Delaware, 1985), http://www.udel.edu/communication/web/thesisfiles/leslie-bole.pdf

16. Larry Bossidy and Ram Charan. *Execution: The Discipline of Getting Things Done*. New York: Crown Business, 2002.

CHAPTER 6

1. Laurens Van Der Post. *Jung and the Story of Our Time*. New York: Vintage, 1976.

2. "Employee Outlook Spring 2012," Chartered Institute of Personnel and Development, 2012, http://www.cipd.co.uk/binaries/5837%20Employee%20Outlook%20(WEB).pdf.

3. Ian Chisholm, Bradley Chisholm and Mark Bell. "Coach vs. Mentor: Designing the Finest Meanings of Words," *International Executive Development Programmes: Developing Leaders*, no. 3 (2011).

4. David Halberstam. *The Best and the Brightest*. New York: Ballantine Books, 1993.

5. Beth Tootell et al., "Metrics: HRM's Holy Grail? A New Zealand case study," *Human Resource Management Journal* 19, no. 4 (2009).

6. Bob Lundin and Stephen Lundin. *Ubuntu!: An Inspiring Story About an African Tradition of Teamwork and Collaboration*. New York: Crown Business, 2010.

7. Kelly Martin, in discussion with the author in 2012.

8. Henry Mintzberg. *Managers not MBAs: A Hard Look at the Soft Practice of Managing and Management Development.* San Francisco: Berrett-Koehler Publishers, 2004.

9. Louis V. Gerstner. *Who Says Elephants Can't Dance?* Waterville, ME: Thorndike Press. 2003.

10. Ken Olsen, speech delivered at the World Future Society in Boston, Massachusetts, 1977.

11. William H. Middendorf. *Design of Devices and Systems,* 3rd Ed. Boca Raton, FL: CRC Press, 1997.

12. Michelle Obama, speech presented at the 2012 Democratic National Convention, Charlotte, North Carolina, September 4, 2012.

13. Jim Collins. *Good To Great: Why Some Companies Make the Leap . . . And Others Don't.* New York: Harper Business, 2001.

14. Euan Semple, in discussion with the author in 2012.

15. Foster W. Cline and Jim Fay. *Parenting with Love and Logic: Teaching Children Responsibility.* Colorado Springs: Pinon Press, 1990.

16. Stan Garfield, in discussion with the author in 2012.

CHAPTER 7

1. Stan Brakhage, "Metaphors on Vision," *Film Culture* 30 (1963).

2. Benjamin Franklin, "Franklin to Benjamin Webb," *Wikisource,* April 22, 1784, http://en.wikisource.org/wiki/Franklin_to_Benjamin_Webb

3. "Reciprocity," *Cambridge Dictionary Online,* 2011, http://dictionary.cambridge.org/dictionary/british/reciprocity.

4. Nancy Bonvillain. *Cultural Anthropology,* 2nd ed. Toronto: Pearson, 2009.

5. Charles Lee. *Cowboys and Dragons: Shattering Cultural Myths to Advance Chinese/American Business.* Chicago: Dearborn, 2003.

6. Barry Wellman, Wenhong Chen and Dong Weizhen. "Networking Guanxi" in eds. Thomas Gold, Douglas Guthrie and David Wank, *Social Connections in China: Institutions, Culture and the Changing Nature of Guanxi,* Cambridge: Cambridge University Press, 2002.

7. Aquiles Limone and Luis E. Bastias, "Autopoiesis and Knowledge in the Organization: Conceptual Foundation for Authentic Knowledge Management," *Systems Research and Behavioral Science* 23, no. 1 (2006).

8. J. F. Keane et al., "Autopoiesis in Disneyland: Reassuring Consumers via Autopoietic Brand Management," *International Journal of Advertising* 18, no. 4, (1999).

9. Mark S. Granovetter, "The Strength of Weak Ties," *American Journal of Sociology* 78, no. 6 (1973).

10. Ronald S. Burt. *Neighbor Networks: Competitive Advantage Local and Personal*. Oxford: Oxford University Press, 2011.

11. Pearl Jam, "Satan's Bed," in *Vitalogy*, 1994, http://youtube/gGup0BWv-ng

12. Lynn Wu et al., "Value of Social Network: A Large-Scale Analysis on Network Structure Impact to Financial Revenue of Information Technology Consultants," paper presented at the Winter Information Systems Conference, Salt Lake City, Utah, February 2009, http://smallblue.research.ibm.com/publications/Utah-ValueOfSocialNetworks.pdf

13. Stephen Downes,"Collective Intelligence? Nah. Connective Intelligence," *Stephen's Web*, February 18, 2008, http://www.downes.ca/cgi-bin/page.cgi?post=43456

14. Robert Cialdini. *Influence: The Psychology of Persuasion*. New York: HarperCollins, 2006.

15. Deborah Richards and Brad Dalton, "Collaboration in Research Protocol Design: A Case Study Exploring Knowledge Creation for the Pharmaceutical Industry and Prescribing Physicians," *Journal of Medical Marketing* 9, no. 3 (2009).

16. Tanya Roscoria, "Collaboration, Leadership Key in Oakland, Calif., School Turnaround," Center for Digital Education, July 11, 2012, http://www.centerdigitaled.com/policy/Collaboration-Leadership-Key-in-Oakland-School-Turnaround.html

17. Lynn Wu et al.

CHAPTER 8

1. Niccolò Machiavelli. *The Prince. Discourses on the first ten books of Titus Livius. Thoughts of a statesman*. Boston: J.R. Osgoode and Company, 1882.

2. Stephen Rhinesmith, "Capitalism 2.0 Leadership and Paradox Management," *Drucker Exchange Blog*, August 28, 2012, http://www.druckerforum.org/blog/?p=154

3. James Manyika et al., "Big Data: The Next Frontier for Innovation, Competition, and Productivity," McKinsey Global Institute, May 2011, http://www.mckinsey.com/insights/mgi/research/technology_and_innovation/big_data_the_next_frontier_for_innovation

4. Jon Husband, "Wirearchy," *Wirearchy*, 2012, http://www.wirearchy.com

5. Jon Husband, interview by Traci Fenton, "'Do You Know About Wirearchy' Interview (From 2007)," *Wirearchy*, http://wirearchy.com/2011/09/18/do-you-know-about-wirearchy-interview-from-2007

6. "Working beyond Borders: Insights from the Global Chief Human Resource Officer Study," IBM, September 2010, http://www-304.ibm.com/businesscenter/fileserve?contentid=221519

7. Cam Crosbie, in discussion with the author in 2012.

8. Aristotle. *Politics (Book Three)*, trans. Benjamin Jowett, 350 B.C.E., http://classics.mit.edu/Aristotle/politics.html

9. Warren Bennis and Burt Nanus. *Leaders: Strategies for Taking Charge.* New York: HarperCollins, 2003.

10. Ibid.

11. Marlene Caroselli. *Leadership Skills for Managers.* New York: McGraw-Hill, 2000.

12. Larry Bossidy and Ram Charan. *Execution: The Discipline of Getting Things Done.*

13. Ibid.

14. Linda Barrington, "CEO Challenge 2010: Top 10 Challenges," The Conference Board, February 2010, http://www.conferenceboard.ca/e-library/abstract.aspx?did=3477

15. "NSS Robert A. Heinlein Memorial Award," National Space Society, 2012, http://www.nss.org/awards/heinlein_award.html

16. "Recognize Achievements, Not Just Anniversaries." *Maritz Connections.* April 2011.

17. Rodd Wagner and James K. Harter. *12: The Elements of Great Managing.* New York: Gallup Press, 2006.

18. Darren Entwistle, speech presented at a TELUS internal leadership forum, 2011.

19. Lynda Gratton, "Results Through Collaboration," Books24×7 Quick-Talks, 2011.

20. Kristin Burnham, "TD Bank Gets Social, Cashes In on IT-Business Teamwork," *CIO,* July 24, 2012, http://www.cio.com/article/711859/TD_Bank_Gets_Social_Cashes_In_on_IT_Business_Teamwork

CHAPTER 9

1. James Boswell. *The Life of Samuel Johnson.* New York: Everyman's Library, 1993.

2. Nicholas Carr. *The Shallows: What the Internet is Doing to Our Brains.* New York: W. W. Norton & Company, 2011.

3. "Transforming BC's Curriculum," B.C. Ministry of Education, August 2012, http://www.bced.gov.bc.ca/irp/transforming_curriculum.php

4. Ralph Waldo Emerson. *The Conduct of Life.* Boston: Ticknor and Fields, 1860.

5. C.S. Dweck. *Mindset: The New Psychology of Success.* New York: Random House, 2006.

6. John Seely Brown and Paul Duguid. *The Social Life of Information.* Boston: Harvard Business Review Press, 2000.

7. Santiago Budría and Pablo Swedberg, "The Shadow Value of Employer-Provided Training," *Journal of Economic Psychology* 33, no. 3 (2012).

8. Cagri Bulut and Osman Culha, "The Effects of Organizational Training on Organizational Commitment," *International Journal of Training and Development* 14, no. 4 (2010).

9. Karen Kocher, in discussion with the author in 2012.

10. Michael M. Lombardo and Robert W. Eichinger. *The Career Architect Development Planner.* Minneapolis: Lominger, 1996.

11. D. Scott DeRue and Christopher G. Meyers, "Leadership Development: A Review and Agenda for Future Research," In *Oxford Handbook of Leadership and Organizations,* D.V. Day, ed. Oxford: Oxford University Press, 2012.

12. *GSV Capital,* http://gsvcap.com

13. "Growing the World's Best Leaders," Deloitte University, 2012, http://careers.deloitte.com/uploadedfiles/US/pdf/DUStudent_Flyer_Winter2012_nonprintready.pdf

14. Karie Willyerd and Jeanne Meister. *The 2020 Workplace: How Innovative Companies Attract, Develop, and Keep Tomorrow's Employees Today.* New York: HarperBusiness, 2010.

15. Jathan Janove, "To Know the Business, Start in the Trenches," *HR Magazine* 57, no. 4 (2012).

16. Aaron Silvers, "Blueprint for Social Learning," *T+D Magazine,* January 2012.

17. Marcia Conner, "Where Social Learning Thrives," Fast Company, February 11, 2010, http://www.fastcompany.com/1546824/where-social-learning-thrives

18. "Welcome to the CompanyCommand Forum," Company Command, http://companycommand.army.mil/index.htm

19. Hennessy

20. Jane Hart, "Social Learning: Are you starting from the right place?" *Learning in the Social Workplace,* January 30, 2012, http://www.c4lpt.co.uk/blog/2012/01/30/social-learning-are-you-starting-from-the-right-place

21. Mitch Resnick, "Rethinking Learning in the Digital Age," in *The Global Information Technology Report: Readiness for the Networked World,* G. Kirkman, ed. Oxford: Oxford University Press, 2002.

22. John W. Gardner. *Self-Renewal: The Individual and the Innovative Society.* New York: W.W. Norton & Co, 1995.

CHAPTER 10

1. Daniel Kligerman, in discussion with the author in 2012.
2. Henry Ford and Samuel Crowther. *My Life and Work.* New York: Doubleday, Page & Company, 1922.
3. Bert Sandie, in discussion with the author in 2011.
4. Euan Semple. *Organizations Don't Tweet, People Do: A Manager's Guide to the Social Web.* Hoboken: John Wiley & Sons, 2012.
5. "Email," *Oxford Dictionaries,* 2012, http://oxforddictionaries.com/definition/english/email
6. "Interconnected World: Communication & Social Networking," *Ipsos,* March 27, 2012, http://www.ipsos-na.com/news-polls/pressrelease.aspx?id=5564
7. *CNN iReport,* http://ireport.cnn.com/
8. "Speakers Give Sound Advice," *Syracuse Post Standard,* March 28, 1911.
9. Yan Huang, Param Vir Singh and Anindya Ghose, "A Structural Model of Employee Behavioral Dynamics in Enterprise Social Media," *Social Sciences Research Network,* July 18, 2012, http://ssrn.com/abstract=1785724
10. *Mozilla Open Badges,* http://www.openbadges.org *Badgeville,* http://www.badgeville.com
11. Ibid.
12. Judd Antin and Elizabeth F. Churchill, "Badges in Social Media: A Social Psychological Perspective," paper presented at CHI 2011, May 7–12, Vancouver, British Columbia, http://gamification-research.org/wp-content/uploads/2011/04/03-Antin-Churchill.pdf
13. Jerry Nine, in discussion with the author in 2012.
14. Linda Stone, in discussion with the author in 2012.
15. Tony Bingham, in discussion with the author in 2012.
16. Sherry Turkle. *Alone Together: Why We Expect More from Technology and Less from Each Other.* New York: Basic Books, 2011.
17. Deborah Hedstrom. *From Telegraph to Light Bulb with Thomas Edison.* Nashville, TN: B&H Books, 2007.

CHAPTER 11

1. "A Review of Leadership in the NHS," *The King's Fund,* 2012, http://www.kingsfund.org.uk/projects/review-leadership-nhs
2. "Leadership and Engagement for Improvement in the NHS," *The King's Fund,* 2012, http://www.kingsfund.org.uk/publications/leadership-and-engagement-improvement-nhs

3. Beverly Alimo-Metcalfe and John Alban-Metcalfe, "Engaging Leadership: Creating Organisations That Maximise the Potential of Their People," The Chartered Institute of Personnel and Development, September 2008, http://www.cipd.co.uk/NR/rdonlyres/F72D3236-E832-4663-ABEC-BCC7890DC431/0/4585EngageleaderRIWEB.pdf

4. "Employers Say They Are Unprepared for Retiring Boomers: Survey," Canada Newswire, October 7, 2008, http://www.newswire.ca/en/story/340973/employers-say-they-are-unprepared-for-retiring-boomers-survey

5. Iain Marlow, "RIM's Market Share No Longer Among Top Five Global Smartphone Makers," July 30, 2012, http://www.theglobeandmail.com/technology/business-technology/rims-market-share-no-longer-among-top-five-global-smartphone-makers/article4445300

6. Kara Swisher, speech presented at Women in Film and Television event, Toronto, Ontario, September 20, 2012.

7. "Open Letter to Blackberry Bosses: Senior RIM Exec Tells All as Company Crumbles Around Him," BGR, June 30, 2011, http://www.bgr.com/2011/06/30/open-letter-to-blackberry-bosses-senior-rim-exec-tells-all-as-company-crumbles-around-him

8. Thorstein Heins, "RIM Will 'Empower People Like Never Before:' Heins," The Globe and Mail, July 3, 2012, http://www.theglobeandmail.com/technology/rim-will-empower-people-like-never-before-heins/article4385940

9. Nick Howe, in discussion with the author in 2012.

10. Shazia McCormick, in discussion with the author in 2012.

11. Tony Hsieh, "Your Culture Is Your Brand," Zappos Blogs: CEO and COO. Blog, January 3, 2009, http://blogs.zappos.com/blogs/ceo-and-coo-blog/2009/01/03/your-culture-is-your-brand

12. "10 Steps to Zappos's Success," Inc., 2010, http://www.inc.com/ss/zappos-struggle#8

13. Vineet Nayar. Employees First, Customers Second: Turning Conventional Management Upside Down. Boston: Harvard Business Press Books, 2010.

14. Ibid.

15. "HCL Named "Best Employers" in Asia and Ranked No: 1 in India by Hewitt in Its 2009 Study," HCL, April 7, 2009, http://www.hcltech.com/press-releases/it-infrastructure-management/hcl-named-best-employers-asia-and-ranked-no-1-india

16. Jena McGregor, "Coming Up Fast: Companies to Watch," Businessweek Magazine, December 10, 2008, http://www.businessweek.com/stories/2008-12-10/coming-up-fast-companies-to-watch

17. Tony Bingham and Pat Galagan, "TELUS Reveals Its Secret to Success," *T+D Magazine*, September 7, 2012, http://www.astd .org/Publications/Magazines/TD/TD-Archive/2012/09/ TELUS-Reveals-Its-Secret-to-Success

18. Ibid.

19. Dee W. Hock. "The Chaordic Organization: Out of Control and Into Order," *New Horizons for Learning*, 1996, http://jtp.ipgkti.edu.my/ppy/ ppismptmk/sumber/KB/NewHorizon/www.newhorizons.org/future/ hock.htm

20. "Atomic Education Urged by Einstein," *The New York Times*, May 25, 1946.

CHAPTER 12

1. George H. Stonehouse and Jonathan D. Pemberton, "Learning and Know-ledge Management in the Intelligent Organisation," *Participation and Empowerment: An International Journal* 7, no. 5 (1999).

2. "Organisational Culture," The Hofstede Centre, 2012, http://geert-hofstede.com/organisational-culture.html

3. Robert A. Cooke and Richard Sharpe. "Employee Engagement: Is It Really 'The Holy Grail' of HR?" Human Synergistics International, 2010, http:// www.humsyn.be/EmployeeEngagement.pdf

4. Edgar H. Schein. *Organizational Culture and Leadership*. San Francisco: Jossey-Bass, 2004.

5. Colin Powell and Tony Koltz. *It Worked for Me: Lessons in Leadership and Life*. New York: Harper, 2012.

6. Marcel Proust. *In Search of Lost Time, Vol. II: Within a Budding Grove*. 1919

7. Amy Edmondson. *Teaming: How Organizations Learn, Innovate and Compete in the Knowledge Economy*. San Francisco: Jossey-Bass, 2012.

8. Ibid.

9. Lisa Brummel, in discussion with the author in 2012.

10. Steve Cadigan, in discussion with the author in 2012.

11. Ajay Mehra et al., "The Social Network Ties of Group Leaders: Implica-tions for Group Performance and Leader Reputation," *Organization Science* 17, no. 1 (2006).

12. The Tragically Hip, "At Transformation," in *Now For Plan A.*, 2012, http:// youtu.be/5Ost6Eupxss

13. Leo Tolstoy. *War and Peace*. New York: New American Library Classics, 1968.

14. Warren Bennis, *An Invented Life: Reflections on Leadership and Change*. New York: Basic Books, 1993.

15. Rolf Kleiner, "Ayers Leadership Series: Purpose-Driven Leadership," The Ayers Group, 2010, http://www.enewsbuilder.net/theayersgroup/ e_article001667707.cfm?x=bdF7Pqq,b9Ww7kIv,w

16. Macon Phillips, "Osama Bin Laden Dead," *The White House Blog*, May 2, 2011, http://www.whitehouse.gov/blog/2011/05/02/osama-bin-laden-dead

17. *Nisga'a Lisims Government*, http://www.nisgaalisims.ca/welcome

AFTERWORD

1. Bernard Bass and Bruce Avolio, "Transformational Leadership and Organizational Culture," *International Journal of Public Administration* 17, no. 3–4, 1994.

2. Henry Mintzberg. *Managing*. San Francisco: Berrett-Koehler, 2011.

About the Author

Dan Pontefract is Head of Learning & Collaboration at TELUS (www.telus.com). He is responsible for the overarching leadership development, learning & collaboration strategy for the company. He has driven a philosophical and cultural shift in the way TELUS views and experiences learning called "Learning 2.0"—a shift to a social, informal and formal learning and collaboration model for all 40,000+ team members, bringing TELUS to the forefront of learning leadership. In parallel with these actions, Dan championed the introduction of the TELUS Leadership Philosophy (TLP), an open and collaborative based leadership framework for all TELUS team members, along with a comprehensive list of social collaboration technologies.

Dan and his team were recognized with ASTD BEST Awards in 2009, 2011 and 2012. In 2010, Dan was also acknowledged by *CLO Magazine* as a Vanguard Award winner. Dan is also a two-time winner by the Corporate University Best in Class Awards of the Leader of the Year in both 2010 and 2011. He is the 2012 winner of Skillsoft's Learning Leader of the Year award. Also in 2012, *CLO Magazine* bestowed the Learning in Practice Innovation Award and BrandonHall Group awarded him the Gold Award in Strategy & Governance. Dan is a frequent speaker and writes about leadership, technology, learning and culture at www.danpontefract.com. He was recruited into TELUS in Q4 of 2008, previously holding senior positions with SAP, Business Objects, Crystal Decisions and the British Columbia Institute of Technology (BCIT).

Surrounded by love, Dan is the proud father of Claire, Cole and Cate (who are proficient bloggers themselves) and Denise—the most patient woman on the planet. When he's not writing, speaking, working, supporting Manchester United, parenting or being an annoying husband, you'll find him cycling. You can reach him at www.danpontefract.com.

Index